CIVILIAN CONTROL
OF THE MILITARY

CIVILIAN CONTROL OF THE MILITARY

Theory and Cases
from Developing Countries

Edited by
Claude E. Welch, Jr.

State University of New York Press
Albany 1976

Published with assistance from
the University Awards Committee
of State University of New York

First published in 1976 by
State University of New York Press
99 Washington Avenue, Albany, New York 12210

Printed in the United States of America

Library of Congress Cataloging in Publication Data

Main entry under title:

Civilian control of the military.

Includes bibliographical references and index.
1. Civil supremacy over the military.
2. Underdeveloped areas—Politics and government.

I. Welch, Claude Emerson.
JF195.C5C58   322'.5'091724   76-40278
ISBN 0-87395-348-7

CONTENTS

PREFACE

One hundred fifty years ago, in his noted book *On War*, General Carl Maria von Clausewitz penned perhaps the strongest justification for civilian control over the military. Armed forces, he noted, are created by states to engage in war; war itself is an instrument of state policy, a continuation of political intercourse by other means. Accordingly,

> The subordination of the political point of view to the military would be contrary to common sense, for policy has declared the War; it is the intelligent faculty, War only the instrument, and not the reverse. The subordination of the military point of view to the political is, therefore, the only thing which is possible.[1]

What is *possible* in the realm of theory, and what is *actual* in the contemporary world, may be far removed. Clausewitz believed in the supremacy of politics, and left to political leaders the key decisions regarding the use of force. He did believe that no professional military officer should arrogate the reins of power, for his duty was obedience to constituted political authority. Clausewitz's maxims seem to be increasingly disregarded. Military intervention in politics has escalated since World War II, and especially in the past fifteen years. Of the independent states in 1961, 12 percent were headed by governments whose leaders had seized power by coups d'etat. By 1966 the percentage had risen to nineteen, by 1972 to twenty-seven.[2] The "man on horseback" has become increasingly prominent; military intervention provides a quicker and surer path to the presidential palace than electoral politics.

The questions that arise are myriad. Can the recent eruption of coups d'etat be attributed primarily to the weakness of civilian control? Or may they be attributed more to the growing strengths of armed forces, its officers aware of the power they wield? Or do conditions exist, particularly in states marked by low levels of economic development, that facilitate intervention? The greatest increase in military involvement in politics has occurred in the Third World, namely, those states marked by limited industrialization, by relatively brief histories of independence (many African and Asian states) or by lengthy histories of military intervention (Latin America), and often by serious problems of ethnic, linguistic, or religious fragmentation. Of seventy-five countries with per capita gross national product under $252 per annum, fifty-eight experienced coups d'etat in the 1960-72 period—in other words, nearly 80 percent.[3] These are the countries in which officers have most readily become political leaders, in the process subordinating the political point of view to the military. Clausewitz has not been vindicated in the contemporary Third World.

Yet there are obvious exceptions to the apparent dominance of the military in Third World politics. This book explores some of these exceptions, in the process illustrating means for civilian control that might be adopted by individual states and adapted to local circumstances. These means are varied—international pressures (as in Japan and the Philippines), domestic political revolution (as in China and Mexico), manipulation of ethnic or class factors (as in Guyana, Malaysia, and India), development of legislative institutions (as in Lebanon and Finland), or "pay-off" to the armed forces (as in Chile in the initial months of Allende's presidency.) But the chief instruments for insuring civilian control are 1) that rare phenomenon, a legitimate, widely supported political institution, such as a parliament or political party, coupled with 2) a self-imposed and maintained sense of restraint by officers and politicians alike in which the military is not actively solicited for resolving domestic political conflicts, but is assigned to carry out relatively restricted, internationally oriented responsibilities.

The examples of civilian control chosen for detailed study range widely. Some are now developed countries, such as Finland or Japan, whose historical subordination of the armed forces provides pointers for the Third World of today. Others, such as Chile, stand on the threshold of industrialization, but have a heritage of coups d'etat and "corporatist" politics that facilitates intervention. Still other states, notably Guyana, India, Malaysia, and the Philippines, experienced colonial administration and the imposition of patterns of civil-military relations designed to insure the subordination of the armed forces, patterns that have been both continued and adapted. Finally, some countries experienced violent political revolution, from which emerged a politicized military nonetheless responsive to civilian direction.

It should be noted that a large part of the Third World is excluded from this volume. The continent of Africa is not represented in this collection, for a simple reason: with a handful of exceptions (Tunisia, Senegal, Kenya, the Ivory Coast, and Zambia as of late 1975), newly independent African countries have yet to establish means of civilian control that have stood the test of time.

I wish to express my gratitude to the State University of New York at Buffalo, and to the Inter-University Seminar on Armed Forces and Society, for making this book possible. Their financial support for a conference, "Civilian Control of the Military: Myth and Reality in Developing Countries," led to the commissioning of the following chapters, which have been revised extensively since their initial presentation in October 1974. The pressures of space and time precluded the publication in this volume of more than half the papers presented at the conference; nonetheless, these papers stimulated a great deal of thoughtful discussion. The monetary assistance of SUNY/Buffalo and the Inter-University Seminar does not tie them to the accuracy or substance of the views subsequently expressed; these are obligations laid on the editor, obligations I gladly accept, with thanks to those who made the conference and this book possible.

Claude E. Welch, Jr.
Buffalo, New York
July 1975

Notes to Preface

1. General Carl Maria von Clausewitz, *On War* (London: Routledge and Kegan Paul, 1966), Vol. III, pp. 424-5.

2. Figures calculated by Franklin D. Margiotta.

3. Calculated from figures in Gavin Kennedy, *The Military in the Third World* (New York: Scribner's, 1974), p. 29. GNP is calculated on the basis of 1968 dollars.

CIVILIAN CONTROL
OF THE MILITARY

Civilian Control of the Military: Myth and Reality

Claude E. Welch, Jr.

Professor of Political Science at the State University of New York at Buffalo, Claude E. Welch, Jr. received his B.A. and D. Phil. degrees respectively from Harvard College and Oxford University. His publications on civil-military relations include *Soldier and State in Africa* (1970), *Military Role and Rule* (1974), and articles in *The Journal of Modern African Studies*, *Africa Today, International Studies Newsletter,* and *Military Review*.

Scholars of civil-military relations appear far more effective in listing causes of military coups d'etat than in prescribing steps for civilian control.* Far easier, it seems, to examine why civilian governments fall than how they are maintained.

The contrast may be attributed, in part, to the clarity and suddenness of military intervention. A coup d'etat is a sharp, clear event, easy to date and (if successful) possible to document. With clarity of hindsight, an enterprising scholar can discern its causes—for example, organizational strains, factionalism or personal rivalries, waning legitimacy of political institutions. Civilian control, however, is more a *set of relationships* than an individual *event*. It lacks sharpness. Although collisions

---

*This chapter has benefited from the comments of many, including Lowell Dittmer, James Dolian, Paul Guinn, Jerome Slater, and Ronald Stupak.

I

between civilian and military authorities may provoke crises, as in budget disputes or in changes of personnel, other day-to-day interactions—the stuff of which civilian control is made—may be routine. Civilian control is not a matter of precluding overt intervention, for a coup d'etat may be the proverbial tip of the iceberg. The heart of civilian control occurs within the corridors of government, far removed from the usual ambit of scholars.

Adding to the conceptual fuzziness of civilian control is its changing nature over time. The nature and extent of civilian control reflect shifting balances between the strengths of civilian political institutions on one side, and the political strengths of military institutions on the other. Civilian control is a matter of degree. All armed forces participate in politics in various fashions. They cannot be precluded from the political arena, given their organizational identity, autonomy, and functional specialization. Any military has an impact on its political system, with its political roles being "a question not of *whether*, but of *how much* and of *what kind*."[1] No military, in short, can be shorn of political influence, save through the rare step of total abolition.

The key issue in civilian control is one of setting limits within which members of the armed forces, and the military as an institution, accept the government's definition of appropriate areas of responsibility. Put in this perspective, civilian control means that the military lobbies as do other parts of the government; seeks to carry out a relatively specific set of policy objectives; and employs channels of decision-making within the military that do not breach its integrity as an institution, or, alternatively, ensures that this organizational integrity is subordinated to political institutions such as parties. The armed forces thereby accept subordinate roles in the political system. Civilian control, as defined by Huntington, is thus "governmental control of the military."[2]

Finally, the diffuseness of civilian control reflects uncertainty as to how it is in fact implemented, in particular the ways in which intramilitary factors and the relationships between governments and armed forces interact. Should the analyst examine the subordination of the military largely in terms of internal factors, such as widespread acceptance of an ethic of subordination? Or should the analyst focus on the institutional means available to the government to ensure compliance, such as constitutional strictures, on-going legislative practices, or purges of military personnel? The first approach tends to focus on the internal workings of the military, with particular reference to psychological factors incorporated in "professionalism." The second approach starts from the perspective of government and stresses devices through whose working those ill-disposed toward governmental policies can be bypassed, replaced, coopted, or otherwise neutralized. One should not simplistically assume, however, that only one avenue of analysis can be adopted; outstanding examinations of civil-military relations consider both what may be termed internal and environmental factors.

As should be clear from the preceding paragraphs, civilian control always occurs within a context of some form of military involvement in politics. A continuum of relationships exists between the power of the military and the power of civilian institutions relative to the enunciation, development, and implementation of policy. Schematically, the continuum of military involvement in politics may be presented thus:

Military Influence (civilian control)	Military — Participation—	Military Control (with partners)	Military — Control (without partners)

Military influence in politics constitutes what many scholars consider the "normal" form of civilian control, as manifested in several Western, democratic states, and in some developing countries. Members of the armed forces are not excluded from politics. However, significant degrees of involvement remain limited to those holding ranking positions. Clear and integral boundaries exist between military and political roles, with officers shying away from the latter. Political influence is exercised through regularized and accepted channels. Contacts between the military and civilian political leaders occur at the top rungs of the military hierarchy; lateral contacts at lower levels are discouraged to preserve the integrity of the chain of

3

command and the integral nature of institutional boundaries. (Exceptions, to be certain, exist where civilian control, as in the Peoples Liberation Army (PLA) of China, results in the deliberate mixing of political and military roles.) Be it through budget lobbying or (more important) providing information regarding strategic decisions, military leaders proffer advice. This advice naturally carries the weight of expertise and cannot readily be disregarded by civilian leaders. The influence that exists thus depends upon specialized knowledge and technical responsibilities, not upon the fact of naked coercive power.

Military participation in politics differs in degree, not kind, from military influence in politics. Legislative enactments may provide the armed forces a secure and extensive area of policy autonomy. The lobbying mentioned in the previous paragraph may turn into lightly veiled pressure or into "blackmail,"as Finer has suggested.[3] The initiative for greater military involvement in politics may come from civilians rather than officers. Political leaders, beleaguered by conflicting demands, turn to the armed forces as props for their power. Such moves convert military influence in politics into military participation in politics. Leaders of the armed forces may be coopted, placed in cabinet positions, to provide the tottering regime a veneer of stability and support. (Chile in the year prior to Allende's overthrow was in such a position.) Alternatively, policy choices may be liable to military veto. Civilian leaders must carefully avoid options that might result in inexorable pressure from officers. The perception of potential veto or even displacement from office thus differentiates participation from influence. There exists in effect, a dual power. Political decisions are made by a combination of civilian and military leaders.

With military control of politics, civilian control of the military has disappeared. No longer can the government oversee the military, in terms of defining its functions and functioning. The armed forces decide basic issues—and woe to those in official positions who would resist what the armed forces consider their prerogatives. Infringements on these prerogatives, in the absence of general acceptance in the military both of the appropriateness of subordination to government control and of the legitimacy of the government, readily explode into intervention. Military control of politics results. The displacement or supplantment of governments (to use Finer's terminology)[4] differentiates control from participation.

Speaking broadly, two varieties of military control of politics can be distinguished. The armed forces govern in the first variety by means of extensive partnerships. In such coalitions, the armed forces may, in fact, remain partly behind the scenes, relying upon trusted allies to maintain policies they support. Alternatively, a military junta may draw leaders entirely from within its own ranks, utilizing civilians in minor and subordinate positions. Allies thus exist on sufferance, as uninfluential advisers; they remain subject to the whims of their mentors.

Civilian control of the military has received far more extensive scholarly attention in "developed" than in "developing" countries. One crude measure comes from Lang's bibliography, *Military Institutions and the Sociology of War.* Of the fifty-six titles listed under the general heading "Civilian Control," twelve deal with Germany, ten with the United States.[5] Brazil, Burma, China, the Koreas, pre-Moghul India, and Tanzania are the only developing states listed—a reflection of the incomplete state of existing research. Studies of the military in developing countries have tended to focus on the immediate drama of the coup d'etat. Military control of politics has been far more characteristic of developing countries than has military influence in politics. Yet there remain exceptions—Mexico, the Philippines, Malaysia, and India, among others—in which the man on horseback has not become (at least in recent years) the leading political figure. The reasons peculiar to these states will be examined in following chapters.

Five means of civilian control have been devised and utilized by governments:

1) constitutional constraints on the political impact of the military;

2) ascriptive factors (e.g., class, ethnicity) affecting relationships between civilian and military leaders;

3) utilization of party controls, possibly through the creation of parallel hierarchies of command;

4) geographic and historical factors permitting the maintenance of relatively small armed forces with narrow responsibilities;

5) delineation of clear spheres of military responsibility, leading to widespread acceptance within the armed forces of an ethic of subordination. Each must be examined in detail.

Constitutional Constraints

Underlying most definitions of civilian control is a time-honored distinction between "military"and "political" matters. Armed forces, as branches of the state, are constituted and funded to carry out specific objectives. The armed forces are instruments; war is "politics by other means," with the military itself a tool. Since it is the responsibility of politicians to determine objectives, as Clausewitz wrote, "the subordination of the military point of view to the political is, therefore, the only thing which is possible."[6] So much for the theory of subordinating the armed forces to civilian control. What are the realities?

Since the French Revolution, civilian control has often been constitutionally enshrined through asserting popular sovereignty over government institutions.[7] The formulas differ little: "all power . . . belongs to the people" (People's Republic of China, Article 2); "national sovereignty belongs to the people" (France, Article 3); "national sovereignty resides essentially and originally in the people" (Mexico, Article 39). But a principle so broad and diffuse requires precise implementation. Hence, specific prescriptions are added—and it is in these specific prescriptions that civilian control receives constitutional backing.

Vesting of command responsibilities in the head of state occurs with great frequency: "the Chairman of the People's Republic of China commands the armed forces of state" (Article 42); "the President of the Republic is head of the armed forces" (France, Article 15); "there shall be a President of India. . .in whom the supreme command of the Union Defense Forces is vested" (Part V, Chapter I, Articles 52-53 [27]); "the President shall be Commander-in-Chief of the Army and Navy of the United States, and of the militia of the several States, when called into the actual service of the United States" (Article II, Section I). As long as the head of state is drawn from a civilian background, his personal command over the military provides a veneer of civilian control.

6

Powers vested in the legislature provide a second set of constitutional constraints. The three most prominent, in ascending order of importance, appear to be legislative investigative powers, reservation to elected assemblies of the powers to declare war and states of emergency, and general budgetary supervision.

Linked to legislative forms of civilian control is the assumption that popular sovereignty is exercised through representative institutions, often with detailed supervision carried out by committees. The obvious question, to which no uniformly satisfactory answer can be provided, rests in the division between "political" and "military" matters. During the American Civil War, for example, did the Joint Committee on the Conduct of the War push so deeply into the conflict as to deny Union generals the possibility of making their own professional decisions? Conversely, have legislative committees at other times and places been so chary about examining the internal operations of the armed forces as to make civilian control through legislative committee investigation a non-entity? Committee oversight may become farcical because of close sympathy developed between the purported supervisors and would-be supervisees. Absence of research staff presents serious obstacles to effective committee supervision. US congressional committees, caught upon the horns of a classic dilemma—attempting both to maintain close ties with professional officers and to provide responsible supervision through the committees' lack of major staff assistance—have, in the words of Clotfelter, "acknowledged the difficulty of trying to oversee the Pentagon."[8] This dilemma is by no means confined to the USA.

Declaration of a state of war represents a grave political act. Almost all written constitutions reserve this power to legislative bodies. In the Federal Republic of Germany, for example, the Basic Law stipulates that a "state of defense" requires a two-thirds vote of the combined houses or of the Joint Committee. In the United States, Congress retains the right to declare war and to "raise and support armies." In India, by contrast, once the president has determined "that a grave emergency exists whereby the security of India is threatened whether by war, external aggression or internal disturbance," he may proclaim an emergency, which must be laid before Parliament for approval (Part XVIII, Article 352 [1]). Since such proclamations are rare, however, their import as a means of civilian control appears negligible.

If "he who pays the piper calls the tune" accurately summarized civil-military relations, then budgetary supervision would indeed be the most powerful weapon for civilian control. As a senior civil servant under Franklin D. Roosevelt indicated, "the budget is one of the most effective, if not the strongest, implements of civilian control over the military establishment."[9] Strong, yes, but crude in many respects. Budget debates normally occur annually, yet the rhythms of military life may require assured funding over longer periods. Tensions thus can readily erupt in the appropriations process between long-range military needs and immediate political exigencies. The circle cannot be squared. Nonetheless, efforts have been made to enshrine civilian control through budgetary supervision, while providing the armed forces extensive autonomy. A prime example is furnished by the Septennate, passed by the Prussian legislature in 1867. This enactment set the armed forces as equivalent in size to 1 percent of the population; funding would be automatic on the basis of a per capita grant. With various modifications, the law continued for several years and became a major item in Bismarck's championing of a strong military establishment versus the legislature—a major question in the politics of executive-legislative competition.

In the absence of other means of civilian control, legislative budgeting supervision may introduce serious strains. Part of the conventional wisdom among scholars of civil-military relations in Latin America is that (as McAllister asserts) "dissatisfaction with budgetary allocations has been a primary factor in precipitating military coups."[10] Graphic evidence has been provided by Villaneuva, who (on the basis of evidence from Peru) asserts that an administration which reduces the percentage of the national budget devoted to the military is invariably deposed, while a government installed by a *golpe* inevitably increases the percentage.[11] Unwisely or summarily exercised, the power of budget review may thus undercut civilian control by leading to its total rejection—that is, to military seizure of

8

power and hence to military control of politics. (The possible exacerbation of interservice rivalries might be a consequence more salutary to the maintenance of civilian control; however, since many developing countries rely almost totally on infantry, and have small navies and air forces, the more likely result of budget reduction is army dissatisfaction than competition among military branches.) Accordingly, civilian leaders who move rapidly to reduce the perquisites of the armed forces may (history shows with the clarity of hindsight) dig their own political graves.

Budgetary control may thus be overrated as a device for ensuring the political subordination of the armed forces. Officers might become the most skillful practitioners of budgetary politics, achieving by pressure and threat what may be a grossly disproportionate share of national resources. Favorable budgetary treatment may enhance the loyalty of the military. However, abrupt reductions in levels of military expenditures can precipitate intervention. Developing countries with high levels of military expenditure have customarily manifested less civilian control than countries with lower allocations.[12] Whether this is cause or effect remains to be determined.

A focus on constitutional constraints, in summary, risks confusing shadow and substance. Effective supervision through governmental institutions does not depend upon formal prescriptions, for the constitutions of most states contain formulas of popular sovereignty, policy supervision, and budgetary control. The exercise of the prerogatives of control may in fact arouse antagonisms within the military, knocking to shreds the grandiloquent declarations of the constitution. Covenants without swords being but words, the acquiescence of those who are armed must be ensured in advance. In defense of constitutional constraints, however, one must recognize that legal prescriptions do help legitimate civilian control—and this legitimation may give pause to potential coup-makers when they consider the act of intervention.

Ascriptive Factors

In his survey, *The Ruling Class*, Mosca warned, "the class that bears the lance or holds the musket regularly forces its rule upon the class that handles the spade or pushes the shuttle."[13] Nineteenth-century western Europe seemed to escape such dominance, which Mosca attributed to class ties binding military commanders and civilian leaders. This "most fortunate exception" depended on "an exceptionally favorable sequence of historical circumstances."[14] The points Mosca raised draw attention to means of subordination based on links between civilian and military leaders.

Ties based on class form part of a broader grouping of means of civilian control, deemed "subjective civilian control" by Huntington. According to him, few marked barriers exist between the military and society. Subjective civilian control, defined as "the product of identity of thought and outlook between civilian and military groups," stems from the close coordination of existing political and military ways of thought. To quote Huntington further, members of the armed forces both reflect and embody "the dominant social forces and political ideology" of the society. [15]

How great is the probability that armed forces can be effectively subordinated in this fashion? Arguments based on history cut in totally opposite directions. On the one hand, civilian control has been aided by identity of thought and background of civilian and military leaders, while on the other, civilian control has been assured by deliberate isolation of the military from integration with civilian social forces. Let us turn to each.

INTEGRATION WITH SOCIAL FORCES

Three markedly different arguments can be distinguished within the more general assertion that civilian control rests upon an integration of existing social forces with the armed forces. The first variant, explicit in Mosca, relies upon the similar backgrounds of the members of the ruling and commanding elites to ensure the political subordination of the armed forces. The second argument, linked to the development of mass- and class-based parties, draws its substantiation from the French and Russian revolutions and is examined at greater length in the following section. The third form of integration with social forces is the nation-in-arms, a means of military mobilization infused with a sentiment we may loosely term "nationalistic."

The argument of class and ethnic congruence diminishing the likelihood of active military involvement in politics has been argued (if not necessarily proven) from Western European history. Before the late nineteenth century, the "ruling class" coupled political and military responsibilities. Even with the growth of standing armies, command positions were often held by the kith and kin of political leaders. The ascriptive ties of consanguinity, in a country such as Great Britain, helped to keep the armed forces in subordinate positions—as did the explicit prohibition after 1688 of standing armies on English soil. The practice of primogeniture abetted civilian control. The eldest son of a noble family gained the title, with its attendant prestige and political power. While not disputing the undoubted existence of sibling rivalry, is it not plausible to argue that those sons who entered the armed forces would accept the political primacy of their titled elder brothers? The absence of clear lines of succession has touched off thousands of disputes and probably hundreds of coups d'etat; primogeniture offered a way out.

One of the striking facts of nineteenth- and twentieth-century colonial history was the relative loyalty of troops stationed overseas (recognizing, to be certain, the military-inspired demise of the French Fourth Republic and the Moroccan base from which Franco moved to Spain). In colonial armies, European-dominated officer corps, in combination with a politically malleable and isolated rank and file, produced (by contrast with Spanish-ruled Latin America) agencies of coercive control unwilling to use their weapons to overturn external rule. The ascriptive and ethnic ties thus important in colonial history were those that linked *officers* to *their* homeland, not the ties that bound the rank and file to their homeland.

In France and Russia prior to their respective revolutions, the officer corps were dominated by nobles, often of doubtful military accomplishments. In 1788 in France, for example, of the 19,578 officers on actual duty, 6,633 were noble; they, plus approximately 2,500 inactive officers carried on the payroll, consumed more than half of the government's annual expenditure![16] The identification of officers with the *ancien régime* and the international repercussions of both revolutions necessitated the development of new armies, led in part by officers of the deposed government under the surveillance of political commissars. Ascriptive ties based on shared aristocratic blood were in part supplanted by ascriptive ties based on bourgeois or proletarian origins. Since these changes were subsumed in the broader development of political parties, they will be examined subsequently.

A distinctive format of civil-military interaction occurs in the nation-in-arms. Though confined historically and geographically to a handful of states in this century—Switzerland, Sweden, Finland, Israel, possibly North Vietnam—the nation-in-arms assures security by means of total participation. Stover has identified four characteristics: universal military training taps the entire eligible population; roles are juxtaposed, in that a citizen becomes a soldier in times of crisis but does not set aside his civilian occupation, role, or ties;[17] government-encouraged civic education is tied closely to military training and defense; organization of the total social and political system, in period of conflict, provides military support.[18]

Given that such total mobilization rests heavily on shared cultural sentiments and historical interactions—in less pretentious terms, on the existence of a "nation"—one might expect the nation-in-arms to arise only in relatively homogeneous societies. The evidence is by no means straightforward, however. Many years ago, Bagehot suggested that "in the early ages of man, war makes nations."[19] In other words, in arms, a nation. Examples ranging as far afield as Sparta, France during the *levée en masse*, and the Zulu kingdom under Shaka furnish apt examples. Rapoport cites the ancient Greek *polis* of Sparta as using a military regimen to achieve civic ends:

> The demands of war and politics can be so similar that if it is possible to teach a man to be a good soldier, he can also be taught how to be a good citizen . . . . By the same token, the good citizen should find it easy to become a good soldier. In all periods of history, many states, especially those which require the full participation of the citizen body in politics utilized the military experience as the best way to educate the citizen to his public responsibilities.[20]

The French mass mobilization of 1793 echoed through that country's history as the most suitable means of inculcating citizens' responsibilities, with Jean Jaurès providing the strongest rationale.[21] Finally, the military innovations of Shaka resulted in basic social alterations. Enhanced fighting effectiveness went hand-in-hand with political centralization and ethnic integration. The most striking consequence of the migrations and conflicts of southern Africa in the nineteenth century was, in the words of one scholar, "the change from the small clan-based tribe to the large kingdom uniting peoples of diverse tribal origin."[22]

The logistical demands of contemporary warfare might appear to obviate the potential political and social advantages of a nation-in-arms. Military efficiency is difficult to maintain with part-time soldiers, the bulk of whose time is passed in civilian pursuits. The success of Israel in its combat and the ability of Finnish troops to fight the Russian army to a standstill in 1939-40 winter war counteract that impression.

A relatively high degree of popular political awareness, enhanced by military service, is central to the nation-in-arms. Thus it should not be surprising that strategists of guerrilla warfare emphasize political mobilization, for successful guerrilla warfare requires an infrastructure of popular support. Mao Tse-tung has frequently spelled out the interlocking nature of military and political organizing. "The Chinese Red Army," he commented in 1929, "is an armed body for carrying out the political tasks of the revolution . . . The Red Army fights not merely for the sake of fighting but in order to conduct propaganda among the masses, organize them, arm them, and help them to establish revolutionary political power."[23] Combining the attractive political objective of land reform with resistance to the Japanese enabled the Chinese Communist Party to establish a foundation of popular support, in the process achieving party control over the armed forces.

Perlmutter has argued that the Israeli combination of a high military participation ratio and role expansion by the armed forces has not resulted in military ascendance over the civil.[24] Although Israel devotes the world's second highest portion of its GNP to the armed forces (25.5 percent in 1972, surpassed only by South Vietnam[25]), and despite the armed forces' extensive involvement in domestic economic, political, and social functions, civilian control has become institutionalized. The long-term influence of David Ben-Gurion (both premier and minister of defense for most of the 1947-63 period) abetted such institutionalization.[26] Implicit in Perlmutter's argument, but meriting further consideration, are certain distinctive features of the Israeli example. Not only was there extraordinary stability in leadership (Ben-Gurion; the Labor party; the Zahal staff); Israel confronted an obvious external challenge, its army was rooted in a series of Jewish self-defense units active in the mandate period, and few significant differences emerged (with the exception of the 1949 resignation of ex-Palmach officers and the 1953-54 Lavon Affair) between civilian and military leaders in the first quarter century of independence. Zahal's political strength was far outstripped by the institutionalization of civilian leadership, which politically ambitious generals sought to join by election rather than intervention. The Israeli example thus presents a distinctive amalgam of high political involvement of the armed forces and its members within a context of civilian control; of a movement away from personalized leadership toward institutionalized control; of high military effectiveness within a setting of reserves; of a nation-in-arms in which military and political imperatives seem not to collide. The Israeli armed forces are integrated with Israeli society and in the process help the society's further integration. Civilian control thus has become institutionalized through the nation-in-arms—though under idiosyncratic circumstances in Israel that cannot readily be generalized to other countries.

SEPARATION FROM SOCIAL FORCES

Colonial history provides support for the assertion that civilian control is enhanced by deliberately isolating the armed forces from the society they defend. Especially in British-ruled areas, recruitment of soldiers often centered on so-called martial peoples, not necessarily drawn from the territory they were to defend. For example, the Indian army under the British Raj drew heavily on Pathans (many from Afghanistan) and Gurkhas (many from Nepal); conversely, some major Indian groups were bypassed on grounds that their members lacked fighting qualities. Certain groups thus became closely linked with the maintenance of British power, which they upheld without questioning the external government control of the military. (That this lack of awareness was sorely tested after World War II with the naval mutiny and the trial of INA soldiers cannot be examined here, for reasons of space. The fact remains that the Indian army was a primary prop of British control up to 1945.) The overriding ethos of obedience undergirded alien rule. Cohen expresses the matter aptly:

> The very fact that the army was drawn from particular castes and classes set these classes well apart. This status brought them into a close relationship to the British and the government, and some groups were encouraged to regard themselves as above the rest ... by the beginning of the twentieth century, the British dominated India and had created a military organization which was reliable, efficient, and relatively immune to external disturbances. ... Its organizational integrity was due to two major accomplishments: the development of a highly competent officer corps and the recruitment of suitable soldiers ... in terms of geographical distribution, the army was grossly unrepresentative .... Most soldiers were middle-class peasants; the camp followers, menials, and porters were composed entirely of the depressed classes and untouchable castes.[27]

In a similar vein, the army of colonial Nigeria remained immune from political involvement. Not questioning British policy, the army of Nigeria "came very near" to carrying out the "ends decreed by its political masters without sentiment or complaint."[28] Miners attributes this loyalty to the British government to four factors: the dominance of British soldiers in the commissioned and non-commissioned ranks; the recruitment of the rank and file from areas untouched by "nationalist agitation"; rotation of units to reduce ties with the local populace; and the isolation of politically conscious Nigerians within the armed forces.[29]

In a callous fashion, one might call "mercenaries" those individual (such as the Gurkhas) drawn to the armed forces by the promise of relative wealth, who were willing to obey without heed to the fate of their supposed fellow countrymen. The epithet is not fully accurate. Their plight has been characterized by van den Berghe (writing on the armies of colonial Africa) as one of "armed and somewhat privileged helots, more or less compelled by circumstances to serve their foreign masters in conquering and subjugating their fellow Africans, usually from other ethnic groups." Consequently, members of such armies "were often regarded by the local civilian populace as hated and despicable tools of the white conquerors."[30] The civilian control thereby maintained rested in the hands of a foreign minority benefiting from the coercive strength of soldiers schooled in obedience and often little else.

Similar processes are by no means unknown in independent countries. The armed forces can be isolated from extensive contacts with civilians and hence isolated from many political and social tensions. As a consequence, the views of officers are paramount in importance, as Chorley noted:

> Experience shows that the process of politically sterilizing the rank and file can be carried through, given favourable conditions of service, to an astonishing degree of success . . . As a result, an enormous reservoir of power is in effect placed at the disposal of officers and can be used by them without let or hindrance to further their own political aims.[31]

Thus presuming integral boundaries between military institutions and social forces, the isolation of the armed forces might not run counter to civilian control, if officers' interests are recognized and protected. With fragmented boundaries between military institutions and social forces, the military cannot be isolated. Under these circumstances, civilian control may well require shared sentiments of class or nationality affecting the behavior of the officer corps and the rank and file alike. (Integral boundaries characterize armed forces whose roles and structures are sharply differentiated from those of other organizations in the social system; interchanges across such boundaries are limited in volume and are controlled by established procedure. Fragmented boundaries, by contrast, mark armed forces with considerably less coherence and autonomy, and whose institutional roles and values are relatively undifferentiated from those found in the environment.)

From the evidence thus far noted, how well do ascriptive factors uphold civilian control? The answer is mixed and more likely negative than positive. Latin America was marked in the nineteenth century by a high degree of ethnic and class identity among the members of the ruling oligarchy and commanders of the armed forces—yet 115 successful changes of government resulted from military uprisings. In the merry-go-round of power, changes occurred only in personnel; "for the masses all that occurred was a change of masters."[32] "Throughout the nineteenth century [successful coup leaders] continued to identify themselves with the propertied elite, often making use of their political offices to amass fortunes and become land owners themselves."[33] Even ethnically homogeneous countries such as Thailand have experienced military intervention. Ascriptive ties provide an unsubstantial foundation upon which to erect a structure of civilian control. The diffuse claims of region, of kinship, or of class affinity must be buttressed by other means of control.

Party Controls and the Impact of Political Revolution

Political revolutions are rare phenomena. Equally rare is civilian control through direct party surveillance of the military establishment and party dominance of decision-making, the party being a product of revolutionary upheaval.

Studies of political party dominance in military affairs have concentrated on the Soviet Union and the People's Republic of China (PRC). Both are governed by single-party systems; both espouse Marxist-Leninist ideologies; both experienced violent revolutions and extensive civil wars; both have attempted to infuse political awareness into the armed forces.

Institutions potentially competitive with the dominant communist party must be subordinated. In instances of party-military conflict, the party should triumph. As Mao Tse-tung asserted in 1929, "Our principle is that the party commands

17

the gun, and the gun must never be allowed to command the party." Translating this conception into reality has never proven easy.

As many scholars have demonstrated, civil-military relations in the USSR and the PRC have fluctuated.[34] The extent of policy autonomy left the armed forces has not been constant. While military effectiveness may be seen by officers as necessitating a high degree of autonomy, political effectiveness may be seen by party leaders as requiring communist party involvement in the internal affairs of the armed forces. Kolkowicz has delineated several factors of "contradictoriness and incompatibility" between party and military:[35]

"Natural" Military Traits	*Traits Desired by the Party*
Elitism	Egalitarianism
Professional autonomy	Subordination to ideology
Nationalism	Proletarian internationalism
Detachment from society	Involvement with society
Heroic symbolism	Anonymity

Like ascriptive ties as opposed to ascriptive isolation, party controls fragment the armed forces' boundaries. Institutional autonomy is reduced. Political criteria interact with strategic considerations in determining military priorities. However, there exist important differences in the impact of ascriptive and party means of "subjective" civilian control. With ascriptive ties extensively utilized, the autonomy of both military and civilian institutions is circumscribed. The claims of kinship and class take precedence over the claims of impersonal criteria. Civilian institutions and military institutions are equally weak, lacking the autonomy and coherence that form important parts of "institutionalization."[36] With party surveillance subordinating the armed forces, it can be argued, political and military institutions have gained some degree of autonomy from ascriptive factors. (This statement, to be certain, presumes that political institutions are staffed more on the basis of achievement than of ascription.) Civilian control based on a dominant political party fragments only the boundary between it and the armed forces.

A successful political revolution, to be won against a determined opponent, requires military as well as political struggle. Either a new army must be created to topple the incumbent government, or parts of the old order's army must be converted to the side of the revolutionaries. Once the new government has been installed, a basic question of control emerges: how can the party command the gun when military accomplishment may have been necessary to topple the *ancien régime* and stabilize the new?

On the surface, Russian and Chinese revolutionary leaders have utilized similar strategies for control. Central to both were 1) political commissars with powers coordinate to, or superior to, "regular" officers in the period of revolutionary combat, 2) recruitment of the rank and file from socially dispossessed groups, 3) election of officers on some occasions, and 4) an ideological aversion (stemming from Marxist-Leninist writings) to standing armies—an aversion not readily harmonized with national defense needs. These factors, in combination, led to distrust of military professionalization. However, contrasts existed and continue to exist between these states; both achieved civilian control by enhancing the power of the communist party, but each gave different scope to the fashions in which the armed forces enjoyed policy prerogatives.

Two strategies of subordinating communist armed forces have been employed: control and education.[37] For the Soviet military, according to Kolkowicz, control affects officers primarily. They must carry out party directives; failure to do so, in the eyes of party leaders, may result in purge.[38] Education is directed more at the rank and file and is intended to secure approval for party policies within the armed forces. This can be approached by recruiting politically reliable individuals, by establishing a hierarchy of party officials parallel to the existing military chain of command, and by avoiding actions that might result in the armed forces' autonomy from party dominance in sensitive matters.

During the Russian revolution, the threats of the Central Powers and later the White armies necessitated the use of "military specialists," selected from officers of the former Imperial and Provisional Government armies. Political commissars ensured these former servants of the czar would not defect with their troops. Political and military expertise were thus vested in different persons and command was dual in nature. The civil war over, the Red Army settled down to a period of modernization, reduction in size, adoption of a mixed cadre-militia framework, and promotion of communist officers. Not until the reforms of Frunze in the mid-1920's were substantial numbers of communists recruited into the officer corps, and the duality of command dropped.[39] By that time, it appeared, no major challenge to the Soviet regime would be mounted by the armed forces. The armed forces were not entangled in the collectivization of the early 1930's. However, party control was brutally enforced in the 1936-38 purges. The heavy hand of the purges fell disproportionately on civil war veterans, who may have enjoyed a basis of prestige apart from the party and Stalin. Erikson suggests that the purge initiated in mid-1937 "was dominated absolutely and almost wholly motivated by political consideration . . . In destroying a potential opposition and crashing this final barrier to untrammelled power, Stalin had done himself a monumental service."[40]

In China, the armed forces (PLA) have rarely enjoyed a degree of autonomy vis a vis the party (CCP). One can look historically at the inherent nature of guerrilla warfare, in which popular support may be more important than logistical or firepower superiority. In his 1929 Kutien speech, for example, Mao Tse-tung criticized "erroneous conceptions," such as a "purely military viewpoint" which regarded military and political affairs as opposed to each other. As Gittings noted, the speech "sets the pattern" for CCP control over the military, because politics becomes all-embracing. "Political work was, and still is, regarded as a totality which embraces all aspects of the army's everyday life, of its cultural, educational, and spare-time activities."[41] Periodic shakeups in the PLA hierarchy—the dismissal of Marshal P'eng in 1959, the dismissal of Marshal Lo in 1966, the mysterious disappearance of Marshal Lin in 1971—testify to party unwillingness to grant the army autonomy.

Soviet and Chinese practices regarding military involvement in domestic affairs differ markedly. The Red Army stood on the sidelines during the agricultural collectivization and was itself a major victim of the purges. The PLA, by contrast, has been periodically summoned by party officials into agricultural production.[42] The armed forces, never far removed from CCP leaders, have played major roles. For example, the 1964 campaign, and the subsequent extensive utilization of PLA personnel in the Cultural Revolution, markedly enhanced the military's role in politics. Chang, for example, portrays the PLA since the 1966 Cultural Revolution as "the dominant political force in China," with "direct military rule" shown by the fact that twenty of the twenty-nine provincial-level party committees drew upon military men as first secretaries.[43] In fact, recent periods of Chinese history seem to exemplify military participation in politics, not influence in politics. The extensive involvement of former guerrilla fighters in the present Cuban government [44] suggests that subordination of the armed forces to the dominant party cannot be readily accomplished even in a communist state; where the *ancien régime* has been forcibly evicted, military leaders have a powerful claim. It is only with the development and popular acceptance of new, legitimate political institutions that they may be curbed.

One can turn to noncommunist states to find other examples of civilian control being developed on the basis of political parties embodying a high degree of legitimacy. An alternative format of party control (though again drawn from a country that experienced violent and extensive revolutionary upheaval) is illustrated by Mexico. Civilian control emerged there through the incorporation of members of the armed services into the dominant party which, over several years, became enshrined as the basis of governmental legitimacy. Mexico appears to bear out Huntington's contention, "Sustained military participation in politics may lead a society away from praetorianism."[45]

For many decades, political supremacy in Mexico has been gained on the battlefield rather than on the hustings. The manifest difficulties of succession led General Plutarco Calles, in his last day as president of Mexico, to found the National Revolutionary Party "to establish a formal code of political succession and thus put an end to battlefield contests for the Presidency."[46] Implicit in these changes was a change from military participation in politics. Under General-cum-President Lazaro

Cardenas, the party was reorganized along occupational lines ("sectors") rather than along geographical lines—and the armed forces became one of the four sectors. Lieuwen deems Cardenas's move a "coup," since the military could be outvoted by the other sectors and since Cardenas could control the selection of all military delegates.[47] After World War II, President Avila Camacho (minister of defense under Cardenas) further pared the military's role in politics by expenditure cuts (from 22 to 14 percent of the national budget), by retiring 550 revolutionary generals, by continuing to stress professionalization, and by reorganizing the party to eliminate the military sector.[48] Conjoined with generous salaries and fringe benefits, as documented in the chapter by Margiotta, these alterations helped keep the military politically quiescent. Military participation in politics was transformed into military influence in politics, based on the increasing legitimacy of civilian and governmental institutions. The gradual acceptance of civilian control thus derived from an astute mixing of such means as promotions and retirements, conscious political organizing, and embodying the rhetoric and legitimacy of the revolution within a widely supported political party. The strength of civilian political institutions came in a few decades to outweigh the political strength of the Mexican military. Military control of politics characteristic early in the century yielded to military participation in politics and (by the late 1940s) to military influence in politics.

Crude or hasty attempts to subordinate the armed forces to a political party may backfire. As stressed at several points in this chapter, the crucial ratio is that of the relative strengths of civilian and military institutions. The West African state of Ghana provides an instructive contrast to Mexico. Whereas the major party in Mexico gained strength and legitimacy with the passage of time, the major party in Ghana lost popular support. At independence (6 March 1957) the Ghanaian government inherited an army schooled in the British tradition of political disengagement and staffed by professional expatriate officers. President Kwame Nkrumah initially favored this form of political sterilization. In a 1962 speech to cadets of the Ghana Military Academy, he proclaimed,

You must have confidence that the Government is
doing what is best for the country, and support it
without question or criticism. It is not the duty of
a soldier to criticize or endeavor to interfere in any
way with the political affairs of the country; he must
leave that to the politicians, whose business it is. The
Government expects you, under all circumstances,
to serve it and the people of Ghana loyally.[49]

Note Nkrumah's emphasis on service to the government, a
stress he later changed. Dissatisfied with the pace of domestic
development, Nkrumah tried to subordinate potentially competitive institutions to his chosen vehicle, the Convention Peoples
Party (CPP). He proclaimed "Ghana is the CPP, and the CPP
is Ghana." The result, as Kraus points out, was "an insistence
upon identification of party with state, the corollary of which
was that the military owed loyalty not only to Ghana but to the
CCP and Nkrumah personally."[50] As a prime mover of the coup
later noted, "If the army was made to identify itself openly with
the Convention Peoples Party and its ideology, it was bound to
lose its self-respect and independence of outlook . . . the army
was virtually at the mercy of the politicians who treated it with
arrogance and open contempt."[51] Among the rankling actions
were a June 1964 order that military personnel join the CCP,
the creation of a counterintelligence unit, the forced retirement of ranking officers, and the establishment of competitive
military organs (notably the President's Own Guard Regiment,
with Russian equipment and training). These steps were not
unusual; comparable ones seemed to work in Mexico. However, the political and social contexts were not analogous. The
CPP lacked the legitimacy of the Mexican revolutionary party;
Nkrumah tried to move too rapidly in subordinating military
institutions; grievances internal to the armed forces interacted
with grievances affecting the political system as a whole. Coup
rather than control resulted. Military control of politics came
to Ghana largely through abortive efforts to change the nature
of civilian control.

Taming the military through subordination to a political
party runs the same risk as any other type of subordination.
Those who are to be controlled may be unwilling to accept

inferior roles. Without widespread acceptance within the armed forces of the appropriateness of civilian control, and without strong, countervailing political institutions, would-be subordination to the party apparat brings unintended consequences. It may be wiser to leave undisturbed the limited responsibilities a military exercises, relying on the habit of obedience to maintain subordination—assuming, that is, that no war threatens and that members of the armed forces accept their responsibilities and funding without undue grumbling.

Geographic and Historical Factors

Given little attention thus far in this chapter have been international factors. Yet no state is an island unto itself, able in its security planning to give heed solely to domestic factors. The political salience of a country's armed forces varies with the perceived significance of security threats. The greater the likelihood of invasion, the larger may be the expenditures and the political significance of the military establishment. States blessed with friendly neighbors, or states whose security can be assured by powerful allies or geographic barriers, may be able to maintain relatively small standing forces—over which civilian control may better be exercised. The absence of a clear external threat diminishes the significance of a country's military, which can be subordinated to government institutions. For the United States, Huntington considers civilian control "a product of geographic isolation and the international balance of power."[52] Facing no hostile army on its own soil after the battle of Bannockburn, the British government could concentrate its defenses in the navy; "This earth of majesty, this seat of Mars" could rely upon the Channel, "a moat defensive to a wall," preserved from the invasion "of less happier lands."

States lacking "natural" or readily defensible frontiers have historically expanded their armed forces to reduce the possibility of successful invasion. Paradoxically, such expansion may enhance civilian control, as in Israel. There, the appropriate locus for military action has been viewed as external, not internal. Rotation through the armed forces of large numbers of civilians reduces a spirit of exclusivity that might facilitate military intervention. Professionalism could function better, but the seriousness of the external threat has led the armed forces to recognize the importance of political as well as military steps. Israeli commanders wield "an enormous influence" in defense and foreign affairs due to the country's "unusually precarious position as a garrison-state"; "the officer corps as a professional group is removed, but is not isolated, from politics."[53] Accordingly, the greater the orientation of the military toward international rather than domestic objectives, the easier may be the establishment and maintenance of civilian control.

It is tempting to hypothesize that neighboring states of relatively equal power, if characterized by mutual hostility, may expand the armed forces' strength, make them national symbols, and (in the process) enhance their political roles. Marked disparity between the military strengths of adjacent countries, conversely, may abet civilian control. If the armed forces are not thought capable of repelling an invasion from a markedly stronger neighbor, or if the state has markedly weaker neighbors, the military may not press to bolster its strength in the name of national security. If directly invaded from the United States, the army of Mexico could do little; it includes but 0.8 percent of males of military age, among the lowest proportions in the world. Nonetheless, with a military establishment of 71,000 men, Mexico clearly outweighs El Salvador (with a total armed forces of 5,630) and Guatemala (with a total armed forces of 11,200).[54] Hostile states with relatively matched military strengths (e.g., India and Pakistan, or Chile and Peru) may be caught in a spiral of escalating tensions and expenditures that enhance the political involvement of the armed forces. On the other side of the argument, to be certain, was rivalry between Germany and France, which resulted in one major and two world wars, but which left the structure of civilian control largely unchanged.

Arguments relating civilian control to external conflict continually run across the paradox of nineteenth-century Latin American militarism. Few conflicts between states rocked that continent; yet civilian control was honored in the breach rather than the observance. There are several possible explanations. Armed revolts, of paramount importance in achieving independence, became enshrined as a chief means of altering government personnel. Confined to dull, repetitious garrison duty, officers enjoyed little scope for their professional skills. Employment in external wars keeps the armed forces apart from the domestic arena; enforced idleness can lead, by contrast, to plotting.

Is the size of the military, both in absolute terms and relative to the particular society, a relevant variable in civilian control? Budgetary allocations lead to some tentative generalizations. According to Nordlinger, countries marked by military control of politics disperse 3.4 to 3.6 percent of gross national product on the military; conversely, countries in which coups d'etat have not occurred spend approximately 1.9 percent.[55] More recent research suggests that Nordlinger has found effect, rather than cause. Dolian, for example, has carefully analyzed expenditure patterns of African governments. The one consistent result of military interventions, he notes, is an increase in military expenditures.[56] Successful coups enable the armed forces to steer government expenditures in directions they deem appropriate—and not surprising they become the major benefactors!

Smallness of a military establishment appears not to preclude successful intervention. As tropical Africa in the past decade has shown, an army as small as 200 can successfully unseat a government. Does this mean that larger armed forces can more readily be controlled by civilians? At the other end of the scale, increasing size and organizational complexity affect the planning and execution of a coup d'etat. It becomes more difficult to build the coalition necessary for successful seizure of control. Needler has suggested, for instance, that greater popular political awareness and greater governmental complexity "have meant that a military coup needs itself to be more carefully planned, and to involve more people if it is to be successful."[57] The likelihood of discovery grows. Widespread political participation may place limits on the extent to which officers can assume political responsibilities, as Finer and Lang note.[58] However, large, modernized, military establishments can intervene and—as Argentina, Brazil, and Portugal illustrate—may have such strength and expertise as to move to military control of politics without the entanglement of civilian allies. Organizational complexity does not preclude coups, although they more likely will be initiated from general rather than field-grade officers.[59]

Whatever the causes for the assertion of civilian control, its maintenance over time endows political institutions with strength and legitimacy. The results are dual. First, members of armed forces may internalize the belief that their subordination is appropriate and should not be lightly set aside. Second, the institutions themselves can better exercise control, their members having gained experience and expertise. The strength and legitimacy of civilian political institutions make possible the maintenance of civilian control. This statement, while it appears utterly simplistic, nonetheless points to a compelling fact. Military intervention in politics has been shown, by Putnam among others, to be closely related to historical trends in particular countries.[60] A state in Latin America marked by intervention early in this century was likely to suffer from continued incursion by the military into the political realm in the 1950s. Patterns of military involvement in politics, to reemphasize a point made earlier, cannot be readily or speedily altered. Arguing by analogy, a government able to exercise control over its armed forces for an extended period benefits from the psychological fact of inertia.

One further area, that of transfer of institutional practices and patterns, merits attention. Although military intervention has erupted in many parts of the former British empire (e.g., Pakistan, Sudan, Burma, Nigeria, Ghana, and Uganda), several Commonwealth states (including some that gained independence after World War II, the so-called "Old Dominions," and Great Britain) enjoy military institutions firmly under civilian control. Something more than chance may account for apparent civil-military harmony in much of the Commonwealth. To put the question crudely, can norms and procedures of civilian control developed under distinctive conditions be successfully transplanted to other historical, geographical, and social settings? In other words, is it possible to reproduce conditions that can restrict the military's political involvement?

Institutions include both formal aspects of organization (e.g., the system of ranks, division among branches of the armed forces) and informal expectations of behavior (e.g., relations between civilians and members of the armed forces). At the risk of oversimplification, the former can be transferred far more readily than the latter. Expectations of behavior vary with factors unique to a particular society. The formal trappings of an organization can be moved; the informal roles and interactions cannot be transferred.

Civilian control emerged in England through a series of gradual steps that, it is obvious, would not apply in the far-flung reaches of the British Empire. Abrams has given the process extensive historic sweep: "effective civilian control was guaranteed sometime in the seventeenth century by sanctions deeply rooted in the social structure . . . Britain avoided producing a self-conscious military caste interested in appropriating power and prestige to itself."[61] The struggle between the Crown and Parliament during the seventeenth century resulted in a split between the militia (under Parliamentary auspices) and the standing army (under royal auspices); by the time of the Glorious Revolution, "the Lords, spiritual and temporal, and Commons, resolved that the raising or the keeping of a standing army within the kingdom in time of peace, unless it be with the consent of Parliament, is against law."[62] Class stratification, with its attendant noblesse oblige, reduced potential friction between officers and politicians—for, after all, they were drawn from the same narrow stratum. The English Channel provided an element of protection. The creation of the police force substantially insulated the British army from domestic disorders, a point noted by Sir John Fortescue, who called the creation of the police the "greatest and most far-reaching military reform" of British history.[63] Imperial expansion provided ambitious subalterns the opportunity to test their military prowess on alien soil. This outlet for energies conceivably could have removed from Great Britain those individuals who, under other circumstances, might have turned their abilities to conspiracy. Finally, the long-standing ethos of the "gifted amateur" conceivably abetted the growth of civilian control. Military professionalization was retarded in Great Britain by comparison with its continental opponents. It took the logistical and tactical blunders of the Crimean War to shock the British government into reform, notably the abolition of the purchase system.[64] Even so, the long-term trend was clear; British officers accepted the ethic of civilian control under the slogan, "Politics is not for soldiers."

In the "Old Dominions," officers found a clear task of "pacifying" indigenous populations that were relatively small (South Africa being the notable exception). As a consequence, the military establishments could remain small; though their duties were in some respects akin to those of the police, there was not a large "native" population over which to lord. The armies of Imperial India or British colonial Africa were notably different. In those territories, unswerving obedience was inculcated through the recruitment to the rank and file of politically reliable and pliable individuals and the staffing of the officer corps by expatriates or by a relatively small proportion of carefully selected indigenous personnel who had imbibed British norms. (Cohen notes, for instance, that Indians sent to Sandhurst before 1932 constituted collectively "the most reliable, politically inert, aristocratic, and conservative group the British could select."[65])

The former colonial armies confronted extraordinary problems of transition after independence was achieved. The comforting assurance that soldiers did not dabble in politics was shattered by events of 1958 in Burma, Pakistan, and Sudan. In each, the support of the commanding officer (Ne Win, Ayub Khan, Ibrahim Abboud) was solicited by a prime minister whose own position had been considerably weakened. The three states moved from civilian control to military participation in politics as a direct consequence of the government leaders' ebbing power base. Full-fledged military control of politics was not long in coming, for the "dual control" situation was unstable: the respective militaries' political strengths far outweighed parties' strengths; only as a consequence of divisive civil war could civilians regain the heights of power.

Sorting through the tasks appropriate to the armed forces has occasioned significant strains between military and civilian leaders. The colonial heritage of unquestioned obedience is no longer blindly accepted by the armed forces; on the other side of the coin, political leaders themselves may not consider the passive support of the military sufficient, given the relative costliness of any military establishment. Both alike may press for changes in the armed forces' responsibilities, the final area for preliminary analysis.

Spheres of Professional Responsibility

Put in simplistic terms, the wider the sphere of responsibilities civilians and soldiers consider appropriate for the armed forces, the greater the possibility of their active involvement in politics. Conversely, the more limited the sphere of responsibilities, the greater the potential for their subordination to civilian control.

A marked trend since World War II, especially in recently independent states, has been role expansion by the armed forces. This role expansion can be attributed to several factors. One is the desire of the armed forces, notably in recently independent states, to remove the stigma of once having supported alien rule. Active involvement in "constructive" undertakings may bring the military in closer touch with the populace. In most cases, the impetus may have come from civilian politicians anxious to find a "productive" use for soldiers. In the absence of significant external or internal security threats, why not turn the military toward development? Second, the training received by officers may encourage them to extend their responsibilities. Pye notes that armies in newly emergent countries "can provide a sense of citizenship and appreciation of political action,"[66] a statement I find ironic, for this appreciation of political action frequently leads to the seizure of power. Third, if the armed forces are "the most modernized public organization in an under-developed country,"[67] their emergence as supreme arbiter of politics should not be unexpected. Role expansion may, finally, be assisted by external aid. Unlike the example of the Philippines, where United States military assistance helped create a politically docile army, the more common result of aid has been indirect encouragement of greater political involvement by the armed forces. An unanticipated consequence of the Alliance for Progress, for example, was encouragement of "civic action" in Latin America.

Transplanted to a different cultural context, "civic action" pressed the armed forces into traditionally nonmilitary roles. In fulfilling these roles, members of the armed forces found themselves thrust into political situations far more complex than those of the barracks setting.

"Civic action" south of the Rio Grande came in a context where the armed forces enjoyed substantial policy prerogatives. Latin America, as McAllister has illustrated, is characterized by wide-ranging military autonomy, guaranteed by the *Estado Militar*.[68] This set of legal guarantees, he asserts, (1) provides the military with a sanctuary in which they can plan political action, (2) imposes a substantial degree of social isolation which guards institutionally derived values and attitudes, and (3) leads to political action by the military to improve their institutional status and prevents circumscription of their privileges, immunities, and budgets.[69] Efforts to abridge the corporate responsibilities of the armed forces without prior agreement from the military may result in more than grumbling: they may lead to intervention. More likely than role contraction, however, is role expansion. Having received or requested responsibility for presiding over extensive social change, the military inherently develops vested interests in political action. Its members are no longer content with constitutional subordination. When accompanied by a sweeping image of duty— "the armed forces conceive of themselves as the creators of the nation and the guardians of the integrity of the national territory"[70]—the sphere of responsibility engulfs the entire political system. (That Israel has combined military role expansion with strong civilian control reinforces the uniqueness of this "garrisoned" state.)

Role expansion can also be viewed as a consequence of professionalization. Abrahamsson has developed arguments that are convincing and important in this context. He delineates two varieties of professionalization within the armed forces, organizational and behavioral. The first ("professionalization $_1$") emerged from the centralization of state authority and the industrial revolution and their concomitants, the decline of the nobility as a recruitment source and technological innovations. The second ("professionalization $_2$") is an on-going process of socialization, including the homogenization of outlooks and behavior. Abrahamsson deems the constituent elements of professionalization$_2$ to be nationalism, pessimistic beliefs about human nature, alarmism, political conservatism, and authoritarianism.[71] He notes that professionalization$_1$ "refers to processes which have led to the establishment of the military as a *pressure* group, whereas professionalization$_2$ turns it into a pressure *group*."[72] The increased cohesion and technical capacity of the armed forces can readily escalate military influence into political participation or possibly into military control of politics.

The narrower the range of responsibilities, it can be argued, the easier the establishment and maintenance of civilian control. To some extent, this assertion is circular. A limited set of duties implies the existence of governmental institutions capable of limiting the armed forces' responsibilities. The ancient question, "Quis custodiet ipsos custodes," is thus partially answered in advance.

Focused responsibilities may mean, however, that the armed forces do not conceive of themselves as guardians of the entire political system. No longer general practitioners to the total body politic, they can carry out their duties as specialists, warding off certain types of infection or challenge. The military thus become part of a broader panoply of institutions sharing general objectives, but concentrating on functionally specific responsibilities. Protection against external attack offers their clearest duty, so long as this responsibility remains disengaged from domestic politics. Accordingly, the more focused the international duties of the armed forces and the clearer the differentiation between their duties and those of police or paramilitary units, the greater the likelihood of civilian control.

The professionalization that has marked all armed forces can be utilized to undergird civilian control, should this professionalization result in technical specialization and institutional complexity oriented toward external military arenas. In simplistic terms, the more complex the armed forces, the greater the organizational obstacles to mounting a successful coup. The sharper the degree of technical specialization, the clearer the criteria for individual and unit professional success, and (more conjecturally) the greater the potential satisfaction of officers. Huntington, for instance, emphasized the instrumental nature of a professional officer who, upon receipt of an order from his authorized superior, "does not argue, he does not hesitate, he does not substitute his own views; he obeys instantly. He is judged not by the policies he implements, but rather by the promptness and efficiency with which he carries them out."[73] Such unswerving obedience admittedly can ease the task of those plotting intervention—but can also be drawn upon by those promoting civilian control. The functional specialization of the military thus provides for narrower, more technical criteria of performance, which can be incorporated within an overall framework of civilian control.

Nonetheless, recognition of technical specialization should carry with it a recognition of the specialist's prerogatives. There should exist, in short, an area of policy autonomy, to make decisions appropriate for the nature of expertise. The power to decide what the military decides should remain in civilian hands, as must most decisions of marked impact, such as declaration of war, acquisition of major new weapons systems, or military alliances. Below such key areas lie many points for military decision, such as troop deployment, policies on recruitment and promotion, and internal organization. It is better, perhaps, to trade a sphere of policy autonomy for acceptance of the paramountcy of the state. France provides a case in point. Ralston has suggested that the army of the Third Republic initially traded internal autonomy for a "cult of obedience." Officers could continue to be drawn disproportionately from Catholic and aristocratic backgrounds; in return for preserving this bastion of privilege, the army would remain *la grande muette*. To French officers, "the primary desire was for independence in their own special sphere. This did not necessarily preclude governmental intervention in, or surveillance over, military affairs."[74]

Such a noli-me-tangere attitude may in fact furnish a convenient intermediate point. Institutional values of the armed forces can be preserved, face can be saved, and certain prerogatives safeguarded. Particularly where the majority of a military establishment cannot be replaced in a short period (as occurred in the revolutions noted above), a long-term policy of clearly defining, and thereby delimiting, the armed forces' responsibilities seems in order. Recognition of spheres of autonomy conforms with the impact of professionalization. Expertise and corporate solidarity are enhanced, recognition of which would appear to be the height of political realism.

Problems of subordination are greatest where the armed forces have traditionally exercised wide-ranging political responsibilities, and where changes in military doctrine and equipment have abetted role-expansion. Many states of Africa and Latin America confront the unenviable challenge of reducing the political strength of powerful military institutions though they lack civilian institutions capable of meeting the challenge. The best strategy would be a long-term, patient process of establishing gradually narrowing areas in which the armed forces would exercise their professional prerogatives. Limited rather than broad conceptualizations of the military's role accord better with civilian control. Despite the pleas of those who see the armed forces as unparalleled purveyors of modernization, the resultant role-expansion has profound political repercussions. Involving the armed forces in the building of political institutions moves the camel's nose considerably further inside the tent. Few developing countries share the advantages of Israel, where the military's active intervention is precluded by the institutionalized legitimacy of the civilian-directed political system—backed up by the not inconsiderable factors of the rapid turnover of officers, the absorptive capacity of the economy, the economic and social integration of veterans, the dependence on the reserve system, the identity of civilian and military goals, and the army's professionalism.[75]

Conclusion

More than a third of the member states of the United Nations currently are ruled by governments installed by military intervention. The overwhelming majority of these countries are "developing"—that is to say, characterized by a per capita gross national product well below $1,000, with largely agricultural or enclave industrial economies, with a congeries of languages and a corresponding lack of national integration, and (particularly in Africa and Asia) with a brief span of independence during which political institutions could be stabilized. Civilian control is thus the exception in the Third World.

But exceptions, as the adage goes, prove the rule. The means used to subordinate the military utilized in countries as important and diverse as China, India, the Philippines, or Guyana merit close study. Limits on the extent of military involvement in politics *can* be implemented in developing countries (*whether* they should be is a different question), and by detailed analysis, prescriptions for effective civilian control can be devised. The remainder of this book is devoted to such analysis and recommendations.

Thus far, the following general points have been presented:

1) Armed forces inherently are political institutions.

2) A continuum of interactions exists between civilians and members of the armed forces, with the result that civilian control of the military is never absolute, nor military control of politics ever total.

3) The nature and extent of civilian control vary markedly in accordance with historic, geographic, social, and political factors.

4) Of several potential bases for civilian control of the military, the strongest comes through the legitimacy and effectiveness of government organs.

To amplify and amend these observations, it is necessary to delve into the political histories of individual states. The following pages are written by area specialists, who examine the means of civilian control discussed in this chapter in ten different countries.

External and international pressures directly affect civil-military relations in individual states. Effective civilian control in the Philippines, Goldberg suggests in chapter 4, demonstrated the influence of the United States. However, this result may have stemmed more from encouragement of civil administrative agencies and political parties than from encouragement of civilian supremacy among the armed forces. President Marcos's declaration of martial law in 1972 has expanded the military's size and responsibilities; external pressures played little part. By contrast, Buck argues in chapter 6 that two profound transformations occurred in Japanese civil-military relations as a result of international pressure. The first transformation, in the early years of the Meiji Restoration, paved the way for rampant militarism; the second, immediately following World War II, resulted in strong civilian control and a greatly diminished political role of the armed forces. The Japanese Self-Defense Forces (SDF) exercise a limited mission within strong constitutional constraints. And, to be certain, the British heritage in India and Malaysia supported civilian control.

Several chapters touch on an issue of central importance to many developing countries, ethnic pluralism. Where members of one group dominate the organs of government but are a minority in the society as a whole, "subjective" civilian control (to return to Huntington's terminology) suffers built-in limitations. Guyana and Malaysia are plural societies par excellence. Enloe demonstrates in chapter 3 that civilian control of the military in such settings may turn into civilian dependence on the military—and it is an open question "whether the controlled effectively control the groups that the controllers want controlled." India offers evidence suggesting the limitations on "subjective" civilian control. As outlined by Cohen in chapter 2, the armed forces have stood above the regional and state loyalties characteristic of contemporary Indian politics. The isolation of the armed forces from social and political pressures has enhanced civilian control. For Lebanon, an ethnically and religiously plural middle class has (up to mid-1975) avoided resorting to coercion in maintaining its control. A small and (until recently) volunteer army has remained under close legislative supervision. According to Baaklini in chapter 9, the legislature itself has achieved political legitimacy, now being sorely tested by domestic strife.

Civilian control may arise through political revolution, most notably through party surveillance and infiltration of the military establishment. The People's Republic of China provides a case in point. In chapter 5, Chang discusses the growing political responsibilities of the People's Liberation Army, noting that civilian control can be achieved and maintained only by continuous and diligent efforts. When key party leaders disagree, or become deadlocked in struggle, the political influence of the PLA increases. Personal loyalty given to Mao Tsetung must be supplanted by institutional loyalty to the party.

The need for several simultaneous approaches to civilian control emerges from several countries. In Mexico, analyzed by Margiotta in chapter 8, the governing elite has employed a skillful mixture of pay-off and cooptation. A gradual institutionalization of politics has permitted a gradual transition from military control toward civilian control since the revolution. The armed forces were kept involved in politics, but under the aegis of the dominant party, PRI. The long-term installation of governmental control over the Finnish armed forces did not involve subordination to a strong political movement. Nonetheless, as Stover comments in chapter 7, the interwar history of Finland holds several lessons for developing countries. Widespread political violence—class conflict, civil war, aborted coups d'etat, and external military pressure—complicated the tasks of civilian and military leaders alike. That such leaders do not always succeed in attaining civilian control emerges in chapter 10, in which Michaels illustrates how the Chilean government of Salvador Allende attempted to "buy" the acquiescence of the armed forces at a time of escalating class tension. The military's initial willingness to accept Allende and his policies was followed by politicization of the armed forces, in which several plots preceded the coup d'etat of September 1973.

In the face of these contrasting strategies of civilian control, what strategy might be formulated for developing countries characterized by military control of politics? The final chapter of this book sketches a set of steps—some hortatory and symbolic, others dependent on imponderable social and economic factors—that could make possible the political subordination of the armed forces. But the view expressed in this section, as in the preceding ones, is not optimistic. The problems of creating politically legitimate institutions, capable of achieving and maintaining oversight of the military, are enormous. "Who will guard the guards themselves" remains a question as appropriate in the last quarter of the twentieth century as when posed 2000 years ago.

Notes to Chapter 1
Welch, *Civilian Control of the Military.*

1. Claude E. Welch, Jr., and Arthur K. Smith, *Military Role and Rule* (North Scituate: Duxbury Press, 1974), p. 6.

2. Samuel P. Huntington, "Civilian Control of the Military: A Theoretical Statement," in Heinz Eulau, Samuel J. Eldersveld, and Morris Janowitz, eds., *Political Behavior: A Reader in Theory and Research* (Glencoe: Free Press, 1956), p. 380.

3. S.E. Finer, *The Man on Horseback* (New York: Praeger, 1962), pp. 148-51.

4. *Ibid.*, pp. 158-63.

5. Kurt Lang, *Military Institutions and the Sociology of War* (Beverly Hills: Sage, 1972), pp. 224-29.

6. Carl von Clausewitz, *On War* (London: Routledge and Kegan Paul, 1966), Vol. III, p. 125.

7. Partial texts of the constitutions cited in this paragraph appear in Leslie Wolfe-Phillips, *Constitutions of Modern States* (New York: Praeger, 1968).

8. James Clotfelter, *The Military in American Politics* (New York: Harper and Row, 1973), p. 150.

9. Quoted in Samuel P. Huntington, *The Soldier and the State: The Theory and Politics of Civil-Military Relations* (New York: Vintage, 1964), p. 437.

10. Lyle N. McAlister et al., *The Military in Latin American Sociopolitical Evolution: Four Case Studies* (Washington: Center for Research in Social Systems, 1970), p. 39.

11. Victor Villanueva, *El militarismo en el Peru*, p.298; cited in McAllister, *The Military*, p.40.

12. Eric A. Nordlinger, "Soldiers in Mufti: The Impact of Military Rule upon Economic and Social Change in the Non-Western States," *American Political Science Review* 64, 4 (1970): p.1135.

13. Gaetano Mosca, *The Ruling Class* (New York: McGraw Hill, 1939), p.228.

14. *Ibid.*, p.229.

15. Huntington, "Civilian Control," p.380; cf. *The Soldier and the State*, pp.80-85.

16. Alfred Vagts, *A History of Militarism, Civilian and Military* (New York: Free Press, 1959, revised edition), pp. 53-61.

17. I am tempted to paraphrase George Washington's observation, "When I became a soldier, I did not set aside the civilian."

18. William J. Stover, "Civil-Military Interaction in the Nation in Arms: The Relationship Between Armed Forces and Political Authority in Finland 1917-1939" (Ph.D. dissertation, SUNY/Buffalo, 1974), pp. 15-16.

19. Walter Bagehot, *Physics and Politics*, quoted in *Ibid.*, p. 26.

20. David C. Rapoport, "A Comparative Theory of Military and Political Types," in Samuel P. Huntington, ed., *Changing Patterns of Military Politics* (New York: Free Press, 1962), pp. 79-80.

21. Welch and Smith, *Military Role and Rule*, pp. 207-8.

22. J.D. Omer-Cooper, *The Zulu Aftermath* (Evanston: Northwestern University Press, 1966), p. 172.

23. Mao Tse-tung, "On Correcting Mistaken Ideas in the Party," *Selected Works* (Peking: Foreign Languages Press), Vol. I, p. 106. (Written in December 1929).

24. Amos Perlmutter, *Military and Politics in Israel: Nation-Building and Role Expansion* (London: Frank Cass, 1969).

25. United States Arms Control and Disarmament Agency, *World Military Expenditures 1972*, reproduced in Welch and Smith, *Military Role and Rule*, pp. 280-81.

26. Perlmutter, *Military and Politics,* p. 54.

27. Stephen P. Cohen, *The Indian Army: Its Contribution to the Development of a Nation* (Berkeley: University of California Press, 1971). pp. 50, 54-5.

28. N.J.Miners, *The Nigerian Army 1956-1966* (London: Methuen, 1971), p. 100.

29. *Ibid*, pp. 100-101.

30. Pierre L. van den Berghe, "The Military and Political Change in Africa," in Claude E. Welch, Jr., ed., *Soldier and State in Africa* (Evanston: Northwestern University Press, 1970), pp. 258-59.

31. Katharine Chorley, *Armies and the Art of Revolution* (London: Faber, 1943), p. 241.

32. Edwin Lieuwen, *Arms and Politics in Latin America* (New York: Praeger, 1961, revised edition), p. 22.

33. *Ibid.*, p. 25.

34. See, *inter alia,* John Erickson, *The Soviet High Command: A Military-Political History 1918-1941* (London: St. Martin's, 1962); Roman Kolkowicz, *The Soviet Military and the Communist Party* (Princeton: Princeton University Press, 1967), and D. Fedotoff White, *The Growth of the Red Army* (Princeton: Princeton University Press, 1944); plus John Gittings, *The Role of the Chinese Army* (London: Oxford University Press, 1967), Ellis Joffe, *Party and Army: Professionalism and Political Control in the Chinese Officer Corps 1949-1964* (Cambridge: East Asian Research Center, 1965), and William W. Whitson, *The Chinese Communist High Command, 1928-1970: A History of Military Politics* New York: Praeger, 1972).

35. Kolkowicz, *The Soviet Military*, p. 21.

36. Samuel P. Huntington, *Political Order in Changing Societies* (New Haven: Yale University Press, 1968) pp. 12-24.

37. Gittings, *The Role of the Chinese Army*, p. 105.

38. Kolkowicz, *The Soviet Military*, p. 30. Kolkowicz aptly differentiates among "positive" measures (privileges and allowances for offices; cooptation into highest party councils), "prophylactic" measures (indoctrination, supervision, manipulation, and the deliberate creation of unease and distrust), and "negative" measures (coercion, intimidation, dismissal). *Ibid.*, pp. 29-30.

39. Erickson, *The Soviet High Command*, pp. 174, 191.

40. *Ibid.,* pp. 470, 474.

41. Gittings, *The Role of the Chinese Army*, pp. 103-105.

42. Edward L. Dreyer, "Military Continuities: The PLA and Imperial China," in William W. Whitson, ed., *The Military and Political Power in China in the 1970's* (New York: Praeger, 1972), p. 21.

43. Parris H. Chang, "Changing Patterns of Military Roles in Chinese Politics," in Whitson, *The Military and Political Power*, pp. 65, 62n.

44. Jorge I. Dominguez, "The Civic Soldier: The Military as a Governing Institution in Cuba," in Catherine M. Kelleher, ed., *Political Military Systems: Comparative Perspectives* (Beverly Hills: Sage, 1974), pp. 209-38.

45. Huntington, *Political Order*, p. 243.

46. Edwin Lieuwen, *Mexican Militarism: The Political Rise and Fall of the Revolutionary Army 1910-1940* (Albuquerque: University of New Mexico Press, 1968), p. 102.

47. *Ibid.*, p. 125.

48. *Ibid.*, p. 144.

49. "Politics is not for Soldiers" (Accra: Government Publishing Company, 1962).

50. Jon Kraus, "Arms and Politics in Ghana", in Welch, *Soldier and State in Africa*, p. 183. Also see Valerie Plave Bennett, "The Intransferability of Patterns of Civil-Military Relations: The Case of Ghana" (Buffalo: Council on International Studies, State University of New York at Buffalo, Special Study No. 20, 1972).

51. Col. A.A. Afrifa, *The Ghana Coup, 24th February 1966* (New York: Humanities Press, 1966), pp. 99-100.

52. Huntington, *The Soldier and the State*, p. 189.

53. Perlmutter, *Military and Politics,* pp. 119, 125.

54. Welch and Smith, *Military Role and Rule*, p. 279.

55. Nordlinger, "Soldiers in Mufti," p. 1135.

56. James P. Dolian, "The Military and the Allocation of National Resources: An Examination of Thirty-Four Sub-Sahara African Nations," paper presented at the International Studies Association Meeting, New York, 14-17 March 1973, p. 19: increases marked eight of the eleven states in the group.

57. Martin C. Needler, "Political Development and Military Intervention in Latin America," *American Political Science Review* 60, 3 (1966): 620.

58. Finer, *The Man on Horseback,* pp. 25-28; Kurt Lang, "The Military Putsch in a Developed Political Culture: Confrontations of Military and Civil Power in Germany and France," in Jacques van Doorn, ed., *Armed Forces and Society* (The Hague: Mouton,1968), pp. 202-228.

59. Welch and Smith, *Military Role and Rule*, p. 243.

60. Robert D. Putnam, "Toward Explaining Military Intervention in Latin American Politics," *World Politics* 20, 1 (1967): 83-110.

61. Philip Abrams, "Democracy, Technology, and the Retired British Officer," in Samuel P. Huntington, ed., *Changing Patterns of Military Politics* (New York: Free Press of Glencoe, 1962), p. 150.

62. Reprinted in David B. Ralston, *Soldiers and States: Civil-Military Relations in Modern Europe* (Boston: D.C.Heath, 1966), p. 59.

63. Sir John Fortescue, *History of the British Army*, cited in David C. Rapoport, "The Political Dimensions of Military Usurpation," *Political Science Quarterly* 83,4 (December 1968): 570n.

64. Huntington, *The Soldier and the State*, p. 43n.

65. Cohen, *The Indian Army*, p. 119.

66. Lucian W. Pye, *Aspects of Political Development* (Boston: Little, Brown, 1966), p. 182.

67. *Ibid.*, p. 186.

68. McAlister, *The Military*, p. 9.

69. *Ibid.*

70. *Ibid*, p. 46.

71. Bengt Abrahamsson, *Military Professionalization and Political Power* (Beverly Hills: Sage, 1971), pp. 26-79.

72. *Ibid.,* p. 155.

73. Huntington, *The Soldier and the State*, p. 73.

74. David B. Ralston, *The Army of the Republic: The Place of the Military in the Political Evolution of France, 1871-1914* (Cambridge: M.I.T. Press, 1967), p. 3.

75. Perlmutter, *The Military and Politics*, p. 126.

Civilian Control
of the Military in India

Stephen P. Cohen

Stephen P. Cohen is presently associate professor of Political Science and Asian Studies at the University of Illinois at Urbana-Champaign. He is the author of *The Indian Army* and numerous articles and monographs dealing with South Asian military problems and US foreign policy. He has served as a consultant for ACDA and the Murphy Commission and is now working on a study of regional proliferation, security, and arms control problems. His field work has included three years' research in India and Bangladesh and one year in Japan.

Introduction

According to conventional expectations the presence of firm, stable, and authoritative civilian control over the military in India is an anomaly. Economically, India ranks near the bottom of the less-developed states with a per capita income of $98. Even this meager amount is maldistributed by region, social class, and level of urbanization, skewing Indian society so that the very rich and the very poor are equally conspicuous.

Culturally and socially, it is difficult to understand how India's political system can rest upon such a diverse multilingual and multiethnic society, let alone manage to support a unified and obedient military organization of over a million men. Regional and linguistic differences are further complicated by a unique Indian phenomenon, the caste system, which has thrived and flourished in an era of mass political participation.[1] But this, too, does not seem to hinder civilian control of the Indian military.

Finally, when we turn to Pakistan for comparative illumination, the Indian puzzle grows. Why should one state have been dominated by the military for most of her independent history and the issue barely have arisen in the other when they are so closely matched in a number of ways? India and Pakistan have similar economies, both are culturally diverse nation-states, and above all the Indian and Pakistani armies share a common origin in the British Indian Army.[2] Why, then, were the Pakistan generals so eager to seize control over the state while their Indian counterparts (in many cases personal friends) were content to remain in a position of subordination which exceeded the strictest Western standards of civilian control?

We have two short answers to these questions. First, the Indian leadership was fortunate (as was the Pakistani) in having available a body of doctrine, theory, and control mechanisms which they inherited from their British predecessors. Second, the Indians—unlike the Pakistanis—ruthlessly applied these theories of civilian control in the years following independence and continue to do so today. This chapter will examine both the theories and doctrines which presently justify civilian control over the military in India, and the numerous devices and control mechanisms which have been developed and applied in that state. These mechanisms will further indicate why the Indian system works and indeed how some of its apparent contradictions and weaknesses may have aided in the imposition and maintenance of civilian control. Before taking a detailed look at contemporary Indian civil-military relations, however, it is important to note some salient features of British India, the predecessor of both present-day India and Pakistan.

Historical Antecedents: The Military in British India

The history of civil-military relations in British India is a long and complicated story which we have elsewhere analyzed in detail.[3] Here two processes are worthy of special attention: the establishment of "normal" relations between British civilians and British officers of the Indian army and the induction of Indians into this process prior to British withdrawal from the subcontinent.

Any colonial situation is by definition abnormal or unusual when compared to the home politics of the imperial power. Two general problems must be faced: whether or not colonial subjects are to be granted equal treatment in law or fact and whether the relationship between representatives of the imperial power is to parallel that which obtains at home. The first problem has been the focus of much historical analysis, but the second usually preceded and had some impact on the former.

In British India the issue of civilian control was live and relevant for almost 150 years: it took that long for the British to conclude that civil-military relations in India were to follow the British pattern as closely as possible. The turning point was the notorious Kitchener-Curzon dispute of 1905, in which the arrogant and brilliant civilian, Lord Curzon, was effectively forced from the viceroy's palace by Britain's most distinguished imperial officer, Kitchener (who was not, however, a member of the *Indian* army). Despite the victory of the military in this crisis (or, more accurately, because of it) civilian officials in India and Great Britain obtained effective control of Indian affairs, civil and military. India had been a military preserve in many ways, and elements of this lingered on right until independence. But they no longer dominated after 1910, as civilians established both fiscal and administrative control over the military.

This was a fortuitous development because shortly after the British put their own house in order selected Indians joined them on both the civil and military sides. Indians had been brought into the Indian Civil Service as early as the nineteenth century, but did not appear in substantial numbers until the 1920s and 1930s.[4] While they were kept away from operational military matters per se, they did gain considerable experience in fiscal and administrative aspects of military policy.

On the military side, Indians were increasingly commissioned as regular officers in the Indian army after World War I. As was true of their civilian counterparts these Indians were very carefully chosen by the British. However, whereas competition for the Indian Civil Service was largely nondiscriminatory, the criteria applied to Indians seeking entry into the officer corps were quite special. Not only were candidates required to pass the standard examinations covering intelligence and physical aptitude, but they were also carefully screened according to their social and family background.[5] The British were interested in seeing that the prospective Indian officer conformed to their notion of the "right type" of officer. This man was quite conservative, but not outspoken; he was obedient; he came from a wealthy, landed, aristocratic background, which eased his adjustment to the semifeudal Indian army; he came from a "martial" community, such as the Sikhs, Jats, Punjabi Muslims, or Rajputs; he was a "gentleman."[6] In short, he was a willing, talented, reliable tool, who was not expected to innovate.

The training given Indian officer candidates reinforced their conservative social predilections. Many were initially sent to Sandhurst, where they underwent the same course as the British. Later, when this became politically and administratively impractical, Indians were given an even more rigorous military education at the Indian Military Academy in Dehra Dun. This education stressed loyalty to the regiment, to the officer corps, to the viceroy, and to the king. Once officers reached their units this process of formal and informal socialization continued. Young Indian officers were reminded of their obligations and duties in various service courses and, above all, through the institution of the officers' mess. By and large this process was successful. Given the hypocrisy and racism of many British officers, it is surprising that few Indian officers defected to the Germans and Japanese during World War II.[7]

While the substance of an officer's education specifically excluded consideration of "political" matters, it must not be thought that Indian army officers—British or Indian—were in fact totally apolitical. It was quite clear that British rule ultimately rested on the loyalty of the army, which was, after all, almost entirely Indian in composition. The army itself was being used for a variety of quasi-political tasks, ranging from "aid to the civil" to de facto governance of frontier regions. These activities, however, were usually defined as nonpolitical.

In addition, recruitment to the military itself was a reward to loyal sectors of Indian society, who were in effect collaborating with the British against their more militant and politically active countrymen. The typical Indian officers of the pre-independence period went along with the scheme of things. Some did this because they were genuinely loyal to the British and some because they realized that when freedom came, their services would be useful for an independent India. Most, however, were apathetic, content to pursue a rather pleasurable and rewarding career.

Civilian Control in Modern India

From the very first day of independence, Indian leaders have been privately if not publicly concerned about civil-military relations. Their chief task was to reshape what was a fairly compatible imperial civil-military relationship to suit their new state. While there have been failures in economic and foreign policy, they succeeded in this area beyond all expectations.

Not only does India have civilian "control," it has an almost crushing civilian dominance over a very powerful and large military. This is a situation almost without parallel in the Third World—how is it maintained? What control devices and mechanisms have been employed in India? To what extent has civilian control been the result of chance and luck, and to what extent is it due to deliberate planning and policy? Answers to these questions will emerge as we consider a broad range of means by which civilian control is maintained.[8]

CONSTITUTIONAL CONSTRAINTS

Like virtually all "new" states India has a formal constitution; unlike most of them the written document has been relevant to an understanding of the political system in general and the maintenance of civilian control in particular.[9] Following British practice formal control over the military rests in the monarch-substitute, the president, although de facto control is exercised by the elected prime minister and cabinet. Moreover, the Constitution reserves the defense of India exclusively to the Union government, and no Indian state has ever seriously contem-

47

plated the development of a military or paramilitary force without Union permission. There is no opportunity in the system for ambitious officers to create their own satrapies outside Union government supervision.

To further enhance civilian dominance, steps were taken after independence to create a balance of power among the three armed services. Under the British, the Indian army was numerically and politically more powerful than the Royal Indian Air Force and Royal Indian Navy combined. The commander-in-chief of the Indian army had a special advisory function vis a vis the government of India and was a member of the cabinet.

Not only did the Indian government make the three services legally equal after independence, but it has also striven to exaggerate the relative influence and power of the chiefs of the two weaker services—the Indian air force and the Indian navy—at the expense of the numerically dominant army. The three service heads are all designated chiefs of staff and the Indian government abolished the position of commander-in-chief, which had been held by the senior-most Indian army general, whose responsibilities included all three services. Further, the chairman of the joint chiefs is always the officer with the longest period of tenure, which has often meant that he has been an air force or navy officer.[10] In brief, this has partially redressed the natural imbalance between the army and the two other services, providing civilian leadership with substantial leverage over the army.

ASCRIPTIVE FACTORS

Recruitment to the officer corps in India is done entirely on the basis of standardized written and oral examinations: there are no regional, class, or ethnic restrictions. However, the *medium* in which the recruitment and examination process takes place is the English language; this alone serves as a powerful selective mechanism and restricts the officer corps recruitment base to a fairly narrow segment of the Indian population. The officer class is unrepresentative in social and regional terms, being skewed towards an urban and northern recruitment base.[11]

Further, the potential officer is trained via the English language, and the military have been permitted to maintain a lifestyle and professional environment which closely resembles that of the Indian army forty years ago, complete with swagger sticks and British accents.[12] All of this, which has often been criticized in Parliament as un-Indian, serves to *encourage* differences between the officer and his Indian environment making it more difficult for him to build alliances across the culture gap.

To further prevent the development of monolithic power in the army, some attention has apparently been given to ensuring that officers from "nonmartial" regions of India are overrepresented in higher command positions. This is not entirely due to planning on the part of civilian officials, for such over-representation occurred under the British as a result of the recruitment and examination process (Bengalis, Tamils, and others from areas of high literacy tended to do somewhat better than Punjabis and Rajputs). But this alone does not explain the disproportionate number of South Indians, Bengalis, and other non-Punjabis in senior positions, especially that of the chief of the army staff.[13] No caste, region, or religion can hold a proprietary view of any position with the Indian army. This is especially true for the numerically dominant Punjabi Hindus and Sikhs. When senior positions do open up there is a natural amount of lobbying on the part of various groups within the army, but final decisions are made by civilians.

PARTY CONTROL

Although India is a functioning democracy and does not have anything approaching a monolithic or one-party system, it has had one dominant party since independence, and this has helped maintain civilian control.[14] Obviously, with a great and politically powerful Congress party providing stable leadership since 1947, the military has had little room for maneuver—even if it wished to do so. The contrast with Pakistan is quite sharp. Yet, the dominance of Congress has furthered civilian control in a number of other, subtle ways.

Because it has been secure in its own power, the leadership of Congress has never felt it necessary to impose any ideological or political viewpoint upon the military itself, avoiding a potentially dangerous area of disagreement. The military are merely required to conform to a generalized secular nationalism and remain aloof from internal political affairs.

And because Congress dominates most of the state governments as well as the Union government and bureaucracy it is in a position to offer a wide range of rewards and punishments to individual officers. One of the most important rewards is postservice employment, particularly for officers who retire in the prime of life. The search for a second career can be eased considerably by the right "connections" in the government, which controls an enormous and ever-expanding number of senior executive positions in various state-controlled enterprises. These posts have been liberally distributed to generals with cooperative career patterns, and such men can be found throughout India, smoothly reintegrated into civilian society. A "maverick" officer must be independently wealthy or well-connected if he is to survive the postservice competition for suitable executive positions.

GEOGRAPHIC AND HISTORICAL FACTORS

Since independence a number of functions of the military in India have been reduced or performed so as to actually enhance civilian control. This has happened despite wars between India and Pakistan, India and China, and the Indian occupation or seizures of Goa, Hyderabad, Bangladesh, and Kashmir.[15] One might have expected the expansion, rather than the contraction, of military involvement in politics. Yet civilian control has been maintained — indeed, strengthened — during these conflicts because several geographic and historical factors came together, three of which are worthy of special note here.

The high incidence of conflict in south Asia has meant that the Indian military are continuously circulated throughout India. An average tour of duty will rarely exceed two years in one place; for infantry and other combat units there may be a stretch of absolute isolation in some Himalayan position.[16] North Indian units are shuffled so that they serve an occasional tour of duty in the south, the few units with substantial south

Indian representation see most of their service in the north. This practice began with the British, who wanted to ensure that troops of a particular caste or region were not used to suppress disorders among their kinsmen. Such shifts are part of the ordinary requirements of good military practice as well, but certainly the near-continual movement of officers and individual units has made control somewhat easier.

A second historical factor which has enhanced civilian control has been the large *size* and low sophistication of the Indian military.[17] This has meant that officers can be trained almost entirely within India itself, the only exceptions being routine exchange programs or training in very specialized or advanced equipment.[18] Thus, an Indian military career is highly self-contained, and the bulk of the officer corps in all three services do not often encounter military officers from the major powers. Here official policy is quite clear; it calls for the minimum amount of such contact. Indian civilians were quite impressed by the ties that developed between the Pakistani and American military and the ways in which these ties were used by Pakistani officers to gain power. They have made it very difficult for foreign military personnel to mix with Indian officers except on the most superficial basis; this was true for Americans even during the period when the US was providing substantial amounts of military equipment to India (1962-65).[19] There have been strong public protests over brief contacts between Indian and Pakistani generals during border demarcation talks. Indian civilian officials are very sensitive about this entire issue; they fear "informal penetration" of their own system through military links and the subsequent political contamination of their own officers. Therefore, they have simply reduced contacts to the bare minimum.

A third historical factor is of a different order and magnitude than either of the above two. It is the emergence of India since independence as a unified state with a particular social and political system: in brief, the very environment in which the Indian military are required to function.

It has frequently been noted that India is an extraordinarily diverse and heterogeneous state. It is also a very disorderly one. There is an intimate relationship between the maintenance of national integrity in the face of such disorder and diversity and the military itself.

The armed forces stand as a permanent and effective deterrent against regional breakaway. They are centrally recruited and trained (even though certain regions tend to dominate both the officer corps and the ranks). No region or state in India has the authority to maintain armed forces or even armed police forces on its own. The elites of those large states which might consider autonomy (Tamilnad, West Bengal) cannot escape the simple fact that short of a national breakup for other reasons they could never succeed in asserting even semi-independent status. New Delhi has responded to such assertions in Nagaland and Kashmir with the ruthless and effective application of force; whatever else happens to India it will not break up as long as the ultimate power of coercion remains intact.

In the second place, the armed forces are important for the maintenance of civil order in the states. This is a task they inherited from the British. It is no more appreciated now than before, but it is no less vital. Since independence several layers of police and armed police forces have been established in each of the states,[20] which have usually been adequate to enforce civil order. On occasion, however, the military has been called in when disruptions exceed the capacity of the armed police; at least on one recent occasion the police have rebelled and the military were used to coerce *them*.[21] This may become a common occurrence and emphasizes the importance of the military for the maintenance of an orderly (if not always democratic) political system.

Finally, the military have been politically important in India as a *symbol* of national unity and integrity. They project a powerful image of quiet competence and efficiency. This image is all the more important since the military are one of the truly all-Indian organizations in which caste, class, religion, and race are subordinated (but not eliminated) in favor of a higher national purpose.

In abstract terms these contributions of the military to the Indian political system may have nothing to do with civilian control. The military deter separatism, maintain domestic order, and act as a national symbol in states which are not controlled by civilians; one can argue the fact that if the military does do all these things, and if they are important, it may *enhance* military influence and weaken civilian control. This was the pattern in Pakistan, where the military grew weary of rescuing an allegedly incompetent and ineffective civilian leadership. Here, India may be a unique case. It is so large, diverse, and heterogeneous, and the example of Pakistan is so vivid and relevant, that very few Indian officers have felt that they were competent enough to manage the Indian political system. While it has become a cliche of Indian political life, it is probably true that the only political system that could operate with some success is pluralist democracy, at least for the foreseeable future. While the military themselves are a fairly representative body, have all-India ties, speak the same link language (English), and tend to share a common perspective, they do know their own limitations. Thus there is a connection between the military's state-maintenance functions and civilian control: they willingly carry out such tasks today so that they will not be called on to intervene more deeply tomorrow. And by and large they have permitted civilian leaders to make the determination of when their assistance is required.

SPHERES OF RESPONSIBILITY : CIVILIAN EXPERTISE AND MILITARY ROLE

A final, and perhaps central, factor in the maintenance of civilian control in India has been the role accorded the military since independence. Civilians have systematically attempted to reduce the prominence of the military in Indian public life. Under the British it was clearly seen as a main prop of colonial rule and the symbols and status accorded the military were correspondingly powerful. Since 1947 both have been gradually but steadily reduced. The formal order of precedence has been adjusted so that senior generals rank below cabinet officers; as we have noted, the rank of commander-in-chief was abolished, and the military have no representation in the Indian cabinet. Parades, flypasts, and assemblies are all stage-managed so that civilian officials receive a flow of deference and respect from the military, who are accorded an honorable but clearly subordinate position.

This seems to be the theme of civilian control in India. Grant the military an honorable and respectable position in society, but one which is subordinate to the political and administrative sectors. Reduce and control their status, but do not humiliate them; take away any symbols of near-supreme authority, but not those associated with the performance of their prime, defense functions.[22]

Coupled with the narrow role definition of the military has been the expansion of civilian competence in defense and security matters. However, this expansion has been selective and by no means includes a wide segment of Indian society. In fact, since independence defense matters have been deliberately kept from the public at large, including MPs. Debate on the defense budget is confined to two days per year and often involves the most superficial and trivial issues. MPs are discouraged from specializing in defense matters, and most have no interest in them except through caste or regional ties. There has been an equivalent lack of defense expertise among scholars, journalists, and scientists, who have been content to let the government manage such problems.[23]

This management has done with a vengeance. There are very few nations in the world where such a small cadre of civilian administrators wields comparable power over the military.[24] While this was a pattern established during the last thirty years of British rule, Indians have elaborated upon it in many ways. As before, fiscal responsibility is strictly within civilian hands via the Finance and Defense ministries. The military are routinely called upon to account to civilian administrators for the smallest deviation from budgetary allocations. Perhaps apocryphally, military officers cite the example of the brigade commander who was asked why his unit exceeded its routine ammunition allocation—during the 1965 war with Pakistan.[25] More importantly, all requests for new weapons, force expansion, and structural adjustments are routinely evaluated by civilians from the very earliest stages of the decision-making process. The civilians are usually members of the Indian Civil Service or Indian Administrative Service, but other administrative cadres are involved as well. The general competence of these civilian bureaucrats is high. While outnumbered by their military counterparts, they can draw upon an extraordinarily rich tradition of civilian administrative control, and more often than not they have prevailed when decisions are appealed up to the political level. Here, as we have noted, competence thins out considerably, although the Defense Ministry has been headed by a succession of politically powerful individuals (Krishna Menon, Y. B. Chawan, and Jagjivan Ram) since the late 1950s.

Important operational decisions are, of course, made with full participation by the military. However, even here there is heavy civilian influence, if not dominance. In each of India's wars politicians and civilian bureaucrats have not hesitated to ignore military advice in specific instances or to choose between recommendations when the military has not been unanimous. In 1962 and 1965 the influence of civilian intelligence officials was especially pronounced; in 1971 the military were given very specific and careful instructions as to what was expected of them; it is likely that any future war will also see strong civilian direction and control.[26]

The value accorded to civilian control over the military should be neither exaggerated nor underestimated. There are today a number of powerful groups in India which might favor greater military influence in decision-making or politics, or even military rule. These would include elements of the Jan Sangh (a militant, pro-Hindu and pro-Hindi party found primarily in Northern India), some other conservative politicians and publicists, and perhaps a number of politicians from the groups which tend to dominate the military: Sikhs, Jats, and Rajputs. Even within the officer corps it is not uncommon to hear bitter and derogatory comments concerning the state of Indian politics in general and the venality and corruption of politicians in particular.

However, this undercurrent of promilitary sentiment must not be overstressed. In comparative terms it is certainly no greater than that found in the United States, or Great Britain. The predominant public and private judgment of most Indian politicians, journalists, and the military themselves is that civilian control is a good thing *in itself*, or at least that no alternative is better. As we have written elsewhere, there is an element of civilian militarism in India but this has never implied a willingness to turn matters over to the military.[27]

Conclusion

From the previous discussion it is clear that civilian control over the military in India rests upon a wide variety of traditions, devices, innovations, and practices. Indeed, the presence or absence of strong civilian control is a function of a number of variables. While it is difficult to always relate these variables to each other and to the existence of civilian control in a causal chain, they can be roughly categorized.

One convenient formulation is that which distinguishes among "spontaneous field control," direct field control, and command.[28] Spontaneous field control is the unintended manipulation of wants, desires, gratification, and deprivation through manipulation of the psychological "fields" of officers; direct field control implies an explicit and conscious manipulation of such fields. If these two techniques are successful, there is hardly need for a third, control by command, which is control by the response of a subordinate "exclusively by virtue of a penalty prescribed by the controller for non-performance . . ."[29]

From this perspective civilian control is the result of a long, complicated process of indoctrination, selection, training, and direct and indirect manipulation of the desires, values, and fields of the officer corps. No system can operate by command alone unless other control mechanisms reinforce the command or there are exceptional circumstances, such as a divided military.

What is striking about the Indian case is the relative unimportance of control by command compared with control by manipulation of the psychological field of the military, often overt manipulation. The recruitment, training, and the military/political environment of an officer all "conspire" to present him with a fait accompli: the omnipotence of civilians in policy decisions. Yet these same civilians have wisely refrained from humiliating or cornering the military, according them a role in the policy process and material rewards which conform with the professional self-image of the officer corps.

In India, as in any other political system, the effectiveness of civilian control will be conditioned by two variables: how easy it is for these control mechanisms to be applied and how clearly the problem of control is perceived by those interested in establishing or maintaining civilian control—especially the civilian administrator and politician. In pre-modern systems the fields of civilian and military elites were identical because they came from the same ruling class or caste. This was also the case in most colonial systems (including British India) where an identity of interest existed between civilian and military elites. But, in a heterogeneous state it may prove practically or politically impossible to obtain adequate numbers of officers with suitable belief systems. Then resources must be allocated so that the beliefs of officers can be manipulated to the point where their fields harmonize with those of the broader political system. Very few new nations have the capacity to impart not only technical, professional training, but political, moral, and ideological training as well. India certainly does.

We believe it is of the utmost importance that there are civilian officials who recognize the importance of beginning to socialize the officer at an early stage in his career. The most effective kinds of control involve the most fundamental assumptions about the legitimacy of the state and the role of the officer in it. These cannot be effectively taught late in a career when attitudes have hardened. Fortunately, a military organization already attuned to the prevailing political ideology can usually be trusted to reproduce itself in succeeding generations, but in a new state, or in one with antidemocratic traditions in the military, only careful civilian scrutiny can produce the desired results.

This raises the fundamental question of whether nonmilitary elites have the capacity to supervise and dominate in that area where civilian and military interests overlap. Not only must the military be taught that civilian control is the norm, but civilians must also demonstrate that they are effective. The original Clausewitzian justification of civilian control was, in fact, that political considerations were so important in war that the purely military outlook was inadequate. The same consideration applies to all defense-related problems. This is doubly true of systems in which power is legitimized by rational-legal norms, for here performance is likely to be an important criterion. It is never the absolute magnitude of an external or internal crisis which alone determines a realignment of political forces in a state, but the relationship of such a crisis to the will and determination of key elites. In a state with a vigorous and alert political elite—and, as in India, an attentive civilian administrative cadre—quite severe setbacks will be tolerated by the military if they have confidence in the ultimate good judgment of civilian leadership. However, quite trivial incidents can trigger a coup in systems where such confidence and respect are lacking. Paraphrasing the aphorism, leadership must not only be competent; it must be seen to be competent.

We have until now discussed civil-military relations in India as if they functioned in a stable, albeit very poor and somewhat disorderly, system. On a speculative plane, how would civilian control in India fare if either the economic situation worsened or domestic political disorder grew?

Unless the Indian economy were to suffer some unimaginable catastrophe, it is quite likely that the technique of isolating and rewarding the military for obedience can be continued indefinitely. There are, of course, two parallel Indian economies: a largely rural, peasant-agricultural system and a slowly growing urban, state-dominated industrial one. Virtually all important weapons are produced in state-owned or state-controlled enterprises; these have been remarkably free of labor unrest or other forms of disruption and even have their own protective security force.

The most likely source of difficulty would be the indirect impact of massive economic dislocation. A soldier whose family and relatives are undergoing extreme deprivation is unlikely to be an effective or obedient soldier; this applies as much to the officer corps as it does to the rank and file. This is a classic source of military disintegration. One mitigating factor is that the most prosperous regions of India are the ones which provide the largest amount of manpower as well as the greatest number of officers. A second such factor in the face of economic disruption would be the likelihood that India could appeal to foreign sources for military equipment and, perhaps, even subsidies for salaries and allowances.[30] As long as it retains some political value for one or the other superpower India should be able to trade this off for material support

A substantial increase in *political* turmoil and disruption might have a greater impact on civil-military relations. If the source of such disruption lies in provincial demands for greater autonomy, the military will then find itself on the side of the central government and would willingly collaborate with efforts to suppress such demands. However, if weakness should come at the *center*, there might be some temptation to throw support to one group or another. This in turn would probably depend upon two factors: whether or not the military sees its interests threatened, and whether or not the military is asked to intervene. As things now stand neither circumstance is very likely. There is general agreement among politicians of a variety of beliefs that, whatever their differences, they should never appeal to the military (and no important group of politicians are antimilitary).

Thus, we regard the present system of civilian control in India as quite stable and unlikely to be affected by foreseeable economic or political disruptions. As in the colonial period the military stand as a deterrent to violent attempts to overthrow the government, forcing political activists to work within the prevailing set of rules. It could well be that these rules will alter greatly in years to come, for India is undergoing a period of extremely rapid social and political, if not economic, change. If they do, however, it is unlikely that the nature of civilian control in India will itself be very different than it was four or forty years ago.

Epilogue: September 1975

The central arguments of this paper remain unaffected by the events subsequent to 25 June 1975. The military played no direct role in the arrests of thousands of political figures, scholars, MPs, journalists, and intellectuals; neither were they responsible for the imposition of press censorship, the expulsion of foreign journalists, and the practical suspension of the Constitution of India.

However, the integrity of the military *was* used as a major excuse for all of these actions. In defense of her actions, Mrs. Indira Gandhi and the government's public relations apparatus have repeatedly stressed that the arrests and censorship were necessary because of appeals made to the military to revolt and mutiny. If in fact such appeals had been made, they would have violated one of the norms of Indian politics, as noted above.

The record does not quite support these contentions. The leading figure of the opposition to Mrs. Gandhi, Jayaprakash Narayan ("J.P.") did raise the issue of military obedience several times in June. For example, in a speech at Suri, West Bengal, the press reported that J.P. renewed his appeal to the armed forces not to carry out "illegal orders."[31] A few days later, in New Delhi on the eve of a planned mass civil disobedience campaign, he repeated his appeal to the military (an appeal that apparently piqued Mrs. Gandhi), calling on the army, police, and government employees "not to obey any orders they considered illegal." Narayan added that

> the Army Act lays down that the armed forces must protect the Constitution. If the Constitution is changed legally it does not matter. But the army must oppose any unconstitutional changes.[32]

Mockingly, he dared the government to arrest and try him for treason.

While J.P. thought he was within both the law and the "rules" of Indian politics, Mrs. Gandhi thought otherwise. Even before the arrests, she had responded to Narayan's suggestion that the armed forces disobey illegal orders. On the evening of the 25th, before J.P.'s appearance at a mammoth rally in New Delhi, she claimed that "if a soldier began doubting whether his superior's order was right or wrong or started referring to the rules book then the war would be lost."[33]

After ordering the arrests of thousands of Indian politicians (including Narayan himself), she charged that "certain persons have gone to the length of inciting our armed forces to mutiny and our police to rebel." This is clearly a distortion of J.P.'s words. It remains to be seen whether her distortion was intentional or accidental, and whether in fact there was substantial evidence that J.P. *was* calling on the military and police to mutiny, and not merely disobey illegal orders.

This is a possibility that must not be ruled out, for there has been some concern about the integrity of the armed forces and police. A large number of Indian army personnel had been killed during the guerrilla struggle in Bangladesh during 1971, even before the Indian army launched a major attack on the Pakistanis. There had earlier been a police revolt in Uttar Pradesh, India's largest state, a revolt which had to be crushed (at some cost in life) by the military. Finally, there is the possibility that promotions at the highest level of the army were manipulated to allow Mrs. Gandhi to elevate a fellow Kashmiri to the position of chief of the army staff. This episode revived memories of the rapid promotion of another Kashmiri officer (B.M. Kaul) by Mrs. Gandhi's father, a promotion which was associated with the 1962 disaster in the Himalayas.

Even allowing for these considerations, we do not see any substantial proof of a military plot, opposition infiltration into the military, or any other internal or external threat which would serve to justify the steps taken by the government on grounds of national security. Rather, these actions were based on other considerations, however they may be rationalized or publicly explained. This rationalization is not unimportant, however. By including the "threat" to the military, Mrs. Gandhi is pursuing a line of argument which has been cultivated by a number of Indian political figures in the last decade and grows out of a hitherto subordinate strand of Indian politics. We have discussed this strand elsewhere, and twelve years ago came to the melancholy conclusion that

> a profound threat to democracy in India could arise as much from too much unity as from too little; under the pretext of a national front, or as the incarnation of the national will, a movement following the Bose-I.N.A. prototype might successfully dismantle India's substantial democratic structure, in the name of the nation, and possibly in the name of democracy itself.[34]

It may well be that this prediction has come true in all essential details.

Notes to Chapter 2
Cohen, *Civilian Control of the Military in India.*

1. For an overview of this phenomenon, see Lloyd and Susanne Rudolph, *The Modernity of Tradition* (Chicago: University of Chicago Press, 1967) and W.H.Morris-Jones, *The Government and Politics of India* (London: Hutchinson, 1971).

2. Upon independence the Pakistani army was hived off from the Indian army. Until then the Muslim officers and soldiers who became the Pakistan army had no separate identity (indeed, there were no all-Muslim units as there were all-Hindu or all-Sikh units). See Stephen P. Cohen, *The Indian Army* (Berkeley: University of California Press, 1971).

3. *Ibid.* See also Nagendra Singh, *The Theory of Force and Organization of Defense in Indian Constitutional History* (New Delhi: Asia Publishing House, 1969).

4. For an overview of the Indian Civil Service, see Philip Woodruff (Philip Mason), *The Men Who Ruled India* (London: Jonathan Cape, 1954).

5. The autobiographies of an Indian and a Pakistani general, respectively, convey the atmosphere of those days. See Lt. Gen. B.M. Kaul, *The Untold Story* (Bombay: Allied, 1967) and F. M. Mohammad Ayub Khan, *Friends Not Masters* (Karachi: Oxford University Press, 1967).

6. Cohen, *Indian Army*, pp. 114 ff.

7. *Ibid.*, pp. 138 ff. and the following: K. K. Ghosh, *The Indian National Army* (Meerut: Meenakshi, 1969) and Joyce C. Lebra, *Jungle Alliance: Japan and the Indian National Army* (Singapore: Asia Pacific Press, 1971).

8. We are here following the categorization of Claude E. Welch, Jr. as it appears in chapter 1 of this volume. For a slightly different perspective within a comparative framework, see my *Arms and Politics in Bangladesh, India, and Pakistan* (Buffalo: Council on International Studies, SUNY at Buffalo, 1973).

9. The Constitution of India was enacted in 1949 and is the outgrowth of a British Indian predecessor plus certain features from a number of foreign constitutions. Including amendments, it runs to almost four hundred pages. There are numerous glosses on the text, one being M. V. Pylee's *India's Constitution* (New Delhi: Asia Publishing House, 1971). The Constitution itself is prepared by the Ministry of Law and annually published by the government. Indian Supreme Court decisions, pending as this was written, may have the effect of substantially changing the nature of the Constitution.

10. Proposals to create a separate chairman (and presumably double the representation of the Indian army) have been rejected. For studies of the defense structure, see A. L. Venkateswaran, *Defense Organization in India* (New Delhi: Publications Division, G.O.I., 1967) and Maharaj K. Chopra, *India: The Search for Power* (Bombay: Lalvani, 1969).

11. Exact figures are unavailable for India since independence. This judgment is based upon an examination of casualty figures in various wars,

government statements, and visits to various Indian military establishments.

12. The armed services in India continue to live apart from the rest of society, often in the very barracks and cantonments constructed by their British predecessors. The British wanted to flee the crowds and prevent the political "contamination" of the troops; today, the motives remain identical. One cannot imagine a more effective deterrent to civil-military intercourse than the neat, antiseptic cantonment boundary line.

13. Since independence only one Punjabi has served as chief of the army staff, while four have been south Indians (two Coorgis, two Tamils), one Bengali, one Parsi, one Maharashtrian, and one Kashmiri (as of August 1975).

14. For a comprehensive and authoritative study of the Congress Party, see Stanley A. Kochanek, *The Congress Party of India* (Princeton: Princeton University Press, 1968), and for an important interpretation of the functioning of the party in Indian politics, see Rajni Kothari, *Politics in India* (Boston: Little, Brown, 1970).

15. For a careful look at Indian security problems up to 1965, see Lorne J. Kavic, *India's Quest for Security* (Berkeley: University of California Press, 1967).

16. A masterful description of military life in the Himalayas, as well as an informative account of civil-military relations during the 1962 conflict with China, can be found in Brig. John Dalvi, *Himalayan Blunder* (Bombay: Thackers, 1969).

17. A rough profile of India's military establishment can be obtained from the annual *Military Balance* published by the International Institute for Strategic Studies. For a number of years the army has stood at about 830,000 and the air force at somewhat under 850 combat aircraft. However, India not only services its large armor and air fleets, it is engaged in manufacturing as well.

18. The latter has usually been for the purpose of training in advanced or very new equipment acquired from abroad—most recently from the Soviet Union. The Indian armed forces also routinely trained a large number of officers and technicians from other states, particularly Nepal and several Middle Eastern and African countries.

19. Total figures of foreign military assistance to India can be found in U.S. Arms Control and Disarmament Agency, *World Military Expenditures and Arms Trade, 1963-73* (Washington: GPO, 1974). It might be noted that even when the US decided to terminate major arms programs to India and Pakistan (1965), a decision was made—and supported by Congress—to continue the training of South Asian officers in the US.

20. These include the various state police forces, state armed police forces, Railway Protection Force, Central Reserve Police, Border Security Force, Defense Installation Protection Force, Industrial Protection Force, and Home Guards. They have often been manned and commanded by exmilitary personnel. The *budget* for Union expenditures on police and internal security increased from $4 million in 1951 to $100 million in 1968-69 to $200 million in

1974-75, reflecting this proliferation of security forces. *New York Times*, 24 October 1974.

21. Helping out civilian authorities ("aid to the civil" in British-originated terminology) was a regular duty for the military in preindependence years; in Pakistan too many such operations continued to the military's disdain and distrust of civilian leadership.

22. At times the military themselves have been most concerned about role-expansion. When one ambitious general tried to make a name for himself among the public by constructing houses with military labor, he was thoroughly ridiculed by his fellow-officers and labeled a "political general." For his own account, see B.M. Kaul, *The Untold Story*, pp. 184 ff.

23. This expertise is growing, however, sometimes inspired and financed by the government of India itself. The outstanding example is the Institute of Defense Studies and Analyses located in New Delhi.

24. See Cohen, "The Security Policy-Making Process in India,", in Frank B. Horton III et al, eds., *Comparative Defense Policy* (Baltimore: Johns Hopkins University Press, 1974), pp. 156 ff.

25. Generally, the armed forces are content with present levels of manpower and technology, although they routinely—and naturally—press for more. But there is no feeling today as there was in the mid-1950s that they are being handicapped or unfairly restricted in their defense function.

26. This will be especially true if India should proceed to the development of nuclear weapons.

27. Cohen, *The Indian Army*, p. 197.

28. See Robert A. Dahl and Charles E. Lindblom, *Politics, Economics, and Welfare* (New York: Harper, 1953), pp. 99 ff.

29. *Ibid.*, p. 106.

30. To the extent that resources are interchangeable, India does this today, as the recipient of economic assistance from various states and international organizations.

31. *Times of India* (Bombay), 21 June 1975.

32. *Hindustan Times* (New Delhi), 25 June 1975.

33. Both quotes are from *The Hindu* (Madras), 27 June 1975. The former statement comes from Mrs. Gandhi's broadcast to the nation on 26 June. After this date press censorship was imposed throughout the country.

34. Stephen P. Cohen, "Subhas Chandra Bose and the Indian National Army," *Pacific Affairs* 36, 4 (Winter 1963-64): 429.

Civilian Control of the Military: Implications in the Plural Societies of Guyana and Malaysia

Cynthia H. Enloe

Currently associate professor of Government at Clark University, Dr. Enloe has conducted studies of political development and ethnic politics in Malaysia, Guyana, and Great Britain. Her books include *Multi-Ethnic Politics: The Case of Malaysia* (1970), *Ethnic Conflict and Political Development* (1973), and *Politics of Pollution in Comparative Perspective* (1975). Her degrees are from Connecticut College and the University of California, Berkeley.

Civilian control of the military by itself does not explain very much. What is far more interesting is *which civilians* control the military, with *what resources,* and for *what ends.* The Guyanese and Malaysian cases shed light on some of the subtle variations that civilian control can take when ethnic communalism is interjected.[1]

Certainly civilians are not an undifferentiated lump in the political process. Some are politicians controlling cabinet portfolios and parliamentary majorities, while others are in the electoral and legislative opposition; still others dismiss the existing political structure as illegitimate and seek instead to mobilize the citizenry to adopt an alternative mode of politics. Any one of these groups of civilian politicians conceivably could exert some control over at least portions of the nation's military. Then, too, not all civilians who have cause to impose their authority over military personnel are politicians at all. Many are bureaucrats. Civil servants have their own ideological, careerist, and programmatic concerns to promote and project, all of which can be affected by either military challenge or subordination. And, of course, bureaucrats themselves are diverse, in that some are much better equipped than others to insure military compliance.

In addition to the distinctions among bureaucratic and partisan civilians, there are in many countries ethnic divisions which cut across both categories. In genuinely plural nations, such as Guyana and Malaysia, a civilian is not just a civilian in the political arena; he or she is as well an Indian, African, Portuguese, Eurasian, Chinese, Malay, or Iban. Whether those ethnic identifications assist or limit civilian control of the military will depend on the sort of bureaucratic role or partisan influence that identity conveys. It will also depend on the character of ethnic responses within various parts of the military establishment. Ethnic affinity between certain strategically located civilians and ranking military officers is not, *a priori,* a guarantor of effective civilian control.[2]

As of mid-1975, neither Guyana nor Malaysia have had military coups. By the crudest measure, then, it would appear that civilian control has been effective — or, at least, that there has been a *convergence* of civilian and military interests so as to make a military challenge to civilian authority unnecessary. The lack of coup experiences in both countries is, in fact, one principal reason for these two militaries being virtually ignored not only by students of military politics but by the respective country analysts, who focus overwhelmingly on party conflict and administrative development.[3]

Superficial examination of the two systems suggests that the particular *kind of civilians* who have achieved that rudimentary control and the *means* by which they have done so are quite similar. Furthermore, it would appear that the *ends* for which that civilian control has been exercised are alike in Guyana and Malaysia.

First, in both of these former British colonies civilians leading long-time dominant political parties have been the wielders of authority over their respective military organizations. Though bureaucrats are important political actors in both countries— especially in Malaysia—it has not been the civilian civil services which have kept the colonels and generals in check, (if, indeed, they were straining). Similarly, in each nation these civilian politicians head parties which are intimately identified with the interests of a single ethnic community: the United Malay National Organisation (UMNO) tied to Malays in Malaysia, the Peoples National Congress (PNC) tied to Africans in Guyana. Critical for this discussion is the fact that in the military establishments of both Guyana and Malaysia there are ethnic imbalances and that the dominant ethnic group in each military is the same group which had held sway over the civilian party system since independence.

Finally, despite their electoral and military ascendency, the dominant ethnic groups in both Guyana and Malaysia have reason to feel insecure. Each lacks clear numerical superiority: the Malays represent 46 percent of the Malaysian populace, while Africans are only about 35 percent of the Guyanese populace. Each possesses inadequate control of their nation's economic resources: Chinese and overseas (British, Japanese, American) investors dominate Malaysia's currently thriving economy, while Guyana's shakier economy remains heavily dependent on British and North American ownership of banks, sugar plantations, and bauxite mines. These soft spots in the Malay and Afro-Guyanese hegemony make it all the more important for the furtherance of communal interests that their control of governmental machinery—civilian and military—be tightly *integrated*.

Laid out in this crude fashion, it seems that ruling partisan politicians wield control over their military organizations by means of appeals to ethnic solidarity and anxiety. Thus the means of control coincide with the objectives of control. For the aim in both cases would be the maintenance of communal political supremacy in fragmented and potentially unstable societies. For the military, the results of this sort of civilian control presumably have been the accentuation of ethnic recruitment and promotion imbalances begun by British colonial administrators and military preoccupation with its role as maintainer of internal security. For Guyana's and Malaysia's civilian politicians the results of this pattern of control have been a bolstering of one party's strength and mounting frustration for opposition politicians from non-Malay or non-African ethnic groups.

Such an interweaving of ethnic community, political party, and military can be found in countries other than Malaysia and Guyana. In the Soviet Union, Yugoslavia, Burma, and Trinidad, for instance, civilian control of the military relies on many of the same ingredients. But there is a problem with this sort of analysis. For in practice Guyanese military-civilian relations look rather different than those in Malaysia, their similarities not withstanding. The connection between party and army is much tighter in Guyana. This has had the effect of making the Guyanese army a far more *vulnerable* institution than is the Malaysian military. Second, greater ethnic differentiation within the Malaysian armed forces presents that country's civilian regime with choices not available to Guyanese leaders. PNC politicians can deploy only all-African battalions or an all-African police force, whereas UMNO strategists have police and military branches that differ considerably in their ethnic complexion. Third, while the relation between the military and the other coercive noncivilian institution—the police—is a neglected but still crucial element in the politics of both countries, it is in Malaysia especially that the political implication of the police's role becomes most salient.

The following brief discussions of civilian-military relations in Guyana and Malaysia raise at least two sets of questions. First, they suggest that even where ethnicity plays a crucial part in shaping civilian-military interaction, it can have quite varying political implications. Second, the two cases might prod analysts to be more discriminating in their concepts of civilian control. For the mere absence of palace coups is scarce evidence of effective control, if control is defined as military acquiescence to autonomous civilians whose policy priorities have an integrity of their own. Control can slip into dependence rather easily for a regime that feels unsure of itself. One sees this occuring today in Guyana. These cases also suggest that we dissect more closely the implications of civilian control of the military for ordinary citizens, who, after all, make up the great majority of civilians in any polity.

While civilian politicians' control of the military in a given country may prevent coups, it may be only at the costs of diverting scarce governmental funds away from needed non-military projects and of alienating a substantial number of ordinary citizens from a political system increasingly perceived as an ethnically limited structure. The military, epecially the army, together with the police are among the most visible state institutions. They can provide essential clues to different sectors of citizenry as to just *whom* the state means to represent and protect and just *whom* the state presumes to be threatening or untrustworthy.

The cases are deliberately set here in an historical context. The Guyanese and Malaysian militaries, as well as all modern militaries, are the products not only of contemporary political choices but of decisions made a generation ago. The effects, for instance, of past British colonial priorities and British ethnic stereotypes can still be seen today in the two nations' armies and police forces, though less so in the newer branches such as the air force. Furthermore, a military's ethnic compostion and ethnically designed strategic deployment can change and evolve out of concrete historical experiences. The particular *sequence* of events in which the military was an actor and the current *memories* of the "lessons" of each riot or rebellion all are critical in shaping the given military institution today.

Malaysia

Until the 1930's the British colonial administrators depended on British troops and on a small armed force composed mainly of Indians (Sikhs and Punjabis) and commanded by British officers, just as Indians had been relied upon to staff many essential civilian government services. The traditional Malay sultans, preserved by British administrators who saw them as useful vehicles for indirect rule, were permitted to keep their small armies, but these gradually atrophied into ceremonial guards.[4]

The first indigenous uniformed force created by the British was the police. The British followed the Portuguese and Dutch colonial practice of relying on Malay village headmen, *penghulus,* for law enforcement locally. But in 1876, the British formed the first of several paramilitary police forces which were sent out on special missions to put down warring bands. Regular police units came later.[5] Although by the early 1930s Malaya was a distinctly multiethnic society (Malaysia was formed by adding two Borneo states, Sabah and Sarawak, to Malaya in 1963), the Malayan police were recruited overwhelmingly from among the Malay community and training was conducted in the Malay language. In 1933 the British augmented its local armed forces by creating the Malay Regiment. Malay sultans had been pressing for such an indigenous regiment for several decades, but it was only the threat of war in Europe and the financial pressures of the Depression that finally persuaded London to accede to the demands. The Malay Regiment became the core of the Malayan military. As its name implied, it, too, was recruited even more exclusively from among the colony's Malay inhabitants. Although all-Malay, the regiment was drawn from the several peninsular states and thus was seen as a regional integrator.

The rationales that the British rulers had for these recruitment strategies cannot be specified with scientific certainty, but given the running discussions among British colonial officials about their obligation to protect the indigenous community (presumably less aggressive than the Indian and Chinese immigrants), given the policy to form a top-level civil-service class preserved for Malays, and given British distrust of the Chinese and the assumed transitoriness of the Indians, the Malay coloration of the initial police and army units suggests an effort by the often ambiguous colonialists, on the one hand, to insure themselves of armed services whose loyalty and gratitude could be counted upon, while, on the other hand, to further protect the indigenous people's status in Malayan society by giving them primacy in governmental institutions.[6] In Sabah and Sarawak, too, indigenous peoples were preferred over Chinese and Indians in the early uniformed services.

In their initial role the soldiers of the Malay Regiment lived up to British expectations of loyalty. It stood its ground and fought the invading Japanese in 1941 when Malaya was overrun and other British units retreated in confusion to Singapore. Thus at the outset the Malayan army's ethnic composition was of little real consequence, since officer posts remained in the hands of British personnel and adversaries were foreign invaders.

It was during the postwar, preindependence Emergency (1948-1960) that the ethnic character of the Malayan army became politically salient. The adversary against whom the army was now mobilized was domestic, the Malayan Communist Party, and it was largely drawn from only one of Malaya's three major ethnic groups, the Chinese. The various communities were becoming more politically aware as the British talked more immediately about the prospects for independence and parties were being formed to express interests in constitutional debates and to provide candidates for elections. These parties were ethnically defined, though there were efforts at interparty alliances. With the domestic political arena becoming more active and with an insurgency occurring which accentuated communal tensions, the British under the leadership of Gen. Gerald Templer determined that the local armed forces had to be ethnically broadened. On the other hand, there remained an official reluctance to give any Malaysian Chinese access to weapons, a fact that angered Chinese planters and tin mine owners, who felt they were being deprived of adequate protection against the rebels.[7]

Adding a multiethnic Federal Regiment to the existing Malay Regiment and deliberately encourging Chinese to join the police and Home Guard were acts intended to insure that more broadly conceived sort of control. The Federal Regiment (later expanded to become the Malaysian Reconnaissance Corps, MRC) as designed in 1952 was to have a composition of 50 percent Chinese, 25 percent Malays, and 25 percent Indians and others. But it proved difficult to attract non-Malays and not until 1955 was the first battalion formed.[8] The MRC today is multiethnic but is a smaller unit than the Malay Regiment. In 1968 the Malay Regiment (made up of ten battalions) comprised 28,000 of the total army ground troops of 35,000.[9] In a separate decision the Sarawak Rangers, a unit then outside the Malayan army, was formed drawing on Borneo residents, chiefly Ibans.

When the tripartite Alliance Party came to power in 1955, led by a Malay but including Indian and Chinese elites, and independence was granted by the British, the Malayan army was multiethnic, but with a Malay predominance in both the ranks and officer corps due to the earlier start of the Malay Regiment and to the persistent image of the Malays as the most "loyal" citizens. Those officers who today hold commanding positions in the army, like their Alliance and civil service counterparts, were politically socialized in the 1950s by the Emergency, which only officially ended after independence. The colonels and brigadier generals today joined in about 1955-58, after having attended English-language schools and often having come from the "raja" upper class of Malay society. Tun Razak, the present prime minister and dominant politician, shares many of the same experiences.[10] This gives Malaysia's top policy-makers shared notions about what constitutes the principal threat to national stability, which in turn makes civilian relations with the military as much a matter of *convergence* as of control.

The military was again depended upon by the civilian leadership during "Confrontation," the armed dispute (1963-65) with Sukarno's regime in Indonesia over the annexation of Britain's Borneo territories to Malaya to form the new Federation of Malaysia in 1963 (Singapore was originally included as well, but was expelled by the Alliance in 1965). This was a period when the military expanded rapidly. On the peninsula the conflict did not take on explicitly ethnic meaning, except as it concerned the proper role for Singapore Chinese in the federation. But in Borneo, especially in Sarawak, Indonesian-Malaysian warfare was mixed with alleged Malaysian Chinese subversion. During this period the paramilitary police took responsibility for handling subversive threats in residential areas, while the army concentrated on operations in more remote jungle areas. Today the Malaysian police's field force remains a crucial ingredient in the regime's overall defense strategy.

During all three conflicts in which the Malaysian army was

active—World War II, the Emergency, and the confrontation with Indonesia—it was bolstered by military units drawn from other territories in the Commonwealth, especially the Gurkhas, thus muting somewhat the particular domestic ethnic character of the military and reducing the political burden placed on the small force. After the mid-1960s, however, as the British cut their Asian forces, the Malaysian army had to be more self-sufficient. It consequently stood out more clearly in the political arena. On the other hand—and this becomes particularly significant in a comparison with Guyana's military—the Malaysian military had by the 1960s developed a certain institutional integrity of its own, which served to protect it from political buffeting.

The communal riots of May 1969 made the ramifications of the ethnic composition of the military and the extent of civilian dependency on it politically central for the first time. Malay-Chinese hostilities broke out in Kuala Lumpur, the capital, just after the returns from the 1969 parliamentary and state elections showed a dramatic slippage in Alliance support nationally and serious challenges to Alliance hegemony in several state assemblies, including that of Selangor, the state in which Kuala Lumpur is located. In the confusing first days of the hostilities both the police and the army were called into the capital. While rumors quickly circulated among frightened Chinese blaming both forces for exhibiting tolerance toward Malay rioters, the army eventually became the chief target for such charges. For after an initial use of the Sarawak Rangers, known for the alleged ruthlessness but impartiality of its Iban troops, the government relied chiefly on the Malay Regiment. This meant sending an all-Malay army unit, including many inexperienced recruits, into an intensely ethnic and admittedly chaotic situation. The police, on the other hand, while also heavily Malay in its rank and file, still had numerous Chinese and Indian officers and had a reputation for being more sophisticated in the handling of disputes.[11]

Ever since the 1930s there had been the belief among officers (and perhaps among the citizenry as well, though we have no survey evidence) that the police recruited the brighter, more cosmopolitan sort of Malay, leaving the less educated, more parochial Malay youths to join the army, where pay was lower and individual responsibilities lighter. Among Malaysian police, it is said, there was a widespread assumption that wherever the army was stationed there would be more disorder, due to the troops' unruliness, and it would always be left to the police to restore the public order.[12] What is important here is not whether these convictions were accurate, but that they bred a distrust between the government's two coercive branches. This distrust was not between a Malay and a non-Malay service, but between services both led by Malays. It exacerbated tensions during the 1969 riots and thus weakened the hand of the Alliance party leadership as it tried to restore order and secure its own delicately balanced position. While there has been virtually no suggestion of coup intentions by the Malaysian military during 1969, civilian control *was* weakened insofar as the subordinate uniformed forces could not agree on how to handle the communal violence.

The 1969 elections and subsequent riots were a watershed in postindependence Malaysian politics—one Malaysian political scientist compared it to the Sputnik "shock" in postwar US politics.[13] First, it left the Malay partner in the ruling Alliance—UMNO—in a more tenuous position with its own ethnic followers, but in a far stronger position vis a vis the other two Alliance partners. The Malayan Chinese Association (MCA) suffered serious electoral losses and seemed powerless to protect Chinese during the riots. The Malayan Indian Congress (MIC) had always been the frailest of the three parties and now faced ever stiffer competition at the polls. In addition, the riots were interpreted by the Malay elites as a testimony to the growing impatience of the Malay rank and file, particularly those who had left rural areas to look for jobs in the city, with the existing strategy of ethnic accommodation, in which non-Malays were assured of commercial primacy while the Malays were guaranteed to be first-among-equals in government affairs. With this interpretation of the electoral-cum-riot "mandate" in hand, the Alliance leadership, now more firmly than ever a *Malay*-led regime, began reshaping its political priorities.

One focus for the postriot reassessment was a new estimate of just how far Malays were lagging behind in enjoying the

benefits of national growth. To emphasize Malay underdevelopment, the government published figures breaking down the
ethnic composition in precisely those areas of the job market
where allegedly and constitutionally Malays enjoyed privileged
access—government service. Looking only at Division I officers, those at the top, the government reported that, while
Malays did comprise 57.8 percent of Division I Administration
Services and non-Malays only 42.2 percent, in the governmental professional services (excluding education), Malays provided only 19.2 percent of the Division I officers, whereas
non-Malays amounted to a full 80.8 percent.[14] It should be
noted, however, that by 1968 in the most elite section of the
civil service, where bureaucrats have the greatest opportunity
to actually shape policy—the Malayan Civil Service (M.C.S.)—
there were more than six Malays for every non-Malay.[15] This
put Malays in senior bureaucratic policy-oriented posts in most
ministries, including the civilian sections of the Defense Ministry. Thus ethnic convergence was likely to occur not only
between top-ranking politicians and uniformed officers, but
between the latter and the civil service elite in the ministry.

In the official report's data on the police and armed forces
again only data relating to senior officers were supplied.

Table 1
Top Ranking Officers[16]

Police	%	Armed Forces	%
Malays	38.76	Malays	64.5
Non-Malays	61.24	Non-Malays	35.5

An independent study conducted to test the accuracy of the
government's assertions found that they were generally accurate for Division I. It is also concluded that "only in education and the police have the Malay proportions increased more
rapidly than those of the other groups since 1957."[17] In the
police this meant that it had been Malays chiefly who had
replaced the departing British in top posts. In both the police
and education it was believed that Malays progressed with

particular rapidity because these were essentially nontechnical services and it was nontechnical careers that Malays since colonial times had been most inclined to pursue.[18] The Alliance regime's official report concluded: "The Malays who already felt excluded in the country's economic life, now (on the eve of the 1969 election) began to feel a threat to their place in the public services."[19] The impact of the ethnic composition of the police and military was not mentioned except to note that the prevalence of Malays in the upper ranks was the consequence of the long-time "avoidance" of these careers by non-Malays.[20]

The National Operations Council (NOC) became the governing body in Malaysia following the riots and throughout the period of the parliament's supension, 1969-74. Its composition more clearly perhaps than any other body's suggests the close cooperation between Malay politicians, Malay senior civil servants, and Malay security officers that occurred during precisely those months when political power was undergoing a major shift. Specifically, ten of the twelve members of the National Operations Council were Malays, several of them also active in UMNO party politics.[21] The things that these men shared made civilian control in the sense of overt constraint or knocking heads together seem unlikely. More likely was a natural convergence of style and viewpoint. All were English-speaking; this was a significant point in a pluralist society where English-medium education separated elites from non-elites in all three major ethnic groups and at a time when Malay activists were pressing for the adoption of Malay as the national language in practice as well as in law. All were secular, cosmopolitan men, many of whom had received training overseas. Most NOC members had shared in the political lessons of the Emergency, the Alliance's decade of tenuous but successful electoral victories, and control of governmental machinery.

The Armed Forces come under the authority of the Minister of Defense. Between 1957 and 1969 the minister of defense was Tun Razak, the number two man not only in UMNO but in the Alliance then headed by another Malay, Tunku Abdul Rahman. In his political career, however, Tun Razak gave much more publicity to his actions in his other ministerial capacities, which he carried simultaneously, especially his pragmatic and efficient approaches to development planning and field implementation. This meant that military officers could be confident that their senior civilian administrator had independent power and that their views would carry considerable weight in party circles.

The principal operational body overseeing command, discipline, and administration of the military is the Armed Forces Council. It is chaired by the minister of defense and includes the chief of the Armed Forces Staff, the secretary general of the Ministry of Defense and other senior civilian and uniformed defense officials. According to the Malaysian government's own *Official Year Book* in 1971, of the total ten members of the Armed Forces Council, eight were Malays, one was Indian (Chief of the Naval Staff) and one was Chinese (an appointee of the king).[22]

The questions that most preoccupy the Malaysian military currently do not insure a lack of friction with the civilian party leadership. On the other hand, they are not yet questions which generate such profound disagreement that there would be charges of bad faith on either side. In working out these policy questions Malay civilians in the cabinet, Treasury, and Defence Ministry appear to hold authority firmly.

First, there is the question of the military's budget. Budgetary allocations have to consider: 1) Britain's withdrawal of its traditional defense umbrella in the region and the somewhat uncertain future of Australian and New Zealand defense commitments in Southeast Asia; 2) the warning flags raised by the 1969 riots suggesting that internal security is likely to remain a potential problem for some time to come; 3) the increasing technical sophistication of career officers, not only in the army but in the newer branches of the navy and air force.

On the other side of the ledger there is: 1) the need for the government to give priority to economic growth and income redistribution for the sake of intercommunal peace; 2) the end of hostilities with Indonesia and the increasingly close cooperation between Indonesian and Malaysian military officers; 3) the diplomatic rapproachment between Kuala Lumpur and Peking which has taken some of the tension out of Southeast Asian regional planning.

The federal government's expenditure on defense rose steadily after independence, with an average annual increase between 1960-1969 of 12.1 percent, measured in terms of government expenditure on goods and services together with capital expenditure undertaken directly by government agencies.[23] In these same terms, the government's nondefense allocations rose only 9.9 percent during that decade, while the Malaysian GNP rose 6.7 percent.[24] Civilian authorities have taken steps to avoid the unintended military inflation that comes from lack of demobilization by imposing strict retirement schedules. Enlisted men must retire by age 45, officers below colonel by age 50, and colonels and above by 55. A new Veterans Affairs Department in the Defense Ministry has been established specifically to ease this demobilizing process and to curb growth of an alienated core of Malay veterans. Rumors that retired Malay sergeants are being recruited—perhaps hired is more accurate —with lures of good pay to go into the jungle to train communist guerrillas cannot help but increase government efforts to insure smooth demobilization.[35] Moreover, Malaysia's industrialization together with its increasing revenues from offshore oil are giving further impetus to the military's push for higher defense outlays.

Table 2
Malaysian Defense Budgets[26]
(in US dollars)

	$ million
1968	— 182
1969	— 132
1971	— 186
1972	— 314.7
1973	— 287
1974	— 311

During the same period armed forces manpower grew from less than 40,000 in 1969 (preriot) to 66,200 in 1974.[27]

The Malaysian Budget of 1974 allocated M$ 887 million to security forces (military and police). This amounted to 25 percent of the government's expenditures in a country that had prided itself on giving highest budgetary priority heretofore to education (in 1974 Budget, education represented 24 percent of expenditures).[28]

These budgetary expansions were not yearly. They were responses to specific conditions, such as the need to replace British protection and to bolster antisubversion forces after the 1969 riots. They do not prove or disprove civilian control. Malaysia's party leaders have shown themselves just as concerned as their military men that another Emergency of the 1950s sort never recurs. In addition, they have demonstrated their interest in asserting a new international autonomy for Malaysia and that requires armed forces capable of backing up such a claim. Both determinations divert funds from social development efforts.

A second question that apparently has concerned Malaysian military officers more than their civilian superiors has been the proper distribution of responsibility between the police and the army. The police, which is under the Home Affairs Ministry, has its regular police units in charge of local law and order; but as a legacy from the British period it also has a police field force, which is essentially a paramilitary unit. Paramilitary forces in 1973 included 54,000 men,[29] Field force brigades have had the chief responsibility for patrolling the northern Malaysian border where remnants of Malaysian Communist Party insurgent forces have remained since the end of the Emergency.

Since defense policy as articulated by both civilian politicians and military commanders is based on the assumption that the primary threat to security will be internal, the police and the army have overlapping responsibilities. The army, which is the first-among-equals of the three military branches, looks after the Borneo territories and the police field force gives its primary attention to peninsular security. When the two carry on joint operations, the PFF comes under overall army command. Given the traditional disdain with which at least some police officers have viewed the army and given the more multiethnic character of the police, one might expect that there are disputes over approaches to potential security matters and over priorities in budgetary allocations which presumably would have to be worked out by the civilian party leaders. The Home Ministry, like the Defense Ministry, has been headed by a UMNO Malay politician ever since independence. The forum for such coordination is the National Defense Council created in 1963. Its members and senior staff personnel have been overwhelmingly Malay.

Postindependence national security in most countries has come to depend on naval and air force power and technical expertise as well as army ground units. In Malaysia the air force and navy, as well as the army's technical services, have been the principal channels for Indian and Chinese recruitment and promotion. Chinese are especially prominent in the air force, a situation which has caused some anxiety among Malay politicians. Today the Navy is headed by an Indian commander. Nevertheless, the primacy of the army and, within it, of the Malay Regiment, as well as the tendency for non-Malay officers to be denied direct command of troops, greatly reduces the possibility that non-Malay officers will influence policy.[30]

The most recent nationwide elections were held in August 1974. They were followed by no riots. There was no apparent overt use of either the police or the army to conduct the elections, though there were criticisms from the opposition candidates that their campaign activities were sometimes curtailed, especially in Sabah. The Alliance was expanded in this election, however, to swallow up most of its organized opponents of 1969. Tun Razak was the architect of the new National Front that included UMNO, MCA, and MIC (though with the latter two playing far less prominent roles than they had in the past), as well as UMNO's principal Malay party challenger, PI, and two largely non-Malay parties, Gerakan (based in Penang) and PPP (based in the Perak city of Ipoh). The National Front won control of all 13 state assemblies in the federation and of 135 of the 154 House of Representative seats. The only opposition to survive was the largely Chinese Democratic Action Party (DAP).[31]

By revising the Alliance's old national integration formula, the party leaders in UMNO have at least for the moment reduced their immediate dependency on the military and police. They have absorbed their party rivals and thus secured their parliamentary majority. They have announced the Second Malaysian Five-Year Plan, which pledges to give Malays, the most critical element in their electoral coalition, a larger slice of the economic pie, while at the same time promising a thriving economy in which non-Malays will also continue to be rewarded. Should either pillar of the new formula prove unsteady, the Malay leadership of UMNO may find it necessary to lean on its security forces.

In late 1974 there were demonstrations by Malay rice farmers in one of the northern peninsular states protesting the low price of rice and the inadequacy of the governmental subsidies. When 12,000 peasants took to the streets and were joined by sympathetic Malay university students, it required government forces to restore order. This presented a potential situation which would make any UMNO-led regime uneasy: Malay uniformed forces called out to quell peasants. These were not at all the circumstances for which the uniformed forces were ethnically designed. The significant questions, should the development strategy falter, would be:

1) to what extent do the Malay senior officers, especially in the army, have faith in the political wisdom of their Malay counterparts in the cabinet?;

2) how effective would police-army cooperation be in putting down any possible civil disturbances?;

3) to what extent would the army's capability to maintain civil peace be undermined by the division of the army into the Malay Regiment and the multiethnic Federation Reconnaissance Corps with few non-Malay officers having charge of troops?;

4) how would non-Malay officers and ranks in air force, navy, and police jobs react?;

5) to what extent would the image of the armed forces as a largely "Malay" institution limit its ability to implement civilian policy?

Guyana

The dilemmas and resultant vulnerability of Guyana's military are even more acute than those of Malaysia. It is not just a matter of ethnic distortions shaping the Guyanese military, but of party and personalism so infiltrating the Guyanese army that it lacks the institutional autonomy that exists to some extent at least for its Malaysian counterpart.

Discussion of the Guyanese military is necessarily briefer. It is a much newer institution, created in 1965 by the British on the eve of their departure. It is also a smaller force, with only two army battalions, and a less complex organizational structure. Perhaps most important, Guyana's politics are less complicated than Malaysia's, if only because Guyana is a newer nation, its party system is less ethnically elaborate, there are no federal states to act as independent power bases, and power is less veiled than in Malaysia.[32] As one Guyanese historian (who later became Guyanese ambassador to Canada) remarked, "When a man is in power here he has a whole set of levers at his disposal. Out of power, he has nothing at all."[33] Power is also more personal. This is seen in the character of civilian control exercised over the Guyana Defence Force (GDF).

The GDF was launched in 1965 and legally instituted by a parliamentary act in 1966. Thus it was born after the country's most serious interethnic riots between East Indians and Africans from 1961-1964, and after the breakup of the biethnic nationalist movement led by Cheddi Jagan and Forbes Burnham, but before independence in 1967. This timing was important, for it meant that Guyana's first regular military force was created at a time of both accelerating politicization and growing party-encouraged ethnic polarization. It would be *as if* the Malaysian military had been founded after the 1969 postelection riots, when threats to security were presumed to be communal in character and when the party in power felt most shaky about its ability to maintain power in the face of organized rivals.

As in Malaysia, the British had treated the several ethnic communities in Guyana differently with regard to government service. The sparsity and remoteness of Guyana's indigenous people, the Amerindians, however, led the British to recruit that overseas group which had been there the longest, left the sugar plantations and migrated to towns earliest, and most readily adopted Christianity and thus gained entrance into the largely church-run secondary schools—the Guyanese Africans. As early as 1925, of the persons employed in the colonial bureaucracy, 84.7 percent were listed as Negroes, while a mere 4 percent were listed as East Indians. This, despite the fact that the East Indians, brought as indentured laborers to work the sugar plantations after slavery was abolished, already amounted to 41.97 percent of the population, while Negroes represented only 39.36 percent (Portuguese, Chinese and "mixed" made up the rest).[34] Europeans, Portuguese, and light-skinned persons of mixed parentage continued to dominate the upper reaches of the civil service until the mid-1960s. When Forbes Burnham and his Peoples National Congress, composed largely of Afro-Guyanese, challenged the preindependence regime of Indo-Guyanese Cheddi Jagan and his largely Indian-backed Peoples Progressive Party, the PNC could use an antiregime labor strike by the politicized African-dominated civil service to bring down the PPP Government.[35]

Guyana's uniformed forces in this stormy period were far less developed than was the civil service, but they too were imbalanced ethnically. Police were recruited overwhelmingly from among Africans, presumably because they were more numerous in the towns and because they met the physical requirements such as height and chest measurement, which smaller framed Indians could not. Guyanese political scientist Ralph Premdas tells of Indian boys like himself being teased by other Indian youths for being thin or short. The disparaging epithet the taunting youths tossed at one another was "Gandhi." By 1965 the police force was 80 percent African and 20 percent Indian and others.[36]

The British Guiana Volunteer Force was established in 1948, though some Guyanese had served in World War II as troops in West Indian units. It was organized along the lines of territorial battalions, but its members served part-time. Cadets were recruited from urban secondary schools, such as the prestigious Queens College in Georgetown. Its task was to assist police, provide static guards at installations, and assist in the restoration of law and order. In this last capacity the Volunteer Force encountered criticism along with the police for its handling of racial disturbances during the Jagan regime in the early 1960s.

Only the Special Service Unit, a paramilitary organization created in 1964 to assist in maintaining civil order, escaped serious criticism; it was the only armed force with a large contingent of Indians.[37] The PPP's East Indian leadership charged that one reason it was not able to govern effectively during its brief time in office (1964) was that security forces—which were under British command, not PPP control—were incapable of coping with such communal tensions.[38] The Volunteer Force included some Indians who managed to gain entrance into such schools as Queens, but it was composed mainly of Africans. Not until 1964 were military recruits taken in from rural areas, where the majority of Indians resided.[39] The GDF's first two Guyanese commanding officers—both Afro-Guyanese—have been products of the Volunteer Force, one having joined as a volunteer in 1948, his successor having joined in 1956. Both men were also at that time employed as government civil servants.[40]

In 1965, just prior to the founding of the GDF, the government of British Guiana, now under Forbes Burnham and the PNC, invited the International Commission of Jurists to study the controversial ethnic situation within the government's civil and uniformed services. The ICJ report found considerable ethnic imbalance in both and traced those imbalances to deliberate recruiting practices as well as historical circumstances. It recommended that steps be taken, especially in light of the 1961-64 disturbances, to redress these imbalances by accelerating the recruitment of non-Africans.[41] Its recommendations were akin to those actually implemented by Templer in Malaysia during the Emergency.

Since 1965 there has been little evidence in the army and the police that Africans are any less dominant. The ICJ report has remained a basis on which the PPP for the past decade has criticized the ruling PNC. Firsthand observers estimate that the GDF in both its ranks and its officer corps is now between 90-95 percent African.[42] In a three-year survey of the GDF's public organ, *The Green Beret* (a publication intended both as a promotion piece and as a vehicle for transmitting government policy to the troops), one rarely finds a non-Anglo-Saxon name, indicating the scarcity of non-Africans. *The Liberator,* a Georgetown middle-class political paper which prides itself on access to sensitive government information, voiced stinging criticism of the Burnham regime and published the following figures in spring 1972 to demonstrate government failure to pursue the ICJ recommendations:

Table 3
East Indian Membership[43]

	1965 %	1971 %
GDF		10
Public Service	33	28
Police Force	20	15

Senior Police Officers[44]

	Number of Officers	Number of Indians
Senior Superintendents	11	1
Superintendents	17	1
Assistant Superintendents	49	1
Chief Inspectors and Inspectors	81	9

The GDF, despite its African composition, was not ethnically designed. It differs from the Malaysian army in that no subunits are officially intended for one group or another, as were the Malay Regiment, the Sarawak Rangers, and the Federal Regiment. Furthermore, there is little evidence that a status disparity exists between the police and army as one finds in Malaysia. In fact, the Guyanese police are the target of frequent criticism and even humor for their alleged inability or unwillingness to tackle petty crime, much of which occurs in busy sections of town in daylight. Finally, and more significant for this analysis, there is less effort in Guyana to build institutional barriers between either uniformed service and the ruling party.

The GDF comes under the administration of the Guyana Defence Board. The board is chaired by the prime minister, presently PNC leader Forbes Burnham. Unlike Malaysia, there is no separate Ministry of Defense. The chief of staff, always an African since the departure of British-seconded officers, also sits on the Board. The constitutional commander-in-chief is a civilian, the president of the Republic. But the President, Arthur Chung, a Chinese-Guyanese, has been a man without effective power or an organizational base.

The power that the prime minister exercises over the GDF is such that he takes a direct hand in promotions—a power important in a force that is too small to have a very elaborate assortment of senior rankings. Such intervention has been much less apparent to the political public in Malaysia, though there has been speculation that Malaysian civilians weed out officers, even Malay officers, deemed too ambitious and potentially threatening to civilian authority. The most significant reshuffling of senior GDF personnel occurred in late 1971. Since those forced to retire or to take positions further removed from operational command were the GDF's most senior officers, it can be safely presumed that the reshuffle was dictated by the prime minister. Those retired or "kicked upstairs" (the GDF commander was promoted from colonel to brigadier and made a "defense adviser" within the prime minister's office) were Africans who had served in army units prior to the GDF's formation and who had nonmilitary careers as well. Since they were still in their late forties or early fifties, several of them returned to civilian jobs, for example in the customs service; some left Guyana to go abroad. It is not perfectly clear what motivated the reshuffle, but some close observers believed that it was a combination of the prime minister's desire to push aside those senior officers who objected to the increasing interweaving of PNC and GDF operations and his awareness of the growing career frustrations of young officers who saw their chances for promotion stymied by the relative youth of their superiors.[45] The announcement of the reshuffle sparked political speculation among Guyanese, but there were no signs of any overt support for one group of officers or the other.

PNC and specifically Prime Minister Burnham's own efforts to tighten relations between the party and the GDF suggest that civilian politicians see the armed forces as crucial for maintenance of power, despite their succession of electoral victories under a proportional representation system that gives the PNC special advantages. PNC attention to the GDF implies also that the reliability of the GDF is not certain without such increased partisan supervision.

The first form of party penetration into the military was, of course, the quadruple role played by Forbes Burnham: prime minister, chairman of the Defence Board, president of the ruling party, and best known spokesman for the ethnic group that comprised 90 percent of the military. But in the early 1970s when the PNC secured a firm electoral grip on the parliamentary system, the party's penetration began taking more elaborate organizational forms. A council, called by its acronym SPEC, was formed to bring together the leading PNC policy planners and the top security officers of uniformed services. According to observers—for SPEC's operations were not open to media coverage—only persons considered loyal to the PNC were given membership.[46] It was headed by a minister brought home from overseas by Burnham who argued that there should be more "social analysis" behind PNC's rule, if only to tighten the regime's grip on power. But by mid-1974 SPEC was disbanded, and some Guyanese speculated that SPEC no longer served a purpose for its members, since those who had joined it from the GDF had done so principally to further their own careers, which depended increasingly on being deemed politically loyal. By 1974 most of those SPEC officers who had not been retired in the 1971 reshuffle had gained the promotions they sought and no longer needed SPEC to give them leverage.[47] Also there may have been some concern in the prime minister's office that the minister who had designed SPEC was using it too much to build up his own power base. In a political system where party heads of both the PNC and PPP exert tremendous personal power over their own ranks, any such autonomous power base is deemed intolerable This personal anxiety on the part of Jagan and Burnham seriously undermines any nascent institutionalization in governmental organization.

Patronage has become a more and more important vehicle for party penetration. It affects recruitment into the police and the GDF. In a nation such as Guyana, where unemployment among the society's burgeoning younger generation is estimated at 20 percent, the police and the army are important potential employers.[48] Entrance into the noncommissioned ranks of the GDF does not appear to require actual party membership, merely African identity and a record showing no affiliations with such opposition groups as ASCRIA, an African movement headed by a disaffected former government official, Eusi Kwayana. Lack of Indian recruitment into the ranks is probably a combination of the selective recruitment uncovered by the ICJ and the reluctance of Indian youths to pursue a career in a now largely African institution to which there is little traditional Indian attachment.

Entrance into the GDF's officer corps appears to require more explicit PNC affiliation, preferably a party card.[49] This is not peculiar to the army. As the PNC's patronage hold on the political system seems progressively unchallengeable, there may be a tendency for Guyanese—both Indians and Africans, both political and apolitical—to take out *pro forma* PNC membership just to insure job security, ease in obtaining a passport, entrance into the university, and avoidance of income tax harrassment. Thus, in the GDF, as in the civil service or the nationalized bauxite company, GUYBAU, one should be wary of assuming that extensive PNC membership is equivalent to genuine party loyalty. Still, in the military the dependence on party clearance for job security and promotion cannot help but make officers sensitive to partisan priorities. Whether this "sensitivity" takes the form of officers becoming more partisan or more restive is a question still unanswered.

The external rationale for the military's existence might seem to come from Venezuela, which since the colonial period has made claims to as much as half Guyana's national territory. The threat appeared greatest in the late 1960s when a ranchers' rebellion along the Venezuelan and Brazilian borders suggested that internal subversion might give Venezuela an opportunity for penetration. The ranchers, mostly Scottish and mixed in racial origin, and their few Amerindian allies were easily put down by the army. Aside from the army, neither Africans nor East Indians played crucial roles in the short-lived uprising. Today one battalion of the GDF is stationed at an interior post, while the second is barracked on the outskirts of Georgetown. The threat of any overt intervention from Venezuela seems unlikely at present, for that country is now attempting to win itself recognition as a leader in Caribbean affairs and in that role has been offering development assistance to the Burnham regime. Furthermore, Guyanese official spokesmen have been increasingly frank to admit that Guyana's small army could be no match for Venezuela. Its role would thus seem strictly domestic.

At present the GDF's principal military role relates to potential internal disorder among the coastal populations. The domestic orientation of the army became more blatant than ever during the 1973 parliamentary elections. The elections occurred after moves had begun to tighten PNC relations with the GDF. They also came at a time when Burnham and the PNC had acquired more power over the economy—through government industries, licensing, patronage, cooperatives—than ever before, though the economy itself was in serious trouble due not only to domestic policy errors but to international dislocations beyond Guyana's control. In addition, the 1973 election took place when criticism of the regime was mounting but when the organized opposition was falling into greater disarray, particularly as the Jagan-led PPP appeared to offer a less and less viable alternative.

It is open to question just how the PNC would have fared had the government not been able to call upon the GDF. It is possible that the PNC still would have won. However, in an open election the PNC might not have been able to capture the two-thirds majority which gave it the ability to amend the Constitution. Furthermore, an untampered poll might have shown a far lower voter turnout, indicating substantial political alienation, something that has occurred in neighboring Trinidad's one-party-dominant system. In largely black Georgetown the PNC carried by only 60 percent, with only 70 percent of the city's electorate turning out to vote.[50] In the area outside of Georgetown the army was more active.

The precise character of the GDF's operations is of course difficult to ascertain because of those very conditions which dampened political competition at the time. Spokesmen for the PPP charged that the army was active in breaking up opposition campaign rallies, often held near coastal sugar estates, traditionally the heartland of the PPP's East Indian support. The PPP also claimed that GDF troops tampered with sealed ballot boxes, which the regime charged them to carry from scattered polling places to Georgetown for official tabulation.[51] Foreign commentators have voiced identical charges. After the 1968 elections there were similar domestic and overseas accusations of ballot-box stuffing and fake overseas proxies, but the army was not then a prominent pillar of support for the PNC.

The accelerated politicization of the Guyanese army could have several consequences, not all of which necessarily insure continued civilian control. Drawing the GDF into electoral campaigns and making it an object of sharp public criticism could make GDF officers politics-shy and place them at increasing odds with their PNC superiors. On the other hand, the party's penetration could convince not only the current officers but the rank and file as well that the GDF's interests are in fact so intertwined with the PNC regime that the army should continue to assist in the regime's maintenance of power for its *own* sake.

One unknown quantity is the African opposition to the PNC. If the army, with its overwhelmingly African composition, believes that PNC interests, Afro-Guyanese communal interests, and Guyana's national interests are all coterminous, then the GDF may become an ever more important vehicle for keeping the present civilian regime in power. If, however, that formula is fractured by the emergence of a credible African-led opposition to Burnham, the army's position may become very awkward. The awkwardness would be exacerbated by the fact that Guyana is such a small country. Even a 2,200-man army* has family and friendship contacts throughout the society, which would make it almost inevitable that many acquaintances of

---

*The GDF may in fact be larger, closer to 3,000 according to some Guyanese.

army personnel would be involved in any African opposition. In the spring of 1975, in fact, the GDF was used to break up a sugar workers' strike which had African as well as East Indian support.

The Burnham strategy for wielding control over the GDF has increased the likelihood that the army could not effectively be insulated from any such political conflict. Indeed, the prime minister has been surprisingly explicit in warning GDF personnel that he expects them to be loyal not just to the nation as an abstraction, but to him personally.

The *Green Beret* (an official GDF publication) featured the following message from the prime minister in its eighth anniversary issue: "As Prime Minister, I expect you to be loyal to this government. If there is any other government, it is a matter for you to decide about that, but so far as I am concerned, I don't want any abstract loyalty. It must be a straightforward loyalty from the top down, and it must be based on an appreciation of the philosophy of this government."[52]

No Malaysian prime minister has so explicitly inhibited military institutionalization. Burnham has also, however, encouraged the GDF to break down the barriers which isolate armies from the civilians they are meant to serve. He and his ministers have encouraged the GDF to think of itself primarily as a vanguard in the country's drive toward socialist and cooperative development. Soldiers and their commanders are expected to be models to other Guyanese in their service to the nation by growing their own food—part of the government's campaign to cut down costly imports of foreign foodstuffs—and in contributing labor to the construction of the ambitious interior highway which will link the Brazilian Amazonian road network to Guyana's coastal port. Soldiers take part in national parades, not in tanks, but on floats heralding agricultural cooperatives. Troops have been instructed to drop the British-inherited "sir" and instead to cultivate more egalitarian relationships.[53]

To insure that this interpenetration of civilian and military spheres does not produce weak or even ambiguous political allegiance, Burnham has also given his military special personal attention in public pronouncements and in attendance at military weddings—all of which are important in a country where political power has such a personal dimension.

More concretely, the government has increased the GDF's budget substantially. Army and civil service salaries have been raised steadily. On the eve of the 1973 election the GDF's budget was boosted 60 percent.[54] The greatest increases have occurred when the Guyanese economy is most shaky but when the GDF's official political role has been most blatant. Although official figures are not available, close observers believe that the GDF has been greatly expanded beyond its 1972 strength of 2,000 men. Prior to 1973 GDF manpower expenditures were relatively stable.[55] Prime Minister Burnham has also used budgetary negotiations to play the police and GDF off against one another, prompting each branch to surpass the other in demonstrations of loyalty to the PNC.

The Guyanese military remains one of the world's most modest in both size and equipment. But in the context of Guyana's domestic politics it wields formidable force. While control of the GDF is consequently of relatively little interest in determining the balance of power in the now fluid Caribbean international arena, it will be a weighty factor in determining the future distribution of power in multiethnic Guyana. But the more important the control of the army becomes for the PNC, the more questionable becomes the actual balance of power between the civilian party leaders and the military officers. The army's increasing importance to PNC politicians gives it leverage its members have never had before. Simultaneously, the interdependency and penetration raise doubts about the long-range fate of the GDF if the political regime in Georgetown should change. There are at minimum three possible alternatives to the current PNC, Burnham-led regime: 1) an anti-PNC African-led regime; 2) a multiethnic anti-PNC regime; 3) an Indian-led regime. In *any* of these possible futures the GDF will be the object of hostility and suspicion or, at best, will be thrown into internal confusion; that is, unless GDF personnel themselves take an active role in shaping the future regime, in which case its political base may be secured but its institutional foundation will be left as insecure as ever.

Conclusion

Civilian control of the military does not mean merely the prevention of coups d'etat—if that *is* all the phrase implies, then it is of little use in political analysis. Genuine control refers to the capacity of civilian authority to mobilize uniformed coercive organizations to serve short- and long-term political objectives set by civilians. Coups do not appear imminent in either Guyana and Malaysia; yet in both states civilian control in a more basic sense is limited.

If "civilian authorities" refers only to a specific regime, rather than to impersonalized enduring institutions,then "control" again is curtailed. For civilian control would refer only to *certain* civilians and would leave open to serious doubt the reliability of military compliance during the transition from one regime to another. In neither Guyana nor Malaysia, for instance, has this test of civilian control been passed. Both the Malaysian armed forces and the younger GDF have served under only one independent regime. Furthermore, both have served under only one ethnic community's political control. Perhaps both militaries would remain compliant to civilian authority in a new ruling party *if* the new party in Malaysia remained Malay-dominated, and the new ruling party in Guyana were African-dominated.

The ethnic factor poses problems as to whether the armed forces can carry out a regime's program. If one were a riddlemaker perhaps the question would be posed thus:

Can the controlled effectively control the groups that the controllers want controlled?

Can the GDF maintain control over a now largely non-African citizenry as Burnham's PNC wishes it to? In Malaysia, can the army work in cooperation with the police so as to curtail guerrilla recruitment in the jungles and to quickly terminate communal hostilities in the cities? The ethnic composition of the Malaysian and Guyanese armed forces puts them at a disadvantage in carrying out these civilian-designed objectives. It undermines nongovernmental civilian confidence, thus reducing military authority and ultimately military effectiveness. The Malaysian armed forces are more organizationally and ethnically elaborate; politicians can draw on different units with varying ethnic images. But the Malay Regiment still remains the core of the armed forces. The Alliance government (now National Front) seems to be aware of the problems created by defining the military's primary mission as maintenance of domestic peace and order while recruiting chiefly from one ethnic community. It has made deliberate efforts to bring more Chinese and Indians into the various branches, although with limited success except in technical services. Yet the Malay civilian leadership remains ambivalent, for at the same time that it desires a military force capable of maintaining civil order, it wants a military command it deems reliable and compliant— i.e., a military led by Malays.

The dilemma is even more severe and seemingly less recognized in Guyana. There, the choice between a military capable of commanding civilian respect and a military firmly loyal to the politicians in power is scarcely seen as a dilemma. Indeed the greatest weight clearly is being assigned to the latter need. This is so much so, in fact, that civilian control in Guyana may—since the 1973 elections—have become civilian dependence on the military, to a far greater degree than in Malaysia.

Civilian control could turn quite sour if:

1) Civilian control refers merely to military compliance with only one political regime.

2) Civilian control relies on such an ethnic symmetry between regime and army that the army loses its legitimacy as a truly national institution and thus generates hostility among the very communal groups it is supposed to "pacify."

3) Civilian control involves a costly *quid pro quo* with the army that diverts scarce government resources at a time when the nation's economy is faltering.

Notes to Chapter 3
Enloe, *Civilian Control of the Military.*

1. This comparison is part of a larger study of the impact of ethnicity on military organizations supported by a grant from the Council on Foreign Relations. During the period of the paper's revision I enjoyed the hospitality and intellectual stimulation of the Richardson Institute for Conflict and Peace Research, London.

The present paper could not have been written without the generous assistance of Stanley Bedlington of Cornell, Percy Hintzen of Clark University, H. A. Zakaria of MIT, Ernest Chew of the University of Singapore, Anthony Short of the University of Aberdeen, Stephen Milne of the University of British Columbia, and officers in the Malaysian and Guyanese embassies in Washington. Of course, they should not be held responsible for any faulty interpretations of the data. That responsibility lies with the author alone.

2. Elsewhere I have discussed the impact of ethnicity on African military development. See: Enloe, "Ethnicity and the Myth of the Military in African Development," *Ufahamu,* 4, 2, (Fall 1973): 35-56; also: "Military Uses of Ethnicity," *Millenium: Journal of International Studies* (LSE, London), (Winter, 1975-76): 220-34.

3. An exception is a paper by James F. Guyot, "Ethnic Segmentation and the Functions of the Military in Burma and Malaysia," presented to the Inter-University Seminar on Armed Forces and Society, University of Chicago, 11-13 October 1973.

4. Stanley Bedlington, a political scientist, but formerly a British police officer serving in Malaysia, supplied much of the historical information in an interview with the author, Northampton, Mass., 18 September 1974. For the histories of both the Malaysian police and armed forces, see also: John Henderson, *et al., Area Handbook for Malaysia* (Washington, Government Printing Office, 1970), pp. 531-582. For an interesting comparison, see Stanley Bedlington's "The Singapore Malay Community: The Politics of State Integration" (Ph.D. Diss., Ithaca, Cornell University, 1974), especially pp. 238-248 on ethnic changes in the Singapore military.

The Malay sultan who maintained the most visible military force was the sultan of Johore. See, "Johore Military Forces," *Malaysia in History,* 14, 1, (October 1971): 37-38.

5. Henderson, *et al., Malaysia Handbook,* pp. 532-533.

6. For a detailed account of early recruitment into the Malay Regiment, see Dol Ramli, "History of the Malay Regiment 1933-1942," *Journal of the Malayan Branch of the Royal Asiatic Society* (July, 1965): 204-216. Also see: William Gutteridge, *Military Institutions and Power in the New States* (New York: Praeger Publishers, 1965), p. 74.

7. For an account of the military aspect of the Emergency, see Harry Miller, *Jungle War in Malaya* (London: Arthur Barker, Ltd., 1972). The most

complete analysis of the colonial government's approach to police and military recruitment and deployment is: Anthony Short, *The Communist Insurrection in Malaya, 1948-60* (London: Frederick Muller Ltd., 1975).

8. Henderson, *et al., Malaysia Handbook,* pp. 561-562.

9. Malaysia, *Official Year Book* (Kuala Lumpur: Government Printer, 1961), p. 113.

10. One of the few biographical sketches of Tun Abdul Razak appears in an interview with him by Dom Moraes, "The Quiet Leader," *The Asia Magazine,* 10 October 1971, pp. 3-12. Early in 1976, Tun Razak died and was succeeded by another UMNO Malay, Hussein Onn, who also has close ties to the top Malay military leadership.

11. John Slimming, a former British police officer in Malaya, reports this in his detailed account of the 1969 riot, *Malaysia: Death of a Democracy* (London: John Murray, 1969), pp. 30-31, 36. For a Malaysian academic account of the May 1969 riots, see Goh Cheng Teik, *The May Thirteenth Incident and Democracy in Malaysia* (Kuala Lumpur: Oxford University Press, 1971). The author herself was in Kuala Lumpur during the 1969 riots and witnessed this effort by local Chinese to try, in the midst of fear and confusion, to determine which was a more reliable protection, the army or the police.

12. Bedlington, "Singapore Malay Community." See also: Zakaria Haji Ahmad, "Police Forces and Their Political Roles in South East Asia," unpublished manuscript, MIT, 1975.

13. H. A. Zakaria in an interview with the author, Cambridge, Mass., 17 September 1974.

14. National Operations Council, *The May 13 Tragedy: A Report* (Kuala Lumpur: October 1969), pp. 22-23.

15. David S. Gibbons and Zakaria Haji Ahmad, "Politics and Selection for the Higher Civil Service in the New States: The Malaysian Example," *Journal of Comparative Administration* 3 November 1971, pp. 337-338.

16. National Operations Council, *May 13 Tragedy,* p. 23.

17. Gibbons and Zakaria, "Politics and Selection," p. 338.

18. *Ibid.*

19. National Operations Council, *May 13 Tragedy,* pp. 23-24.

20. *Ibid.,* p. 23.

21. Slimming, *Malaysia,* p. 82.

22. *Malaysia, 1971: Official Year Book* (Kuala Lumpur: Government Printer, 1972), pp. 105-106.

23. Ron Huisken, "Federal Government Expenditure in Malaysia, 1960-69," *Kajian Ekonomi Malaysia* 3, 2 (December, 1970): 31.

24. *Ibid.*

25. "A Double Wedge in the Communists' Ranks," *Far Eastern Economic Review,* 15 November 1974, pp. 20-21; "S.A.S. in Malaysia," *Race Today* (June, 1975), p. 127.

26. Based on the yearly estimate published by London's International Institute of Strategic Studies in its *Military Balance* (1969-70, 1971-72, 1972-73, 1973-74, 1974-75).

27. *Ibid.*

28. Malaysia, *1974 Budget Report* (Kuala Lumpur: Government Printer, 1974), pp. 26-27.

29. International Institute of Strategic Studies, *Military Balance 1973-74* (London, 1973), pp. 54-55. The 1974-75 *Military Balance* lists (on p. 57) paramilitary personnel as numbering only 13,000 men, but this drop seems questionable, especially when the number of police field force units increased.

30. In 1969 Chinese made up 50 percent of the air forces' officer corps, while Malays comprised 33 percent of the officers. Yet among air force enlisted men, Malays were numerically dominant. Henderson *et al., Malaysia Handbook,* p. 558. Regarding efforts to maintain a "correct" ethnic balance in the air force and technical branches of the army, see also David Hawkins, *The Defense of Malaysia and Singapore* (London: Royal United Services Institute, 1972), p. 62.

31. *New York Times,* 9 October 1974. See also Harvey Stockwin, "Malaysia: Electing to be Moderate," *Far Eastern Economic Review* 6 September 1974, pp. 10-12.

32. Among the most thorough analyses of Guyana's ethnic party system are by Professor Ralph Premdas. See his: "Elections and Political Campaigns in a Racially Bifurcated State: The Case of Guyana," *Journal of Interamerican Studies and World Affairs* 14, 3 (August 1974): 271-296; "Competitive Party Organizations and Political Integration in a Racially Fragmented State," *Caribbean Studies* 12, 4 (January 1973): 5-35. For a graphic and sophisticated journalistic account of Guyana's political climate in 1974, see Jane Kramer, "Letter from Guyana," *New Yorker* 16 September 1974, pp. 100-128.

33. Kramer, "Letter from Guyana," quoting Professor Bobby Moore, p. 128.

34. Harold A. Lutchman, "Race and Bureaucracy in Guyana," *Journal of Comparative Administration* 4, 2 (August 1972): 227.

35. Robert B. Dishman, "Cultural Pluralism and Bureaucratic Neutrality in the British Caribbean," paper presented at the Annual Meeting of the American Political Science Association, Chicago, 29 August-2 September 1974, pp. 26-40.

36. International Commission of Jurists, *Report of the British Guiana Commission of Inquiry: Racial Problem in the Public Service* (Geneva, International Commission of Jurists), p. 36.

37. *Ibid.,* p. 48.

38. Lutchman, "Race and Bureaucracy in Guyana," p. 243.

39. International Commission of Jurists, *Report,* pp. 46-47.

40. For biographies of Brig. Clarence Price and Col. Ulric Pilgrim, see the Guyanese Defense Force's newspaper *Green Beret* 2, 1 (1972): 1-5.

41. International Commission of Jurists, *Report,* pp. 43-48.

42. Interviews by the author with Guyanese in Georgetown during 1971 and in the US during 1973 and 1974. Also Kramer, "Letter from Guyana,", p. 121.

43. *The Liberator,* Georgetown, Guyana, May 1972, p. 4.

44. *Ibid.* The PPP newspaper, *The Mirror,* in its 10 June 1973 issue quoted a letter from the general Council of Indian Organizations which estimated that Indians made up 8 percent of the GDF and 10 percent of the police.

45. Interviews by the author with Guyanese with personal contacts on the GDF, Georgetown, February 1972.

46. Interviews by the author with Guyanese in Georgetown, March 1972 and in the US, September 1973.

47. Interviews by the author with Guyanese, US, September 1974.

48. Though from a more cynical viewpoint, induction into the army or into the government's new National Service can seem to be "forced labor" rather than rewarding employment. This is the opinion of Cheddi Jagan as expressed in a speech to the PPP-affiliated youth group, reprinted as "Guyana at the Cross Roads," *The Black Scholar* 5, 10 (July-August 1974).

49. Interviews by the author with Guyanese in the US September 1973 and September 1974.

50. Kramer, "Letter from Guyana," pp. 112-113.

51. The PPP's charges are spelled out in detail in Janet Jagan, *Army Intervention in the 1973 Elections in Guyana* (Georgetown: PPP Education Committee, 1973).

52. Hon. L.F.S. Burnham, quoted in *Green Beret* 2, 10 (1973): 2.

53. See, for instance, articles in *The Scarlet Beret: Journal of the GDF* 1 (May 1971). (Both *Green Beret* and *The Scarlet Beret* are official GDF publications.)

54. Kramer, "Letter from Guyana," p. 120. In his 1974 budget speech the PNC finance minister requested a $G 1.2 million increase over 1973 for defense and an additional $G 7.8 million increase for internal security, "1974 Budget Speech," Georgetown, mimeo, 1974, p. 3.

55. See Gertrude E. Heare, *Latin American Military Expenditures, 1967-1971* (Washington: US Department of State, 1973), p. 12.

The Bases
of Civilian Control of the Military
in the Philippines

Sherwood D. Goldberg

Major Sherwood D. Goldberg, United States Army, is an assistant professor of Social Sciences at the United States Military Academy, West Point, New York. A Ph.D. candidate in international relations, University of Pennsylvania, his chapter is based on doctoral dissertation research that included field research in the Philippines in the summer of 1974. He has recently concluded service as a staff assistant to Ambassador William R. Kintner in the US Department of State in the preparation of "U.S. Policy Interests in the Asian-Pacific Area."

Introduction*

When President Ferdinand E. Marcos declared martial law in the Philippines on 21 September 1972, many deplored what was seen as the end of a democratic tradition in this "showcase of democracy" in Asia.[1] What was less frequently addressed by reporters and commentators on Philippine affairs, especially

---

* This chapter is a revised version of a paper prepared and presented in cooperation with Major James P. Thompson, Jr., US Army Institute for Military Assistance, Fort Bragg, North Carolina. The views expressed in this chapter are entirely those of the author and should not be considered to be representing the views or policy of the United States Military Academy or the United States Army.

during the first twelve months of the martial law period, was the new role of the Armed Forces of the Philippines (AFP). Accepting perhaps the continued applicability of the "American model" for civil-military relations, despite the constitutional crisis which the Philippines was to face and the higher profile of the armed forces in the "New Society" which was to be created, most students and participants of Philippine affairs either focused on the social, economic, and political effects of martial law, or accepted the assurance by President Marcos that civilian control of the military continued in the Philippines, that no military coup had occurred despite the conditions of martial law, and that the military was being used under the constitutional prerogatives of the chief executive, which permit limitations to democratic processes when threats to national security exist.[2] This was "Martial Law, Phillippine Style."[3]

This chapter sets forth those factors which have served as the basis within the Philippine political system for a "unique imposition of martial law"—a regime that was and remains one in which the military adheres to the principle of civilian supremacy. This is not a detailed accounting of how martial law was imposed, nor does it assess how martial law has affected Philippine political development, except as it relates to the new civil-military relations which may evolve if democratic practices continue to be constricted. This chapter suggests the unique combination of factors that from independence in 1946 to martial law in 1972 provided for this developing country a military which has been civil-responsive and which, by all accounts, has yet to present a serious challenge to authority.

Welch, in chapter 1, sets forth five means of civilian control. "Party controls" clearly do not apply to the Philippine model, for, as is most apparent, this has not been a single-party-dominant state. With party elites neither loyal nor subordinate to their own parties, with frequent rotation of national offices between the major political parties, and with neither of the two major parties, the Nacionalistas or the Liberals, professing a particular ideology with which to indoctrinate the state's armed forces, party controls as a factor are irrelevant to the Philippine scene.[4] Historical factors, constitutional constraints, ascriptive factors, and, at least until September 1972, clearly delineated and restricted spheres of military responsibility—these four means of civilian control are identified in the following analysis of civil-military relations in the Philippines.

Historical Factors—Constitutional Constraints— Ascriptive Factors—Limited Sphere of Responsibility: The Bases of Civilian Control

Professor George Taylor, in his brief discussion of "The Political Role of the Military," emphasized that "civilian supremacy" in the Philippines was a value inculcated under American tutelage during the colonial and commonwealth periods. Taylor wrote:

> In the early days of American rule William Howard Taft had demonstrated that the military is subordinate to the civil authority. This lesson was inculcated in the Philippine army so successfully that after independence the Philippine Republic stood in less danger of a military *coup d'etat* than any other country in Southeast Asia. Of all the American contributions to the Philippine value system, that of the military establishment was perhaps decisive.[5]

Further, Taylor suggested that the civilian and military sectors were consistently exposed to the same value system. There was, from his observations, no separate military class or elite which would have caused a divergence in values as of the early 1960s.

> In the Philippines, certainly since 1898, all classes have been exposed to the same value system. There are no violent contrasts in values between the Army officers, the government officials, the professional classes, the politicians, and the intellectual leaders.[6]

As scholars in the Philippines are inclined to suggest, however, this "civil supremacy value" may not have been the sole product of American influence. Rather, if one considers the writings and addresses of the nineteenth century Filipino nationalists, one notes how they stressed the ideals of a liberal democratic tradition which encompassed the virtues of "civilian authority."[7] What is perhaps most important to note for purposes of this discussion is that civil supremacy was a value readily followed by the Filipino upon independence. What the United States' contribution to the Philippines may well have been was to both support the ideal and to encourage its realization through specific actions. The civil administrative agencies and the political party system were so developed as to enable the civilian elite to meet the crises of political development, free from a threat to their legitimacy by the military. Further, the early Filipino nationalists, or evolutionaries, and the American colonial and commonwealth administrators were similarly in concert regarding the development of the Philippines through education rather than through military revolution. This was thus a shared value of both peoples and one held by most of the elite during the first half of the twentieth century. Its salience, though it was important for encouraging the civilian sector, may well have been the major deterrent offered to military intervention.

While Samuel Huntington in *The Soldier and the State* suggests that adoption of the slogan "civilian control" is not satisfactory for continued subjective control as the military profession develops,[8] it is apparent that the first twenty-six years of Philippine independence realized a continued adherence to the more traditional means for insuring civilian supremacy. In the Philippines the value of civilian control was not taken for granted! Despite the paucity of information to date on civil-military relations in the Philippines, the continued enunciation of the "proper relationship" between the military and the elected civilian officials is readily apparent even through the current period of martial law.[9] In particular, the power of particular government institutions was often exercised to demonstrate the subordination of the military to civil authorities and the democratic character of the Philippine constitution was (and is) routinely emphasized as the guideline for "proper" relationships.

Invariably, as one notes through discussion with political and military elites in the Philippines and through a review of public documents, the basis for civil-military relations is grounded in Commonwealth Act Number 1, The National Defense Act of

1935. Article 1, Section 2 of this act states "the civil authority shall always be supreme. The President of the Philippines as the Commander-in-Chief of all military forces shall be responsible that mobilization measures are prepared at all times." The 1935 Constitution indicated that the president was the senior civilian to whom the armed forces owed their loyalty. Responsible for the security of the nation, the president (operating within the guidelines of the "Citizens' Army" concept, which called for a small regular force backed by a large, well-trained reserve force to be called forth by presidential order) was placed over the military to insure civil supremacy. According to the 1973 Constitution, the Philippines is eventually to have a parliamentary system of government with the military responsible to the prime minister.[10]

Military responsiveness to presidential control from 1946 to 1972 did not rest solely on these idealist constitutional expressions. Civil supremacy became part of the political culture in the Philippines through indoctrination or, more appropriately, through the political socialization process which instilled this principle in the people at all levels of military training, including that administered in the schools as primary military training. The press in the Philippines, perhaps the freest of all in Asia until 1972, was consistently used in the socialization process by those to whom the military represented a threat to the nation's liberal tradition. Certainly the opposition in Congress to past administrations employed all of the public media in its expression of concern for "proper" civil-military relations. In addition, opponents attempted to insure that the president employed his constitutional prerogative "correctly" when calling out the military during threats to national security. Congress frequently expressed concern that the executive would use his power for personal ends, such as to influence elections.

The 4th Congress of the Republic of the Philippines (1959) acted typically in its concern that the civilian sector maintain firm control of the military. No fewer than eight pieces of legislation on civil control of the military were introduced in the second session of this Congress. Both to illustrate the continuing concern for civil rule and to note the various foci of legislative efforts to institutionalize this control, several of these legislative proposals are quite instructive. One bill, "To Prohibit Appointment of Any Member of the Regular or Reserve Force of the Armed Forces of the Philippines or a Retired Member Thereof to Positions of Secretary or Undersecretary of National Defense," included the explanatory note by the bill's sponsor that:

> This bill was designed to prevent the growth of the power and influence of the military in this country, in order to spare our country from tragic experiences of our Asian neighbors, recently in Burma and Thailand, where military dictatorship has marred their beautiful history.[11]

Congressman Ligot of Cagayan was sufficiently concerned by the "rumors" of a pending military coup d'etat in 1959 that he urged the death penalty for such acts.[12] A final topic, which remains even today a focus of concern in Philippine affairs, was addressed in 1959 by Congressman Gonzalez of Laguna when he sought to have the Philippine Constabulary separated from the Armed Forces of the Philippines (AFP) in an effort to remove "the threat of the Commander-in-Chief, or the Chief of Staff, or the Secretary of National Defense being too powerful with all the armed forces in the palm of one man."[13]

The Philippine military was, of course, not isolated from these expressions of concern as to proper civil-military relations. Whether to allay fears or to insure that improper conclusions from the experiences of such states as Burma and Thailand were not drawn, the AFP also stressed the "civil supremacy" principle through its "troop information and education program." The "Code of Conduct of the Filipino Soldier" for example includes: "I am a Filipino soldier. I will support and defend the Constitution of the Republic of the Philippines. I will uphold the supremacy of civilian authority over the military in war, or in peace." Again, while most governments may assert this principle, the government of the Philippines has continuously recommended civilian authority to its people.[14] The principle was (and is) clearly not taken for granted.

If the cautious eye of the legislator, the press, and a politically aware populace were not sufficient to enhance civil authority over the military, one should recognize that the military itself was not a viable alternative to civil rule, at least through the period under study. While more recent accounts of Philippine history may rightfully seek to place the armed forces' contribution to Philippine development in a more positive light, Philippine history as taught until 1972, at least, did not place the military in the forefront of Philippine society. Independence from Spain may have been won by militarists, but it was not sustained. Independence from the United States was not the result of a war, but rather of a political struggle among the civil elite, with the military either not politically involved or completely involved with purely defense-related issues. Further, until 1950 when a fairly successful campaign against the Huks was launched, the military did not present itself as a viable alternative to civil rule. Though politicians were corrupt or accused of collaboration, neither the military itself[15] nor the populace thought it had a better right to rule than the civilian elite, despite the heroism of many in the armed forces prior to and during Japanese occupation. More precisely, the army lacked legitimacy not only because of the abuses its soldiers committed, but also because it failed to protect the populace, while the constabulary faced charge after charge of corruption. The prewar civil-political process had to function, for there was no alternative. The open struggle which ensued among the civil elites through the election process may have served to strengthen the civil tradition, and the military was kept at bay due to its commitments, its lack of governing tradition, and its own institutional development problems. These persisted until Ramon Magsaysay became secretary of national defense in 1950.[16]

As important perhaps as any of the above environmental factors was the development of competent civilian institutions during the formative years after World War II. Despite postwar problems of modernization and reconstruction, the government, with its elected officials and trained civil servants, was able to govern. While the collaboration issue threatened to divide the country, the Huk challenge by 1950 threatened the very viability of national and local government, elections often resulted in violence and extensive charges of corruption, and resource allocation was never effected to the complete satisfaction of the peasants and certain minority groups, the political process did continue to function. And it is this continued "effective" rule by the civilian sector which, as one observer noted, "resulted in the military never having a cause for intervening." Military men, unlike in many other developing nations, were not needed to fill the void left by departing colonial administrators. Beginning in 1901 Filipinos were trained and given increasing opportunity to govern themselves. By 1946 "political institutions were well-developed. The civilian bureaucracy and the political institutions manned by elected or appointed officials were able to function without encouraging military involvement."[17]

The Armed Forces of the Philippines, at least through the period 1946-1972, was also relatively small compared to the armed forces in other developing states. While size is not a foremost consideration in maintaining civilian supremacy, largely because small military forces have often assumed political dominance in other states, the size factor does have a bearing in the Philippine system. Despite Department of National Defense efforts to increase the defense budget (note especially the 1970 budget proposal which initially represented a 250 percent increase over previous appropriations[18]), the figures for Fiscal Year 1971 maintained the Philippines among the lowest in defense expenditures. With a GNP over $10 billion and a population of some 38.4 million, $124 million was expended for military equipment and manpower. With armed forces of 55,000, military personnel represented at that time a mere 0.1 percent of the population. Comparable statistics for other states of the Far East placed the Philippines third in GNP, fourth in population, but eleventh in military expenditures, thirteenth in the number of personnel in uniform, and fifteenth of fifteen in the percentage of population in the armed forces. Using the data available on armed forces throughout the world, the Philippines ranked in 1971 among such nations as Haiti, Jamaica, Sri Lanka (then Ceylon), and Zambia as the nations with the lowest percentage of the population in the armed forces.[19]

But the size factor alone is not adequate to explain the

responsiveness of the military to civilian authority. As Welch and Smith have stated in *Military Role and Rule:* "The crucial question is not the absolute measures of these factors but rather how they are weighed within a particular sociopolitical context."[20] What should be noted is that the Philippine military, while remaining relatively small during the period 1946-72, was very active throughout the period developing a "Citizens' Army," fighting the Huk insurgents, conducting extensive "civic action," participating in United Nations operations in Korea, and joining the United States in South Vietnam. The Armed Forces of the Philippines was and is very busy! Resources, compared to tasks undertaken, were utilized apparently with little extra equipment or personnel resources available to "encourage" the less militarily acceptable tasks of governing! Again, size and activity considerations alone do not suggest a very participatory role for the military in the Philippine political process, at least until 1972.

As initially noted, American influence was a factor in establishing Philippine civil-military relations. Although American political and economic influence may have waned since 1946, American military influence did not. From 1946 to date the Philippine military has relied heavily upon the US for both materiel and, decreasingly, for much of its training.[21] This reliance appears to have a correlation with the role of the Philippine military in politics, for in addition to materiel dependence, the mere presence at most command levels (until the late 1960s) of US advisors constantly reminded the Filipino of his dependence upon the US military.[22] This dependent relationship, it is suggested, served to influence the nature of civil-military relations in the Philippines.

That the US military had so penetrated the Philippine military system suggests influence.[23] It is the reality of such a relationship. Americans did not have to exercise the influence relationship. (Nor is there any basis for suggesting efforts were made to "manipulate" the AFP.) What is suggested is that the mere dependence upon Americans created an influence relationship. This material and emotional dependence, called the "JUSMAG factor,"[24] was aggravated by Filipino congressmen, who, desirous of cutting defense appropriations, would frequently suggest to the AFP that if its equipment requests were so necessary, the AFP "should go to your friends at JUSMAG."[25] The AFP was forced into a closer identity with JUSMAG elements than with its own legislative branch, which was unwilling, and in part unable, to meet perceived defense needs. This American context reinforced the experiences learned at Fort Knox, Fort Benning, or other US military centers.[26] If size alone did not inhibit the military, its reliance upon the United States may at least have "blocked out" a more active political role. If the military did have institutional objectives other than those of the civilian elite, there was little prospect for realizing these goals outside the system—a system which often placed the AFP between the Philippine Congress and JUSMAG.

The National Defense Act, legislative proposals and enactments, values, the strength of political institutions, size, the JUSMAG factor—all appear to have inhibited AFP political intervention and enhanced civil control. There are, however, more positive factors which served to encourage military subordination to civilian control. The Philippine civil elites are quite responsive to military interests, as the "malacas"[27] which the AFP has had with two of the most influential commanders-in-chief—President Magsaysay and President Marcos—reflects. The realities of the Philippine military officer's career are also a positive factor.

While the military was at odds with the politicians in 1948 over the granting of amnesty to many collaborators with the Japanese and members of the Huk paramilitary organizations,[28] the Philippine military was not isolated from national decision-making. The most prominent of its acknowledged representatives was Ramon Magsaysay. Initially a congressman involved in defense-related matters, Magsaysay, as the secretary of national defense, was quickly recognized by the military as their man with access to the presidential palace at Malacanang. From 1950 to 1957 military men could all identify this champion of their institutional objectives.[29]

Magsaysay, in addition to serving as a communications and identification link between the civil and military sectors, did politicize the armed forces. He focused on the counterinsurgency effort against the Huks, brought military lawyers into civil suits between peasants and landlords, mobilized ROTC cadets to police national elections, and had the Department of National Defense (DND) respond not only to many military complaints but also to many nonmilitary issues. Crime, land problems, gambling, health, sanitation, water supplies, etc., became military issues as military resources were used in short-term solutions.[30]

Through the person of Magsaysay, both as secretary of national defense and later as president, the military not only "won" the Huk fight by winning the "hearts and minds" of the people for the government, but it also began to receive a great deal of respect and admiration from the people. Instead of political decisions being made over the military's opposition, as was the case with the amnesty issue, political decisions now aided the military in its newly defined primary task of law and order.[31]

The military also was able to identify with President Ferdinand E. Marcos, when he assumed office in 1965. As with Magsaysay, the military came to feel "malacas with Malacanang." Like Magsaysay, Marcos was a former guerrilla leader, who was perceived as having a common interest with men in uniform. The two presidents not only provided the military elite with access to high-level decision-making, but they also brought prestige and honor to the military, along with such tangible benefits as increased pay, allowances, and promotions.

The realities of the military officer's career in the Philippines offer additional positive factors for civil supremacy. First, the Armed Forces of the Philippines, and specifically the officer corps, do not represent an elite military class in society. The regular officer corps, largely drawn from the Philippine Military Academy (PMA), which admits cadets on the basis of congressional appointments, much in the manner presently followed by US academies, provides a cross-sectional representation of Philippine society. The officer corps is neither homogeneous by social or economic class, nor is it homogeneous by geographical background. From statistics a former member of the PMA faculty has provided, we can see that the 1963-66 academy classes were composed as follows:

geographical regions largely (70 percent) represented were Ilocano, Tagalog, and Cebuano, while occupation of parents exhibited greater diversity with 20 percent of the cadets from military families, 15 percent from families in which the father was a teacher, and 30 percent from families in which income was from either a small business or a small farm. "About 79.7% or 105 families (of the 120 cadets' families surveyed) had an income of from 2,000 to 15,000 pesos annually, a range which roughly corresponds to the middle class in Philippine society."[32] Further, 74.2 percent of the sample were born in rural areas, in the provinces, while 25.8 percent were identified with the Manila area. No clear class or ethnic congruence can be discerned. The officer corps is neither homogeneous nor elite in its make-up.

The reserve officer corps is composed largely of officers commissioned through ROTC units at universities, and while additional research is necessary into the composition of the officer corps, the data suggest there were and are cross-cutting cleavages within the armed forces which have enhanced the subordination of the military to civil authority. The AFP has been too heterogeneous to effect a united stand against civilian rule. Regional differences in particular have inhibited greater political activity, as officers have tended to place family ties above professional loyalties.

Military officers have frequently cited the promotion system as having constrained professionalism during the 1946-72 period. While the exact extent of political interference on such issues as promotions and assignments cannot be determined, the impression exists that a large percentage of officers perceived promotion to the rank of colonel and higher as necessitating a personal identification with and subordination to politicians who by law sat on the Commission on Appointments. These officers perceived the system as one based less on ability than on political contacts—a complaint usually couched in terms which suggested that "politicking" was unprofessional.[33] The extent to which the officers had to patronize "their" civil official or officials on the commission is difficult to discern; however, the following reveals that influence-peddling did exist. While issuing a 1936 executive order governing the administration of the officer corps, President Quezon stated:

> ... it is wholly impossible to devise any infallible system of evaluating ability that will permit higher authority to make distinctions on any such particularized basis. But the most serious objection to the selective method of promotion is that it frequently permits political or other extraneous influence to affect an officer's advancement. This is fatal to efficiency! Whenever an army becomes convinced that the promotion of an officer has resulted from favoritism or prejudice, irreparable harm is done to the morale of the whole corps, and the military service is certain to be neglected in favor of political maneuvering.[34]

Apparently President Quezon's warning was not adequate in the postwar period, for by 1951 political interference in officer promotions and the split loyalties of officers between the service and their extramilitary "compadre" or "patron" necessitated a more precise explication of what was to be avoided. General Headquarters distributed a circular regarding promotions which included the following admonition: "The logic behind these regulations is obvious and compelling—an officer who obtains preferential assignment, detail or treatment through the intervention of parties outside the military command channel will feel indebted to his patron and will be obliged to render his allegiance and loyalty first to his benefactor and next to the organization to which he belongs." The circular concluded that "it devolves upon every officer to advise all their kin and friends to desist from 'wire-pulling' because it is only through the elimination of this cancerous vice that an efficient and self-respecting officer corps can emerge."[35] By 1969 political interference had apparently become so extensive, at least by reputation, that a news story concluded: "The officers, even those of them who boast of a purely military education, have become the cringing creatures of politicians. They have become in other words, the lap dogs of Congressmen and Senators."[36]

It is difficult to draw conclusions as to the extent of this political interference. Perhaps the "reputation" of what it takes to attain senior positions is sufficient to suggest to the AFP that civil authorities have considerable power whether it is over promotions or the budget and that to dismiss the civilian elite out of hand may be not only institutionally but personally disastrous.

Political interference does undermine military professionalism, but it also increased lateral identification with the civilian sector. The compadre and patron relationship have made civil authorities accessible to the military, thereby lessening the isolation of the AFP from society. Despite the institutional or professional shortcomings which result from this type of relationship, greater communication does exist between the civil and military sectors, with one military interviewee noting, "the realization of enhanced civil-military relations through less institutionalization and less adherence to the chain of command except during the execution of operational orders."

The Philippine military officer's living arrangements further inhibit the AFP from assuming a posture distinct or separate from Philippine society and the prevailing social forces. The AFP is not set apart from society on expansive military reservations. Housing for most military men is within the civilian communities of middle and lower-middle income occupational groups. Children of most military men go to school with children of the civilian community. Local chapters of the Lions Club, Rotary, or Kiwanis-type associations combine a cross-section of Philippine society, including the military, which does not have a separate, distinct social grouping. The officers' club is not the social organization it once was and occasionally remains for US military officers.

The missions of the AFP have also brought the military and civil society into a closer working relationship than is realized in those nations where district borders are to be manned or distant lands are to be guarded. The AFP, except for units sent to Korea in the 1950s and to Vietnam in the 1960s, has been a "home army." Overseas duty and frequent reassignments are rare. Military families have roots in communities and these communities rarely change. Even if the husband is reassigned, his family often remains in the provinces or in the greater Manila area. In many cases a military family owns property and the transfer of property rights is not as easy as in the US.

Accordingly, the military family becomes identified with the civil community, its goals, and its values. Because of these basic socioeconomic ties, the Philippine political system has not been torn by diverging civil and military goals. The civilian and military sectors in the Philippines have been highly integrated.[37]

Finally, as Taylor noted,[38] mandatory retirement after thirty years of service (with four years at PMA counted towards retirement) has encouraged the military officer to identify with the civilian community in which he not only has associations but which he will join at quite a young age. The retirement system encourages the officer to solicit civilian positions into which he may work upon retirement—another factor inhibiting a more institutionalized and distinct military set of interests. In addition, the brevity of the active military career hedges in one who might have sought to build a military power base. By the time most officers reach senior rank and position, attention turns either to the prospects for future employment or to maintaining the system to which one has devoted thirty years and from which one receives retirement benefits.[39]

Civilian Control of the Philippine Military During the Martial-Law Period

The focus of this chapter thus far has been on the basis for civilian control of the military as it was realized during the first twenty-six years of Philippine independence. The discussion would not be complete, however, without a brief analysis of civil-military relations since 21 September 1972, when a new era in Philippine history was initiated.

The four controls considered most significant in maintaining civil supremacy prior to martial law remain appropriate for assessing the new role for the Armed Forces of the Philippines. The military's new role, or more precisely, its expanded sphere of responsibility, has most significantly changed when compared to its more limited law-and-order and external-defense roles from 1946-1972. While the military already began to have expanded civic-action type missions during the first Marcos administration,[40] it was not until martial law that the chief executive employed the armed forces as his principle operative in "revolutionalizing" Philippine society. For the "New Society" the AFP was "to become a creative force."[41] It was to set the standards for society in discipline and efficiency, as it initially assumed operational control of all means of communication, insured adherence by the populace to proclamations ranging from the prohibition of the private ownership of firearms, to health and sanitation decrees, and assumed all government responsibilities in several of the outlying provinces.

While the military has been withdrawn from the actual management of many agencies within the public and private sector, several of the more senior officers remain, as one interviewee suggested, as "catalysts for efficiency." While no longer temporary directors or supervisors, several officers have remained in businesses (especially those in communications activities) to insure that backsliding does not occur and to insure adherence to the "revolutionary" programs.[42]

One must emphasize, however, that the expanded sphere of military responsibility was not the result of military initiative. Civilian authority was not set aside. Military tribunals were established to try cases involving "enemies of the state," but civil courts remained operative. A military junta was not empowered. Armored vehicles and uniformed servicemen were not conspicuous in the populated areas. This was "Martial Law, Philippine Style," and as with pre-1972 civil-military affairs, the military and civilian communities were assured that actions by the military were in keeping with the president's constitutional powers.[43]

Had the constitutional basis for civilian supremacy over the military not been as ingrained in Philippine political culture as previously asserted, or had the military been less constitutionally conscious, President Marcos's actions from 21 September 1972 might have been less frequently argued on legal grounds. Since martial law has been proclaimed, Ferdinand Marcos and his spokesmen, both from the civilian and military sectors, have repeatedly delineated a growing crisis in Philippine society between 1969 and 1972 which verged on open rebellion. Given such a scenario, the president acted constitutionally under the provisions of Article VII, Section 10, Paragraph (2) in authorizing the imposition of martial law. The rationale for, the legality of, and the style of martial law have become almost an ideology for the Philippine "public" elite.[44]

By the time the real constitutional crisis was to be faced on 31 December 1973,[45] when President Marcos's second term in office was to expire, a new transition period, also described increasingly as "constitutionally correct," was in effect. The military accordingly could continue to follow the "duly constituted" civil authority. Apparently the AFP did so without realizing the divisiveness in its ranks that the opposition to Marcos had expected and sought.[46]

Steps have been taken, of course, which encourage the continued loyalty of the military to the present chief executive. In addition to a more favorable public image, both as described in the more circumspect media and through the frequent encouraging remarks by the chief executive himself, individual soldiers and officers have realized appreciable improvements in pay, housing or subsistence allowances, promotion opportunities, retirement benefits, and educational benefits.[47]

Contrasted to conditions which prevailed for the military when it sought from the late 1960s until 1972 to get Congress to raise military budgetary authorizations and when contrasted with the public abuse to which the military was subject in the late 1960s, it is perhaps understandable why, when the decisions were made to impose martial law and to effect the constitutional transition period under "Constitutional authoritarianism," the AFP remained loyal to the commander-in-chief. The Congress, the press, and certainly those politicians who were the chief critics of the armed forces did not encourage the military to question Marcos's authority. Rather, the opposition to Marcos was in fact driving the military into further alignment with the present regime. As one senior officer reflected about the period prior to martial law, "the politicians had their day!" Conditions in Philippine political affairs were sufficiently critical to necessitate a decision by the armed forces, and they opted to join Marcos with whom many, by virtue of regional, familial, collegial, and/or economic ties, had "malacas."[48]

Since martial law the size of Philippine armed forces has been significantly enlarged,[49] in part to fill the positions which an expanded sphere of responsibility created and in part to meet what may be an expanded threat to the territorial integrity of the Philippines in the southern islands, especially on Mindanao. With this expanded size, however, the military has not become less socially integrated. The military remains part of Philippine society and not apart from it. Despite reports of the "Ilocanization" of the officer corps (selection from members of that ethnic group), allegedly to strengthen its identification and loyalty to Marcos, the officer corps is as representative of society as it was in the mid-1960s. There is no reason to suggest that the values of the military are any different from those of the larger community, though there is justified concern that the longer the military remains the junior partner of an authoritarian regime, the more likely the military will grow accustomed to its prominent position. More critical perhaps is the concern that the longer the civilian political elite remains muted, the less capable it will be of governing when martial law is lifted. By then the military may both perceive itself and be perceived as the only viable governing body. Were such the case, of course, historical factors which contributed significantly to the maintenance of a liberal democratic system would be negated and the Philippines would become comparable to its neighbors in Southeast Asia.

A new Philippine model for civil-military relations is evolving. Whether a new relationship will find "military control with or without partners" or whether the military will lessen its involvement in politics and assume a position of influence with continued civilian control depends upon the success of Marcos's initiatives, especially in the social and economic areas. Future civil-military relations will be influenced by what happens in the southern provinces where the military is facing its most critical test, both politically and militarily. The future relationship will also be influenced by perceived or actual external threats to the Philippines and by the nature of US-Philippine relations as the United States lessens its commitments in Asia and as the Filipinos seek greater self-reliance in defense matters. If the JUSMAG factor becomes less pronounced, the AFP may find its organizational interests best served in a political system less characteristic of pre-1972, when

Congress thwarted its appropriations and "forced" the military into an alliance with Marcos.

Finally, since the situation has developed so rapidly and changed so drastically in the Philippines in a relatively brief period of time, it is appropriate to conclude this discussion by drawing upon Joseph Hayden's noted analysis. Prior to World War II he wrote:

> If the independent Philippines were to sink below a certain economic level, it might easily become a sub-marginal state socially and politically. Then there would be grave danger that the Army would play the same sort of role that the military forces have often acted in other nations of that character. On the other hand, should fundamental conditions remain reasonably favorable for the continuation of a sound government, it seems unlikely that the Army would give rise to either autocracy or instability.[50]

Notes to Chapter 4

Goldberg, *The Bases of Civilian Control of the Military in the Philippines.*

1. For a recent book sympathetic to President Marcos's actions, see Beth Day, *The Philippines: Shattered Showcase of Democracy in Asia* (New York, M. Evans and Company, 1974). For a most comprehensive bibliographical listing of published material on martial law in the Philippines, see Tom Walsh's *Martial Law in the Philippines: A Research Guide and Working Bibliography,* Southeast Asia Working Paper No. 4, Asian Studies Program, University of Hawaii, 1973.

2. See especially Ferdinand E. Marcos, *Notes on the New Society of the Philippines* copyrighted 1973 by Ferdinand E. Marcos. In this book Marcos discusses the rationale for imposing martial law.

3. Brig. Gen. Guillermo A. Pecache, Deputy Chief of Staff for Home Defense, AFP, "Martial Law—Philippine Style", speech delivered at the Conference of School Superintendents, Presidents of State Colleges and Universities and Chiefs of Division, University of Santo Thomas, Manila, 9 October 1972.

4. For an excellent analysis of Philippine political history, see Onofre D. Corpuz, *The Philippines* (Englewood Cliffs, N.J.: Prentice Hall, Inc., 1965).

5. George E. Taylor, *The Philippines and the United States: Problems of Partnership* (New York: Frederick A. Praeger, 1964), p. 181.

6. *Ibid.*, p. 195.

7. The author is indebted to Professor Remigio E. Agpalo, Department of Political Science, University of the Philippines, who suggested that such writings of Jose B. Rizal as *Noli Me Tangere,* among others, be considered to reflect the Filipino value of "civil government." For an excellent discussion of the historical roots for recent (pre-1972) Philippine politics, see Remigio E. Agpalo, "The Philippine Political System in the Perspective of History," *Philippine Journal of Public Administration* 15, 304 (July-October 1971): 239-258.

8. Samuel P. Huntington, *The Soldier and the State* (Cambridge: Harvard University Press, 1959), p. 83.

9. In addition to note 2 above, see "Statement of President Ferdinand E. Marcos on the Proclamation of Martial Law in the Philippines," dated 21 September 1972, in which President Marcos states, after noting Article VII, Section 19, paragraphs (2) of the Philippines Constitution which served as the basis for presidential action: "I repeat, this is not a military takeover of civil government functions. The government of the Republic of the Philippines which was established by our people in 1946 continues." Reprinted in *Proclamation No. 1081,* a compilation of presidential decrees by Office of Civil Relations, Philippines Army, 1973.

10. Section 12, Article IX of the 1973 Constitution of the Philippines states: "The Prime Minister shall be Commander-in-Chief of all armed forces of the Philippines...." The Constitution is reprinted in Office for Civil Relations, Philippine Army, *Proclamation No. 1081: Presidential Decrees, General Orders, Letters of Instructions and Related Matters* 1, 1 (June 1973): 489-507.

11. House Bill No. 2220, introduced by Congressman A.F. Agbayoni, Philippine House of Representative, Fourth Congress of the Republic of the Philippines, Second Session.

12. House Bill No. 2242, introduced by Congressman B.T. Ligot, Philippine House of Representatives, Fourth Congress of the Republic of the Philippines, Second Session.

13. House Bill No. 2224, introduced by Congressman J.Z. Gonzales, Philippine House of Representatives, Fourth Congress of the Republic of the Philippines, Second Session.

14. Hayden noted that "positive efforts have been made to keep the Army out of politics and politics out of the Army. The reservists, the young people in the schools, and the public generally have been systematically indoctrinated with the conception that the army is a nonpolitical instrument of national salvation." Joseph R. Hayden, *The Philippines: A Study in National Development* (New York: Macmillan and Co., 1942), p. 753. As an example of recent efforts to insure that the "civil supremacy" principle was clearly stated, see President Ferdinand E. Marcos, "The AFP—Bulwark of De-

mocracy," address at the 72nd Anniversary of the Philippine Army, Fort Bonifacio, 22 March 1969 in which he stated, "I hereby order every officer, every enlisted man, every airman, and every sailor in all military installations throughout the country to refrain from taking any action that may may mean or may be interpreted as partisan political activity . . . . I want you all to refer to your personal copy of your respective oaths of office, wherein . . . you had sworn to 'support and defend the Constitution of the Philippines.' " Excerpts of address represented in Jose M. Crisol, ed. *Marcos on the Armed Forces* (Manila: Capital Publishing House, Inc. 1971), p. 77.

15. Carl H. Lande makes this point in his "The Philippine Military in Government and Politics," a paper read to the Research Committee on Armed Forces and Society of the Seventh World Congress of Sociology, Varna, Bulgaria, 14-19 September 1970, p. 8.

16. For a discussion of the state of the armed forces as of 1950, see Edward G. Lansdale, *In the Midst of Wars* (New York: Harper and Row Publishers, 1972), pp. 17-31. For the Philippine military's own realization of the difficulties with which it was faced at this time, note the remarks of Maj. Gen. M.N. Castaneda in his 1949-50 "Annual Report to the Secretary of National Defense." Castaneda wrote: "Beset by difficulties within and threatened by forces from without (referring to the Korean conflict) the AFP faces considerably more problems with considerably less means than the Philippines Army of Bataan and Correigidor . . . . It is true that there have been cases of misunderstanding among soldiers and civilians in the past, but these have been relatively isolated cases, and may be attributed to the incomplete training of some of the troops . . . . The later half of the year 1949 found the AFP operating on the same budget as that of the previous fiscal year and with an organization that had become inadequate." Maj. Gen. M.N. Castaneda, *Annual Report of the Commanding General, AFP to the Secretary of National Defense 1949-1950* (Major Goldberg wishes to note the kind assistance of the Philippine Department of National Defense in granting him access to this and other reports).

17. Observation by Raul P. DeGuzman, Dean, College of Public Administration, University of the Philippines, Manila, 31 July 1974 in interview with Major Goldberg.

18. See "Defense Budget Alarms Senate," *Saturday Chronicle* (Manila), 8 March 1969.

19. "World Military—Expenditures and Manpower" reproduced in Claude E. Welch, Jr. and Arthur K. Smith, *Military Role and Rule* (North Scituate, Mass: Duxbury Press, 1974), pp. 278-282 from US Arms Control and Disarmament Agency, *World Military Expenditures 1971* (Washington: Bureau of Economic Affairs, U.S. Arms Control and Disarmament Agency, 1972), pp. 10-13.

20. Welch and Smith, *Military Role and Rule,* p. 38.

21. The Republic of the Philippines received under the Military Assistance Program FY 1950-1972 a total of $440,556,000 worth of equipment, supplies, and services on a grant basis from the United States, plus a total of

$23,914,000 worth of "excess defense articles" during the same period. A total of 14,331 Filipinos were trained under the MAP Training Program from FY 1950-1972. "Military sales" by the US to the Philippines from 1950-1972 totaled $8,182,000. Source: US Department of Defense, Security Assistance Agency, *Military Assistance and Foreign Military Sales Facts,* May 1973.

22. AFP active and retired officers suggested to Major Goldberg during the interviews conducted in the summer of 1974 that the heavy dependence on the US and the close contact maintained between the US military and the AFP served as a constant reminder of their common adherence to "civil supremacy." Commentaries on the AFP "Self-Reliant" Program suggest the psychological dimensions of military dependency as realized from 1946 to 1972. See Colonel Marcario D. Mendoza, "Introduction to the AFP Self-Reliant Defense Posture," *Philippine Military Digest* 1, 2 (1973): 33-35 and Undersecretary Manuel Q. Salientes, "The AFP Self-Reliant Program," *Philippine Military Digest* 1, 3 (1974): 13-15.

23. For a discussion of "influence" through "penetration," see Karl W. Deutsch, "External Influences on the Internal Behavior of States," in R. Barry Farrell, Ed., *Approaches to Comparative and International Politics* (Evanston: Northwestern University Press, 1966) pp. 5-26.

24. JUSMAG is the Joint United States Military Advisory Group, established in the Philippines after World War II to provide material and advisory assistance to the Philippine armed forces.

25. A frequent comment made by officers of the AFP to Major Goldberg. The officers were lamenting the lack of cooperation shown by some congressmen in the past to defense needs. The near frustration expressed by some, who perceived the Philippine Congress as unwilling to lessen the reliance on the US, was expressed already in 1949 in the *Annual Report of the Chief of Staff AFP 1948 to 1949.* Maj. Gen. M.N. Castaneda wrote, "To those who advocate complete reliance on the Military Assistance Agreement (with the US) to buttress our defense structure, I regret that I must say that the best evidences on our hands indicate that beyond what have already been given we cannot expect any further military assistance other that for our internal peace and order campaign . . . . it cannot be expected that the United States will give the bountiful assistance that so many dream of."

26. For the period FY 1964 to 1970 alone, 1,253 officers and enlisted men of the AFP received training in the United States. Figures provided by Ground Forces Division, Joint US Military Advisory Group, Quezon City, Philippines, August 1974.

27. "Malacas"—a Philippine word suggesting a good relationship or more specifically in this case that the military at least had access to the civil elite. Major Goldberg is indebted to the Honorable Manuel Q. Salientes, Undersecretary of Defense for Munitions, for his insight into this "special relationship."

28. Position of the military on this issue discussed with retired senior officer of AFP during interview with Major Goldberg, August 1974.

29. On the role of Magsaysay in this regard, see, among others, Alvin H.

Scaff, *The Philippine Answer to Communism* (Stanford: Stanford University Press, 1955); Col. Napoleon D. Valeriano and Lt. Col. Charles T.R. Bohannan, *Counter-Guerilla Operations: The Philippine Experience* (New York: Praeger, 1962); Robert A. Smith, *Philippine Freedom 1946-1958* (New York: Columbia University Press, 1958); and Lansdale, *In the Midst of Wars.*

30. *Ibid.*

31. The temporary suspension of the writ of habeas corpus in 1952, an action taken in accordance with the constitution when the nation faced insurrection or rebellion, was an aid in the anti-Huk campaign. See Lansdale, *In the Midst of Wars*, p. 65.

32. Benjamin C. Duque, "A Descriptive Analysis of the Successful Cadets at the PMA" (Master's Thesis, Graduate College of Education, University of the Philippines, March 1964). Additional background data on the PMA cadet is also found in Benjamin C. Duque, "The Philippine Military Academy: An Analysis of its Environment and the Characteristics of its Cadets," (PhD Diss. Graduate School of Arts and Sciences, Saint Louis University, October 1972) and Col. B.D. Duque, "An In-Depth Study—The Educational Environment and Characteristics of Cadets in the Philippine Military Academy," *Philippine Military Digest* 1, 3 (1974): 16-37.

33. Major Goldberg's interviews during the summer 1974 with many active and retired officers found most agreed political interference was extensive. Congressmen who were interviewed were not in accord on this matter.

34. Manuel Quezon, "Statement made by the President upon Signing of Executive Order Governing Administration of Officer Corps," *Report on National Defense in the Philippines* (Manila: Commonwealth of the Philippines, Office of the Military Advisor, 1936), p. 51.

35. Circular Number 35, "Soliciting Political Influence to Advance Personal Ends," General Headquarters, AFP, Camp Murphy, Quezon City, 22 May 1951.

36. I.P. Soliongco, "An Astronomical Sum for a Hopeless Army," *The Manila Chronicle,* 2 March 1969.

37. For additional discussion of this point, see Q.R. De Borja, A.N. Gatmaitan, and G.C. De Castro, "Notes on the Role of the Military in Socio-Economic Development," *Philippine Journal of Public Administration* 12, 3 (July 1968): 266-283.

38. Taylor, *The Philippines and the United States,* p. 184.

39. For an excellent discussion of this issue which is based on survey data, see Quinten R. De Borja, "Some Career Attributes and Professional Views of the Philippine Military Elite," *Philippine Journal of Public Administration* 13, 4 (October, 1969): 349-414.

40. De Borja, Gatmaitan, De Castro, "Notes" pp. 266-283.

41. President F.E. Marcos, "The Armed Forces in the New Society," Speech of the President during the Graduation of the Associate Command and General Staff Course Number 5, 1 March 1973 reprinted in *Philippine Military Digest* 1, 1 (First Quarter 1973): 8.

42. For what Marcos saw as the "revolutionary style," see his *Today's Revolution and Democracy,* 1971.

43. See Office of Civil Relations, *Proclamation 1081;* Marcos, *Notes on the New Society.*

44. Interviews, speeches, and articles by civil and military elites retell the crisis of September 1972, explain "Martial Law, Philippine Style," and assure the audience of the legality of the actions taken. See, for example, Marcos, *Notes on the New Society;* Marcos, "Extemporaneous Speech," 29 December 1973; Attorney G.L. Loja, "Martial Law and Peace and Order in the Philippines: An Assessment," *The National Security Review* (Philippines National Defense College) 1, 2 (June 1973): 6-12; and "President Marcos Defends Philippine Martial Law," interview with Marcos by F.T. Chrysler, *The Sunday Bulletin* (Philadelphia), 4 August 1974.

45. For a discussion of the constitutional crisis, see Richard Butwell, "The Philippines after Democracy," *Current History* 65, 387 (November 1973): 217-220 and Butwell, "The Philippines Since Marcos," *Current Affairs Bulletin* (Australia), May 1973.

46. Marcos alleges in *Notes on the New Society,* p. 20, that "the group of former officers of the AFP were conspiring to mount a *coup d'etat....*" Former senator and presidential candidate and Marcos opponent Raul Manglaupus from his exile in the US called on the elements in the military to fill the "constitutional vacuum" on 30 December 1973. See Gerald H. Anderson, "Interview with an Exile," *America,* 29 December 1973, pp. 498-499.

47. Many of these benefits were announced by Marcos in his speech on 29 December 1973, which was made on the thirty-eighth anniversary of the AFP and followed the annual public "pledge of loyalty" by the AFP to the president.

48. For an excellent discussion of the "realignments" which occurred in Philippine politics prior to martial law, see Robert B. Stauffer, "Philippine Martial Law: The Political Economy of Refeudalization," paper prepared for presentation at the 1974 meeting of the Association for Asian Studies, Boston, 1-3 April.

49. Total armed forces in the Philippines: 31,000 reported in *The Military Balance 1972-73,* p. 53; 1974-75 reports reflect total armed forces as 55,000. International Institute for Strategic Studies, *The Military Balance 1974-1975,* p. 59. These later figures do not reflect the integration of the local police into a national police force under the constabulary and thus part of the military force structure in the Philippines. Unconfirmed reports suggest that the army of the AFP has quadrupled in size since 1972.

50. Joseph R. Hayden, *The Philippines,* p. 753.

The Dynamics of
Party-Military Relations in China

Parris H. Chang

Parris H. Chang, who received his Ph.D. from Columbia University in 1969, is currently professor of Political Science at Pennsylvania State University. He is the author of *Power and Policy in China* (1975), *Radicals and Radical Ideology in China's Cultural Revolution* (1973), a contributor to several books, and has published numerous articles and reviews in such journals as *Asian Survey, The China Quarterly, Current History, Far Eastern Economic Review, The New Leader, Journal of Asian Studies, Journal of Politics, Military Review, ORBIS,* and *Problems of Communism.* He did field study in Japan, Taiwan, and Hongkong and visited China in 1972 and 1974.

Since the second half of the 1960s, a number of significant, far-reaching changes have taken place in China's political system. Due to the Great Proletarian Cultural Revolution (GPCR) starting in 1966, for instance, the People's Liberation Army (PLA) has enormously expanded its political power at the expense of the Chinese Communist Party (CCP). Consequently, a new equation has been introduced into the party-PLA relationship.

This essay, in examining this relationship, will attempt to answer a number of questions. What was the relationship before the GPCR? How did the changes in that relationship come about during the GPCR? What were the political roles performed by the PLA during 1966-1971? How did the party leadership control the PLA during and after the GPCR? What resources and mechanisms does the party possess? What is the current state of party-PLA relationships? Finally, what assumptions and conclusions in the previous studies of CCP-PLA relations seem viable or untenable in retrospect, and what seem to be useful areas for further research?

The Historical Legacy

In the history of the Chinese communist movement and until the first half of the 1960s, the CCP had largely succeeded in maintaining tight civilian control over and enforced party priorities within the military establishment. Such a rare accomplishment can be attributed to both internal and environmental factors.

Internal factors include the values accepted by the military and certain organizational arrangements within the military which reinforce the military's political subordination. The values in question refer to the principle of civilian (party) supremacy and control over the military which was set forth as early as 1929 by Mao Tse-tung in a resolution in a party conference in Kut'ien (known as the Kut'ien Resolution) to regulate relations between the CCP and its armed forces. The principle, epitomized in the expression that the party should command the gun and the gun should not be allowed to command the party, gradually acquired legitimacy and, in the course of the communists' struggle of power, evolved into a cardinal rule in the Chinese communists' organization of military power. The principle of party supremacy and control was also given concrete organizational expression in the system of political commissars and party organizations within the military—mechanisms which the Chinese communists adopted from the Bolsheviks to maintain political control over the armed forces.

A number of favorable environmental factors also contributed to the growing acceptance of party supremacy by PLA leaders. First of all, CCP leaders and PLA leaders were united in their life and death struggles against common enemies (Nationalists and Japanese) during the 1930s and 1940s; thus potential conflicts between them were minimized. Second, prior to 1949 party and military organizations were hardly distinguishable, for most Chinese communist cadres held leadership positions concurrently in the party and military organizations. Furthermore, until the 1960s the CCP leadership under Chairman Mao had been relatively cohesive, united, and enjoyed a high degree of legitimacy and popular support—an important factor which reinforced PLA's political subordination.

That the principle of civilian supremacy had secured wide acceptance among the Chinese communists, including the PLA leaders, was demonstrated in the orderly transition of power that took place in the early 1950s. Despite the fact that during 1949-1952 in the wake of the civil war and the early period of communist takeover military leaders ruled the country directly through the Military Control Committee and the Military and Administrative Committee, these military governors of the provinces rapidly "returned to the barracks" and handed the political power over to the civilian party/government officials (in some cases they themselves took up the civilian posts in the provinces and gave up their military status) as the regime appeared to consolidate its control. Thus by 1954 the vestiges of military rule had virtually disappeared. With a few exceptions in border regions such as Sinkiang and Tibet, civilian governing structures, headed by civilians, had replaced the previous military bodies in the provinces and in that year the Peking regime proclaimed its state Constitution. From that time to the mid-1960s, China was governed primarily by civilian authorities, and there was more or less a separation of civilian and military functions, permitting party/government cadres and the PLA officials to become highly specialized in their own spheres of work.

It does not follow that the PLA leaders were excluded from politics. Quite the contrary, many PLA leaders were represented in the party's decision-making bodies, such as the Politburo and the Central Committee (CC), and occupied key posts in the government. It ought to be pointed out, however, the scope of the PLA involvement in politics until the 1960s was largely confined to wielding what Welch in chapter 1 of this book calls "military influence" (i.e. exercising political influence through regularized and accepted channels, which is to be differentiated from other kinds of military involvement in politics such as military participation or military control).

Environmental changes, the division of labor, and the specialization of functions between the civilian and military officials inevitably led to conflicts of interest. Although the top PLA officials took part in the party's most important decision-making bodies, conflict of interest between the party and the military was only mitigated, not eliminated totally. The military, by the nature of its special functions, had its own particularized interests and leaders. Even PLA leaders who were also members and leaders of the party found themselves compelled by the logic of their special responsibilities and the special concerns of their own constituency to fight for the military's priorities and to resist the demands of other party leaders. There had been numerous issues of contention between the party and military leaders during 1949-1966; chief among these were China's entry into the Korean War, the professionalization of the PLA, politicization of the PLA, participation in the economic tasks, the build-up of militia, the Quemoy-Matsu crisis, Sino-Soviet relations, and the Chinese response to the escalation of war in Vietnam.[1]

Without exception, each of these and other discordant issues was settled in favor of the civilian party leaders' policy priorities, a fact which testifies to the general acceptance in the policy of the principle of civilian supremacy and party control over the military. The PLA leaders, despite their control of the instrument of violence, could only "lobby" the party leadership through prescribed channels. Not unlike representatives of an interest group, the PLA leaders participated in the decision-making process as claimants and advisers to the party leadership, advocating certain courses of action in domestic and foreign policy, demanding a greater allocation of resources, and trying to protect and advance their corporate interests. When they could resort only to lobbying and politicking in political conflicts with the civilian party leadership, and when the arena of such conflicts was in the Politburo or the CC where the civilians were preeminent, the military leaders were easily outvoted.

The best illustration of civilian supremacy was provided by the Lushan Affair in the summer of 1959. During an enlarged Politburo meeting held at Lushan in July 1959, Marshal P'eng Teh-huai, a Politburo member and minister of defense, submitted a memorandum attacking Mao Tse-tung's Great Leap and commune policies. A large number of PLA officials signed the memorandum in support of P'eng's action. However, his challenge to the party leadership stopped short of the threat or actual use of naked force (of which P'eng was obviously capable inasmuch as he and his close collaborator, General Huang Ko-cheng, the PLA's chief of staff, had the power to deploy troops), and it was eventually defeated in a CC Plenum that followed the enlarged Politburo session. Marshal P'eng and General Huang were replaced by Marshal Lin Piao and General Lo Jui-ch'ing as minister of defense and chief of staff, respectively.

PLA Intervention in Politics

In the light of the civilian party leaders' ability to beat back the challenge by the PLA leaders at the Lushan showdown and to assert party priorities thereafter, it seems natural that many writers should have stressed PLA loyalty and subordination to the civilian leadership and highlighted the success of the party's system of political indoctrination and control over the PLA in their studies.[2] However, in the course of the GPCR, as will be analyzed below, the political involvement of the PLA approximated what Welch calls "military control," not only in the political arena, but for a number of years the PLA also displaced party and government organizations and enforced a direct military rule.

It should be noted at the outset that initially the PLA did not seek political power for itself and that the initial expansion of PLA's political power falls into the category of what Morris Janowitz calls "reactive militarism."[3] That is, the PLA gained new political power, not through a premediated coup ("designed militarism" by Janowitz's definition) as the military has done in many other political systems, but through circumstances largely not of its own making. Granted that some PLA leaders may have actually contemplated military intervention from the outset to enhance their own personal power,[4] it still remains true that the expansion of PLA's political power had been a direct result of the pressure of party leaders, especially Mao.

Thus, the PLA intervention in the political process can be viewed as the "socialization of political conflict," whereby the politically weak expanded the arena of political conflict and mobilized new participants so as to redress the balance of forces.[5] In the wake of the collapse of Mao's utopian Great Leap and commune programs in the early 1960s, Mao was opposed and politically eclipsed by other party leaders who controlled the party machinery. To overcome opposition within the party and to carry out his will, Mao was compelled to go outside the party organizations to recruit support from other groups.[6] Hence he turned to the PLA, coopted it, and used it as a power base to attack and remove the centers of opposition within the party.

The first sign that the PLA was siding with Mao in the intraparty conflict came on 29 November 1965, when the organ of the PLA, *Liberation Army Daily,* reproduced an article by Yao Wen-yuan (a Maoist ideologue from Shanghai) criticizing a historical play, "The Dismissal of Hai Jui," by Wu Han (vicemayor of Peking), and accompanied it with an "editor's note" which denounced the play as a "big poisonous weed."[7] The reproduction of Yao's article in the *Liberation Army Daily* clearly signalled the PLA's endorsement of Yao's attack; moreover, the severe indictment had the effect of redefining the nature of offenses by Wu Han and his protectors within the party.[8]

From that time on, the PLA steadily broadened its role in the political arena as Mao used the PLA as his instrument of power to struggle with other party leaders who were entrenched in the party organizations. On 2 February 1966 Lin Piao had Chiang Ch'ing (Madame Mao) convene a "Forum on the Literary and Art Work in the Armed Forces" in Shanghai. At the conclusion of the eighteen-day forum, a summary report was prepared under Chiang Ch'ing's guidance and revised three times by Mao personally before its release.[9] The forum summary did not confine itself to literary matters in the armed forces; it spelled out the Maoist position, policy, and intention on the cultural revolution in the nation. Clearly, Mao had secured the full backing of Lin Piao and was using the PLA as a power base to fight P'eng Chen and his allies in the central party apparatus.

In the spring of 1966 *Liberation Army Daily* took the lead in the attacks on Mao's intellectual critics and their supporters within the party hierarchy. For instance, the editorial on 18 April, which paraphrased the PLA forum summary, declared war on the antiparty, antisocialist "black line" in the nation's cultural front. Furthermore, the PLA's organ now openly challenged the party's authority by attacking and ridiculing the editorials of the party's organ, *The People's Daily*. In May Lin Piao was apparently a key figure at the enlarged Politburo session which sealed the fate of P'eng Chen and other top leaders such as Lo Jui-ch'ing and Lu Ting-yi. Addressing himself to the Politburo meeting on 18 May, Lin expressed his wholehearted support for Mao, warned of the danger of a capitalist restoration in China, and strongly hinted that the danger was most acute at the upper levels of the party leadership.[20]

In the summer of 1966 the support of the PLA, or at least some of its leaders, was crucial to Mao's defeat of Liu Shao-ch'i. There were reports that troops loyal to Lin Piao were moved into Peking in June 1966; in fact, Fu Ts'ung-pi, a long-time aide of Yang Cheng-Wu, the newly appointed acting chief of staff, took command of the Peking garrison at this juncture, and the *People's Daily* editorial board was reorganized on 1 June and placed under PLA control. It is not known whether troops were used to intimidate Mao's opponents during the eleventh CC Plenum. Nevertheless, it is quite obvious some PLA leaders played a very vital role in the victory of Mao and the defeat of his opponents in the Plenum. To reward their support, Lin Piao was chosen as Mao's deputy and heir-apparent and three marshals of the PLA—Yeh Chien-ying, Hsu Hsiang-ch'ien and Nieh Jung-chen—were given membership in the Politburo.

The Military Rule: The Expansion of PLA Political Roles

Although some PLA leaders played a substantial supporting role in helping Mao defeat such powerful party figures as Liu

Shao-ch'i and Teng Hsiao-p'ing in the Eleventh CC Plenum in August 1966 and were also instrumental in organizing and providing transport and logistical support for the hordes of Red Guards who journeyed to Peking in the summer and fall of 1966, the extensive involvement of many PLA units in the subsequent "seizure of power" from below by the Maoist rebels was evidently not planned from the outset.

What seems most striking of the PLA intervention in Chinese politics, at least during 1965-1967, was that the scope, objective, and domain of the intervention were structured largely by the civilian leaders, and by Mao in particular.[11] It was the civilian party leadership headed by Mao that expanded or contracted the political roles of the PLA, in response to political exigencies both before and during the GPCR. It is often overlooked that, in the initial stages of the GPCR, the Maoist leadership placed major reliance on the spontaneous forces of the "revolutionary left" (the Red Guards and rebels). Only when this strategy proved unworkable in the face of strong resistance by conservative power holders in Peking and the provinces did Mao and his supporters push the PLA into the mainstream of GPCR to support the "revolutionary left" in January 1967. A central directive to that effect was issued on 23 January 1967. By injecting the military into the GPCR, however, Mao provided the opening for subsequent military intervention in politics and for PLA emergence as the dominant political force in China.

These far-reaching consequences Mao probably did not foresee and could not have foreseen at the outset, for the PLA, having been indoctrinated for years with the thought of Mao, not only enjoyed his highest confidence but also seemed a reliable political instrument. Indeed, soon after the promulgation of the 23 January central directive, PLA leaders in Heilungkiang, Shansi, Shantung, and Kweichow provinces plus the municipality of Shanghai dutifully aided local Maoists in seizing power from existing authorities and in establishing revolutionary committees (RCs), the new organs of power. But in most other provinces the response of the PLA leaders to the directive was at best equivocal. In some, PLA leaders even intervened, knowingly or unknowingly, against the Maoist groups whom they had been called upon to support.

The most important single factor that elevated the military to political prominence, however, was a series of rebel assaults on the provincial authorities in an effort to "seize power from below" (in emulation of the 1871 Paris Commune experience). These assaults paralyzed the party and government machinery in many provinces, and the resultant riots, disorderly demonstrations, and "struggle by force" between rival rebel groups produced public chaos. As the civilian party and government organizations could no longer exercise effective authority, the PLA had to move in to fill the power vacuum; thus, power in many provinces devolved onto the local PLA leaders.

From March 1967 onward the political situation in numerous provinces approximated a military takeover. Not only did the PLA actually supplant civilian party/government officials and set up military governments in the form of "military control committees" to enforce direct military rule, but it also ran agricultural and industrial production in the nation, controlled the mass media, and operated other essential services.

The Wuhan mutiny of July 1967 resulted in still further expansion of military sway in Chinese politics.[12] In fact, the incident was, in retrospect, a major turning point in the GPCR, for it ultimately compelled Mao to change his tack. The mutiny clearly indicated that at least some military leaders supported the anti-Maoist groups in opposition to the radical goals of the GPCR and were even willing to defy the central authorities overtly in doing so; it likewise testified to a direct and sharp clash between the PLA and the revolutionary rebels. Although Ch'en Ts'ai-tao, commander of the Wuhan Military Region, and several of his collaborators were ousted after the mutiny was quelled, the broad conflict between the PLA and the rebels continued, and there was a distinct prospect that other incidents similar to that at Wuhan might occur. Confronted with this situation—and apparently pressured by regional-provincial military leaders who met in Peking in early August 1967—Mao decided to grant the military a new power. A central directive of 5 September 1967 authorized the PLA to use naked force to quell any disobedience.[13]

The effect of the 5 September directive was to make the PLA the determining political element in the provinces. The military authorities soon took advantage of their enhanced power and endeavored to crack down on unruly and protesting rebel groups. They sent the Red Guards and rebels back to schools and factories, enforced stern discipline against troublemakers, and forcefully dissolved many rebel organizations. Moreover, the PLA had a major hand in the formation of the RCs, the organs of "revolutionary power," in twenty-three provincial-level administrative units from August 1967 to September 1968. The very establishment of this new structure of authority politically symbolized the completion of the seizure of power from the former provincial authorities; hence it not only imposed greater limitations on the rebels' activities but also tended to negate their *raison d'être*.

The leading personnel of the twenty-three RCs unmistakably mirrored the prevailing political reality. Thus, of the 46 chairmen and first vice-chairmen, 36, or 81 percent, were high-ranking regional or provincial PLA officers. As of September 1968, 95, or a little more than 43 percent, of the 220 chairmen and vice-chairmen of China's entire twenty-nine provincial-level RCs were military men, with 20 of them holding the post of chairman. Quite plainly, then, most of the twenty-three RCs set up after the Wuhan incident constituted creations of the local military leaders.

PLA Recalcitrance

It seems clear that whereas Mao succeeded during 1965-1966 in coopting the PLA to defeat his opponents (e.g., Liu Shao-ch'i) within the party and was largely able to determine the scope and objectives of the PLA's political involvement up to the beginning of 1967, thereafter the PLA intervention had assumed a logic and purposes of its own and had become less amenable to political control by the civilian party leaders. The reasons are complicated, but quite comparable to those causing military intervention in other political systems.[14]

It is important to keep in mind that the attacks Mao and his Red Guard supporters launched upon the party organizations after the fall of 1966 severely damaged the image and legitimacy of the party. This fact, coupled with a divided leadership in the party and Mao's waning political influence, tended to embolden PLA leaders to defy the party leadership. Moreover, since both the Maoist faction and Mao's opponents vied for PLA support, some PLA leaders were able to play both groups against each other or exact political concessions. The virtual destruction of civilian party and government authorities after January 1967 left the system with only one organizational hierarchy capable of exercising effective authority—the PLA— and this state of affairs severely diminished the capability of the party leadership in Peking to control PLA actions.

In addition to these environmental factors, Mao's attempts to use the PLA both for suppressing his domestic political opponents (whom he labeled capitalist powerholders within the party) and for other political purposes clashed with most PLA leaders' perception of their proper mission and severely strained their loyalty to Mao and to the ethic of party leadership. Thus, when Mao ordered them in January 1967 to help the leftist Red Guards oust *en masse* the party officials, the reaction of most PLA leaders was equivocal and negative.

Moreover, the enormous expansion of PLA roles in Chinese society and the paralysis of Peking's civilian control mechanisms during the GPCR made the PLA totally autonomous. Prior to 1966 civilian party officials headed provincial institutions (except in outlying border regions like Sinkiang and Tibet); after 1967, however, local PLA commanders or professional political commissars headed the party and government apparatuses in most localities and ruled these provinces by fiat. Furthermore, before the GPCR senior secretaries of the party provincial committees or regional bureaus served concurrently as first political commissars in the provincial military districts or military regions to provide party control over the local PLA, but in most cases after 1967 local PLA commanders or professional political commissars functioned concurrently as senior provincial party secretaries, thereby neutralizing the political control mechanism of the party leadership. This interlocking of party, government, and military leadership positions and the concentration of political, military, and financial powers in the same hands greatly enhanced the opportunities for local PLA autonomy and rendered these local PLA leaders more intractable for the central authorities.

It is true that military domination of the provincial power structure is not without precedent in China under communist rule. During 1949-52 PLA personnel ran China's provinces, but the circumstances of the post-1967 years do not appear comparable, for by 1954, with the consolidation of communist control of the mainland and the establishment of civilian institutions of rule, the military administrators had handed their political responsibilities over to civilian officials. In the late 1960s, however, the military administrators of China's provinces showed no sign of a willingness to return political authority to the civilians even though the turmoil and disruptions of the GPCR had ended and there was a fair degree of order throughout the country. On the contrary, they had continued to dominate the political scene despite Mao's apparent wish to circumscribe their political roles.

Thus, when the twenty-nine provincial-level party committees were reconstituted in August 1971 (more than two years after the Ninth Party Congress which politically symbolized the return of political normalcy), PLA commanders or professional military political commissars still headed twenty-one of them; and, among the 158 ranking provincial officials (first party secretaries, second secretaries, secretaries, and deputy secretaries), 95 or 60 percent of them were PLA men. It seems inconceivable that Peking had willed and imposed this heavy military representation on the provincial party apparatus! The truth of the matter is that the local PLA leaders who were already the nucleus of their provincial power structure had played the primary role in rebuilding the civilian party organizations and, in the process, had entrenched themselves in the provincial party leadership hierarchy.

Although the PLA performed nonmilitary (e.g., political) functions prior to the GPCR, such functions had been assigned to it by the party in the first place and were carried out under the close civilian supervision. During and after the GPCR, however, the various political roles the PLA assumed were more decisive and important. Specifically, they included intervention in the resolution of political conflict at the top, administration in the form of direct military rule, running of the economy in the provinces, political institution-building and supplanting the civilian party/government officials at the center (the party's CC and the State Council) and at the provincial leadership hierarchy, and active participation in the policy-formulation process. Moreover, the PLA had played those roles in a drastically different political context, since for many years the party organizations (except those within the PLA) were destroyed, and the new organs of power (the revolutionary committees, and, subsequently, the reconstituted party committees) were heavily dominated by military men. It was extremely difficult, therefore, for the civilian party leaders to exercise any meaningful control and supervision over PLA actions.[15]

Besides the unprecedented political prominence of the PLA was the danger of Bonapartism. Without question, Marshal Lin Piao and his followers had greatly benefitted from the GPCR. Not only had Lin replaced Liu Shao-ch'i as Mao's successor and become the sole vice-chairman of the party, but he had also placed many of his followers in the Fourth Field Army in key positions and substantially expanded his base of power. For example, Lin promoted a fellow Fourth Field Army leader, Huang Yung-sheng, commander of the Canton Military Region (MR), to the post of the PLA chief of staff in March 1968, bypassing many equally, if not better, qualified men, including several incumbent deputy chiefs of staff. In addition, Lin put his followers from the Fourth Field Army and his wife to control the "Administrative Unit" of the Military Affairs Commission (MAC), the regime's supreme military decision-making body. Moreover, Lin also replaced more than 300 senior military officials at various levels with his own men and made considerable inroads into the power base of other military factions.

When the Ninth Party Congress was convened in April 1969, Lin's men packed the meeting. He was the featured speaker, delivering the political report to the Congress, and the Congress adopted a new party constitution containing an unprecedented provision which salutes Lin Piao and sanctions his succession to Mao (a provision which was allegedly inserted at Lin's behest):

Comrade Lin Piao has consistently held high the

great red banner of Mao Tse-tung's thought and has
most loyally and resolutely carried out and defended
Comrade Mao Tse-tung's proletarian revolutionary
line. Comrade Lin Piao is Comrade Mao Tse-tung's
close comrade-in-arms and successor.[16]

In the newly elected CC, approximately 46 percent, or 127,
of the 279 members were career soldiers, and, in the twenty-
five-member Politburo, 13 were military representatives. In
these two highest decision-making bodies of the party, Lin's
supporters constituted the largest and most influential group.
In the post-Congress period, the military continued to dominate the party and, under Lin's stewardship, the army managed
to control nearly every aspect of life in China, defying the
"unified leadership" of the party.

The Purge of Lin Piao and the Reassertion of Party Supremacy

There seems to be no question that PLA domination of
China's political system was the basic cause of the conflict
between Mao and Lin Piao and that Mao came to perceive
Lin's enhanced position as threatening his own power and
leadership. Mao had certainly not anticipated nor desired this
situation, for it was contrary to his dictum of party control, and
after the GPCR a suspicious Mao apparently viewed the whole
situation with grave apprehension.[17] When the party's CC met
in a plenary session at Lushan in late August to early September 1970 to consider, among other things, a draft of the new
state constitution, and Lin Piao spoke in favor of retaining the
post of head of state (to which Lin may have aspired) in disagreement with Mao, who wanted to abolish the post, Mao's
distrust of Lin was strengthened and he apparently decided
shortly thereafter to curtail Lin Piao's power and to reassert
the party's control over the military.

In December 1970 Mao called an enlarged Politburo session
at Pei-tai-ho and subjected Lin Piao and his five top aides,
Huang Yung-sheng, Wu Fa-hsien, Li Tso-p'eng, Yeh Ch'un, and
Ch'iu Hui-tso, to severe criticism. Following the meeting, at the
end of January 1971, Mao reshuffled the commanding officers

of the Peking Military Region and the Peking garrison, replaced Lin Piao's men there, and transferred troop units considered loyal to Lin out of the Peking area. These maneuvers
have been detailed vividly in a secret party document numbered "*Chung-fa* 1972 (12)." In Mao's own words, he adopted
three measures after the Lushan conference:

> One was to throw stones, one was to mix in sand,
> and the third was to dig up the cornerstone. I crit-
> icized the material Ch'en Po-ta had used to deceive
> many people, and I commented on reports of the
> Thirty-Eighth Army and of the Tsinan Military Dis-
> trict on opposing arrogance and complacency. I also
> made critical comments on a document of the long
> forum of the Military Affairs Commission, which
> didn't criticize Ch'en at all. My method was to get
> hold of these stones and make critical comments,
> and then let everyone discuss them—this was throw-
> ing stones. When dirt is too tightly packed, no air can
> get through; but if a little sand is mixed in, air can
> circulate. Not enough people had been mixed into
> the "Administrative Unit" of the Military Affairs
> Commission, so I added a few more men—this is
> called mixing in sand. Reorganizing the Peking Mili-
> tary Region is called digging up the cornerstone.[18]

The intentions and implications of Mao's moves were not
lost on Lin Piao and his top aides. And soon thereafter, ac-
cording to another secret CCP document "*Chung-fa* 1972 (4),"
Lin Piao and his cohorts went into action to prepare a coup
against Mao to which they gave the code name "571 Project."[19]
After the coup was foiled, according to the story released by
Peking, Lin, his wife, and his son were killed in a plane crash in
Mongolia on 13 September 1971, attempting to flee China.

Amid efforts to expose and repudiate Lin's crimes since the
fall of 1971, the Chinese leadership has also renewed an intensive nationwide campaign to curtail the political roles of the
PLA and reassert party control over all spheres of Chinese life.
The arrogance and complacency of PLA men and their tendency as leaders in various party and government organizations

to ignore the principle of democratic centralism and to rule by fiat have been singled out for attack, and the role of the PLA cadres has been subjected to mounting criticism and close scrutiny by their civilian colleagues.

In the wake of Lin's demise, scores of ranking PLA officials, most if not all of them presumably Lin's followers or otherwise implicated in the Lin Piao affair, have been removed. Among these victims were heads of PLA central command and service arms (e.g., Huang Yung-sheng, PLA chief of staff; Chiu Hui-tso, commander of The General Logistics Department; Wu Fa-hsien, commander of the air force, and Li Tso-P'eng, first political commissar of the navy), as well as senior provincial leaders who concurrently held top posts in the local military headquarters (e.g., Liang Hsin-chu, commander of the Chengtu MR and Lung Shu-chin, commander of the Sinkiang MR).

The drive to cut back the political roles of the PLA and to tighten party control over the PLA leaders culminated in a dramatic wholesale transfer of virtually all top regional PLA leaders in December 1973.[20] This major shift moved regional PLA leaders from their long entrenched power bases, which Peking had come to see as intractable "independent kingdoms."

Moreover, through the transfer Peking also relieved the regional PLA leaders of the top provincial party and government posts they had held and filled these posts with civilians. For example, since his shift to the Peking MR, Ch'en Hsi-lien is no longer the first secretary of the Peking Party Committee; the position has been occupied by Wu Teh, a civilian. When Ting Sheng, the former commander of the Canton MR and first secretary of the Kwangtung Party Committee was moved to Nanking as the commander there, Hsu Shih-yu became the new Canton MR commander and Chao Tzu-yang the new first party secretary of Kwangtung. There are still a few provinces in which commanders of the provincial military districts still concurrently head the provincial party committees, but they are likely to be relieved of their top party and government posts in time.

Resources and Tactics of Party Control

The dramatic developments of December 1973 forcefully demonstrated the determination of the party leadership to return the PLA as a whole to "unified party leadership." The smoothness with which Peking has carried out the reshuffle also testifies to its resourcefulness and leadership skill. Clearly, the party leadership possesses several trump cards.

First of all, the central leadership still wields the power of appointment and dismissal. A system of *nomenklatura* enables the center to dismiss and shift recalcitrant officials, civilian and military alike, and effect periodic shake-ups and reorganizations. This is a formidable weapon, for civilian and military leaders' authority to command obedience and to allocate resources stems largely from their possession of leadership positions in the party, government, or military hierarchies, and once such positions are removed from them, their source of power is also preempted.

Furthermore, the party leadership, through the MAC (Mao being its head), controls troops and, when necessary, can use the military force to try to achieve certain political ends. During the Wuhan mutiny in July 1967, Peking actually dispatched superior forces to overpower the rebellious Wuhan PLA leaders. Various regional PLA headquarters also control military units, but the MAC can relieve local PLA authorities of such units and place them under central control, as it actually did on many occasions during the GPCR. There is no evidence that the party leadership has ever hinted any use of military power against regional leaders to forestall opposition in the recent shake-up; this is perhaps unnecessary, for the regional PLA leaders seem well aware of what Peking is capable of doing, so they have muttered in discontent but offered no overt resistance.

In addition, Mao has resorted to divide-and-rule tactics to create and foster rivalry among PLA leaders in order to maximize control. Lin Piao, who knew only too well, exposed the manipulation of Mao and his inner circles in these words:

> Today, they use this group to attack that group; tomorrow they use that group to attack this group

... they manufacture contradictions and splits in order to attain their goals of divide and rule, destroying each group in turn and maintaining their ruling
position.[21]

In fact, Mao himself admitted as much when he spoke of his
maneuver to "mix in sand." The existence of cliques and factions in the PLA and the party leadership appears to have
facilitated the divide-and-rule tactics. Inasmuch as Mao knows
intimately the personal ties and rivalries of Chinese leaders,
who historically belonged to different field army groups, and
since there was strong antagonism toward Lin Piao among
many top leaders, who suffered from his ill treatment and his
encroachment into their "fiefs" during the GPCR, Mao had
little difficulty in mobilizing support to overpower Lin and his
Fourth Field Army group in 1970-1971.[22] In line with the same
approach, Mao has since the fall of 1971 assigned many PLA
officers who do not belong to Lin's faction to various PLA units
so as to strengthen the anti-Lin forces or to dilute pro-Lin
control. The appointment of Yang Yung (a First Field Army
man) as commander of the Sinkiang MR to replace Lung Shu-
chin (a Lin Piao follower) and the transfer of Hsu Shih-yu (a
Third Field Army leader) to the Canton MR, the stronghold of
Lin's Fourth Field Army group, as its new commander are only
two of the examples.

Whereas Mao had allied with the leaders of the Fourth Field
Army group during the GPCR, he has, since Lin's demise,
courted and coopted the leaders of the Second Field Army
group and, to a lesser extent, those of the Third Field Army
group. Thus, the rehabilitation of many party officials who
have close ties to these groups, such as Teng Hsiao-p'ing (former general secretary of the party) of the Second Field Army
and T'an Chen-lin (former Politburo member) of the Third
Field Army group, who were disgraced during the GPCR,
seems politically motivated and not entirely due to their successful "remoulding" as Peking has claimed. The sudden rise in
the political star of Teng Hsiao-p'ing since the beginning of
1974 (he was elevated to the Politburo in January, led a Chinese
delegation to attend a special session of the United Nations in
April, and was elected vice-chairman of the party and first

vice-premier in January 1975, and appointed PLA chief of staff in February 1975) may be another facet of Mao's cooptation maneuver. Reportedly Teng played a vital role in arranging the major reshuffle of regional PLA leaders in December 1973.

With respect to organizational matters, mechanisms of party control over the PLA which were impaired or weakened by the disruptions during the GPCR have been gradually reinstituted or strengthened. At the central level, for instance, the General Political Department (which is the party's watchdog body within the PLA and carries out political indoctrination and control on behalf of the party leadership) was revived in 1969-1970 after having been closed since the summer of 1967. At regional and provincial PLA levels, the system of political commissars, through which the civilian party cadres enforce political control over local PLA authorities, has also been reinforced. It is true that the political commissar's system was never abolished during the GPCR; however the GPCR purges did remove many top regional/provincial party officials who were concurrently senior political commissars, while those political commissars who survived or were newly appointed during the GPCR were military men and tended to articulate military viewpoints. Since the downfall of Lin Piao, Peking has gradually reinstituted the civilian control system by appointing civilian party cadres to these senior political posts.

If all this has enabled the party leadership to elicit PLA compliance and to reassert party control, it is perhaps because the final trump card—is Mao Tse-tung himself. There is no question that Mao possesses enormous personal authority and his charismatic qualities inspire the deep loyalty of many Chinese communists. He has become an institution above the party; he is the source of legitimacy and he alone controls the legitimate political symbols of the regime. Other leaders, civilian and military alike, can only exercise power by claiming conformity to his standards. When necessary, he can (and did) redefine the standards, change the rules of the game, thereby politically undermining those "waving the red flags to oppose the Red Flag." As the linchpin of the Chinese political system, Mao at eighty plus, is precariously holding the pieces together.

The Prospects and Lessons

During the past decade, the sharp turns and abrupt changes in the CCP-PLA relations, and the enormous expansion of the PLA's political power in the GPCR followed by the equally severe contraction in the Lin Piao aftermath, have caught many outside observers—this writer included—by surprise. The events in China since 1966 serve to highlight the inadequacy of our analytical framework. One of the major shortcomings, as Gittings pointed out, is the use of an overly simplistic and static approach to analyze a very complex and ever-changing relationship between the party and the PLA.[23] Such an approach seems to err in seeing the CCP-PLA relationship as one-dimensional—either as one of harmony and civilian (party) control or as one of continuing rivalry and struggle for power, without giving sufficient attention to a host of variables that affect the relationship.

Before the GPCR there was a tendency to overstress the importance of internal factors (e.g., widespread acceptance of party supremacy by the PLA) and the system of external political control, thereby reaching conclusions on PLA subordination. Yet internal discipline and external party control broke down badly in a different political context, the GPCR, when the roles and responsibilities of the party and the PLA had changed drastically.

Likewise, there was an opposite tendency during the GPCR to write off those aspects of the system making for party control and PLA compliance and to overemphasize PLA independence and power. As a matter of fact, the upheavals during the GPCR have demonstrated that factions and cliques do exist within the PLA and party leadership. Western writers who in the past ignored or pooh-poohed the theory of Chinese Nationalist writers that old "field army" ties are salient elements in factional cleavages have found it relevant and useful,[24] for on many occasions during the GPCR the Chinese communists give the unmistakable impression that they think and act in terms of these old ties.[25]

On the other hand, however, the field army theory should be regarded as only one useful tool to explain and predict Chinese political behavior, for political actors must weigh their loyalty to the old field army association against their particular present roles and responsibilities. In this regard, Whitson may have elevated the field army approach too far when he views Chinese politics as a balance of power among five "field army" elite groups.[26] Chinese politics during and after the GPCR certainly has not fit such a model, and the forecasted regionalism or warlordism has failed to materialize. In fact, the developments since Lin Piao's demise in the fall of 1971 forcefully attest to both the power of the party leadership and the resources it possesses to keep the PLA in line—factors to which analysts did not give sufficient attention and which remain to be studied.

Another equally important but unexplored factor may have been the impact of individuals. Undoubtedly Mao's charismatic qualities and personal authority command profound loyalty in China; the willingness of the PLA leaders to accept Peking's control in recent years may have been greatly facilitated by their great personal allegiance to the chairman, which may have overridden their own political considerations or their better judgment. The passing of Mao may drastically change the equation between the party and the PLA. In this connection, the dramatic appointment in January 1975 of two civilian leaders, Vice-Premiers Teng Hsiao-p'ing and Chang Ch'un-ch'iao respectively, as PLA chief of staff and director of the PLA General Political Department (positions traditionally occupied by professional soldiers) seems to reflect CCP leaders' continuing apprehension about PLA insubordination.

In the light of this what political roles will the party-military relationship evolve in the future? If the past can be a guide, then it is possible to predict with a fair degree of certainty that the military's political roles will again expand whenever the central party leadership is divided and bitterly deadlocked in struggle. Under such circumstances, some civilian leaders (just like Mao did on the eve of the GPCR) may enlist the support of the PLA, or some of its leaders, to resolve the political conflict, thereby reintroducing the PLA into the political arena.

Even without the prodding of the civilian party leaders, some PLA leaders are most likely to intervene in the successional struggle following Mao's death. A number of powerful PLA leaders, such as Li Teh-sheng, a CCP Politburo member and commander of Shengyang MR (which encompasses the whole of Manchuria) and Ch'en Hsi-lien, a member of the Politburo and commander of the Peking MR, could conceivably become contenders for the top post. Even if they did not become the "candidates," they, together with other PLA leaders, could function as "kingmakers" or "king-vetoers" to structure the choice of China's future top leader or leaders.

Broadly speaking, the party-PLA relationship in the post-Mao China will be in flux, as there will be frequent changes in the equilibrium between the party and the PLA. This is not to imply that internal factors such as PLA acceptance of the principle of party supremacy will become inoperative, nor does it suggest that the external control measures the party leadership has thus far imposed on the PLA will cease to exist in the future. Rather, the point is that despite them the party-PLA relationship will, as it did in the past, depend on and vary according to the political context and the interactions of the individual actors who operate the system.

In other words, the party-PLA relationship will continue to be shaped to a great extent by the degree of unity or disunity in the leadership, China's international milieu (e.g., presence of war threat), and the dominant political or military priority of a given moment. Moreover, political loyalty in China has focused largely on the figure of Mao Tse-tung rather than on institutions; the working of the system has been highly personalized and not sufficiently institutionalized. In the post-Mao era, things are bound to be different. Undoubtedly, party loyalty and the principle of party supremacy will be invoked, but the concrete relationship between the party and the PLA will have to be determined by the future leaders and conditioned by their perception of what roles they should play and where or to whom they owe their ultimate allegiance.

Notes to Chapter 5

Chang, *Dynamics of Party-Military Relations in China.*

1. Various writers have treated some of these issues in great detail; see, for example, John Gittings, *The Role of the Chinese Army* (London: Oxford University Press, 1967), Ellis Joffe, *Party and Army: Professionalism and Political Control in the Chinese Officer Corps, 1949-1964* (Cambridge: Harvard University Press, 1976), Alice L. Hsieh, *Communist China's Strategy in the Nuclear Era* (Englewood Cliffs, N.J. Prentice-Hall, 1962), and Harry Harding and Melvin Gurtov, *The Purge of Lo Jui-Chi'ing: The Politics of Chinese Strategic Planning* (Santa Monica: RAND, 1971).

2. E.g., Gittings, *Role of the Chinese Army,* Joffe, *Party and Army,* and Ralph L. Powell, "Maoist Military Doctrines," *Asian Survey* (April 1968).

3. Morris Janowitz, *The Military in the Political Development of New Nations: An Essay in Comparative Analysis* (Chicago: University of Chicago Press, 1964), p. 16.

4. In the aftermath of the Lin Piao affair, the Chinese propagandists have strongly made such a point in their efforts to reinterpret past events and rewrite history.

5. This concept is adopted from E. E. Schattschneider, *The Semisovereign People: A Realist's View of Democracy in America* (New York: Holt, Rinehart and Winston, Inc., 1961). Several scholars of Chinese politics, e.g., Professor Tang Tsou of the University of Chicago and Professor Richard Baum of the University of California at Los Angeles, have applied a similar concept to analyzing Chinese politics since the Great Proletarian Cultural Revolution.

6. This tactic has been used over and over again by Mao. See Parris H. Chang, "Research Notes on the Changing Loci of Decision in the CCP," *The China Quarterly* (October-December 1970): esp. 173-74, and Richard Baum, "Elite Behavior Under Conditions of Stress," in Robert A. Scalapino (ed.), *Elites in the People's Republic of China* (Seattle, Washington: University of Washington Press, 1972), pp. 550-52.

7. Mao had harbored resentment against Wu Han, who allegedly wrote the historical play "The Dismissal of Hai Jui" to defend Marshal P'eng Teh-huai's criticisms of Mao at the Lushan Meeting. Although Mao had called for the party to repudiate Wu publicly in a conference in September-October 1965, his demand was resisted by other party leaders, particularly Wu's superior P'eng Chen, so Mao instructed Yao Wen-yuan to write the article, which was published on 10 November 1965 in the Shanghai *Wen-hui Pao,* to attack Wu Han and, by extension, P'eng Chen and others who supported P'eng. Due to P'eng's maneuver, few newspapers reproduced Yao's article, and P'eng apparently succeeded in circumventing the publicity and minimizing the political repercussions of Yao's attack.

8. Bowing to the pressure which the *Liberation Army Daily* obviously exerted, the *People's Daily* reproduced Yao's article the following day (30

November) but added its own editor's note, said to have been written by P'eng Chen, which mentioned nothing of the political offenses of Wu Han's play and described the issues involved as "academic."

9. Editorial, *Liberation Army Daily,* 29 May 1967 in *Survey of China Mainland Press* (Hong Kong), No. 3951 2 June 1967, p. 21. (Hereafter cited as *SCMP.*)

10. Lin Piao, "Address to Politburo," translated in *Chinese Law and Government* Vols. 2, 4 (Winter 1969/70): 46-62.

11. I am grateful to Professor Tang Tsou for this point.

12. The origins of the mutiny go back some months to the actions of Wuhan PLA leaders in support of the local conservative faction against the local revolutionary faction. In July two Peking emissaries—Vice-Premier Hsieh Fu-chih, a member of the Politburo, and Wang Li, a member of the Cultural Revolution Group and acting director of the CCP Propaganda Department—arrived in Wuhan to assess the situation. When they admonished the local PLA leaders for suppressing the revolutionaries, the military officers became enraged, and matters quickly got out of hand. On 20 July, members of the Million Heroes—a group which Hsieh and Wang had denounced but which Ch'en Ts'ai-tao and Chung Han-hua, commander and political commissar respectively, of the Wuhan Military Region, had backed —kidnapped and physically abused the two Peking envoys. For a detailed and excellent analysis of the incident and its consequences, see Thomas W. Robinson, "The Wuhan Incident—Local Strife and Provincial Rebellion During the Cultural Revolution," *The China Quarterly* (London) 47, (July-September 1971): 413-38.

13. The 5 September directive is translated in *SCMP,* No. 4026, 22 September 1967, pp. 1-2. On the same day, Chiang Ch'ing made a speech tacitly admitting that her Cultural Revolution Group lieutenants had erred in advancing the slogan of "dragging out the handful of capitalist powerholders in the army" and enjoining the rebels not to raid military headquarters or seize arms from the PLA. See *SCMP,* No. 4069, 29 November 1967, pp. 109.

14. For an overall analysis of factors in military intervention in politics, see Claude E. Welch, Jr. and Arthur K. Smith, *Military Role and Rule* (North Scituate, Mass.: Duxbury Press, 1974), pp. 8-33.

15. Prior to the downfall of Lin Piao in the fall of 1971, the reconstituted party committees in the provinces were unable to exercise "unified leadership" over local PLA authorities, and the decisions they made had to be "reviewed" by the PLA leaders. Mao was quoted to have complained; "Local party committees had already been established, and they should have exercised unified leadership. Wasn't it just upside down if matters already decided upon by local party committees were still taken to army party committees for discussion?" "Summary of Chairman Mao's Talks to Responsible Local Comrades During His Tour of Inspection" (mid-August to 12 September 1971), translated in *Chinese Law and Government* 5, 3-4, (Fall/Winter 1972-1973): 40.

16. "The Constitution of the Communist Party of China" (adopted 14 April 1969), *Peking Review,* 30 April 1969, p. 36.

17. For an excellent analysis of the causes of the Mao-Lin conflict and its development, see Ying-mao Kau, "Editor's Introduction," *Chinese Law and Government* 5, 3-4 (Fall/Winter 1972-3): 3-30.

18. The text of the document is translated into English in *ibid.*, pp. 31-42. The quoted passage is based on *ibid.*, p. 38, with minor corrections in translation. Ch'en Po-ta, mentioned by Mao in the passage, was a member of the Politburo Standing Committee since 1966 and used to be a Mao brain-truster; Ch'en allegedly plotted with Lin Piao in 1970 and was singled out for attack by Mao.

19. *Ibid.*, pp. 43-57.

20. Ch'en Hsi-lien, who was the former commander of the Shenyang MR and concurrently the first secretary of the CCP Liaoning Provincial Committee and chairman of the Liaoning Revolutionary Committee, has been appointed to command the Peking MR; Chi Teng-k'uei, a member of the Politburo, has now become the first political commissar, while Wu Te, the first secretary of Peking is the second political commissar. Li Te-sheng, elected one of the five vice-chairmen of the CCP at the Tenth National Congress in 1973, is now the commander of the Shenyang MR. Hsu Shih-yu has been transferred from the Nanking MR to Canton, effecting an exchange with Ting Sheng, who went from Canton to Nanking. Similar exchanges have taken place in the Tsinan MR, whose commander, Yang Te-chih, has exchanged posts with the Wuhan MR commander, Tseng Ssu-yu and in the Lanchow MR, whose commander, P'i Ting-chun, has exchanged with his counterpart in Foochow, Han Hsien-chu. Pai Ju-ping, secretary of the CCP Shantung Provincial Committee, and Hsu Li-ch'ing, former vice-director of the General Political Department, are now respectively first political commissar and political commissar of the Tsinan MR. Wei Kuo-ch'ing became a Politburo member in August 1973 and was concurrently appointed the first political commissar of the Canton MR in January 1974; in October 1975, he gave up his post as first secretary of the CCP Kuangsi Chuang Autonomous Region to head the CCP Kuangtung Provincial Committee. Changes in the leadership of the three other regional PLA headquarters, Kunming, Chengtu, and Sinkiang, took place earlier. In the case of the Kunming MR, Wang P'i-cheng was promoted its commander, replacing Chin Chi-wei, who was transferred to the Chengtu MR to succeed its former commander, Liang Hsin-chu, who was implicated in the Lin Piao affair. Lung Shu-chin, commander of the Sinkiang MR, was also purged for his alleged involvement in the Lin Piao affair and was replaced by Yang Yung.

21. Quoted in "*Chung-fa* 1972 (4)," *Chinese Law and Government*, p. 54.

22. Five field army groups, or five major elite factions, are believed to have existed in the PLA leadership. These field armies were developed in the course of the communist movement—each grew from a small armed band operating in a base area, which fought, recruited, and expanded independently, each dominating separate geographical regions in China after 1949. Since the leaders of each field army have had close personal and working ties and have shared a common experience, they were believed to have formed a

faction or clique. The Fourth Field Army group, which was associated with Lin Piao, was the most powerful until 1971.

23. John Gittings, "Army-Party Relationship in the Light of the Cultural Revolution," in John W. Lewis (ed.), *Party Leadership and Revolutionary Power in China* (Cambridge University Press, 1970), p. 374. I have liberally drawn from the article in the discussion of this section.

24. The field-army thesis originated among Chinese Nationalist writers; a foremost representative is the late Huang Chen-hsia who expounded the thesis in his *Mao's Generals* (Hong Kong: Research Institute of Contemporary History, 1968).

25. See, for example, Lin Piao's "Speech at a Meeting of Army Cadres" (24 March 1968), translated in *Chinese Law and Government* 4, 2 (Summer 1973): esp. 3-11.

26. William W. Whitson (with Huang Ch'en-hsia), *The Chinese High Command: A History of Communist Military Politics, 1927-71* (New York: Praeger, 1973).

Civilian Control
of the Military in Japan

James H. Buck
University of Georgia

James H. Buck is associate professor and coordinator of graduate programs in history at the University of Georgia. He served in the US Army 1942-47 and 1949-67 and spent seven years in Asia. He has a B.A. from the University of Washington (1948), an M.A. from Stanford (1953) and a Ph.D. from American University (1959). Editor of *The Modern Japanese Military System* (1975), his articles on Japanese military history and defense policy have appeared in *Monumenta Nipponica, Asian Survey, Asian Affairs, Naval War College Review,* and others. He has taught the Japanese language during summer sessions at the Universities of Michigan, Indiana, and Minnesota.

Most of this volume concerns civil-military relations in "developing nations." Japan is an apparent exception to this general line of research, but it should be instructive to consider the development of civil-military relations in Japan during the first two decades of the Meiji Period (1868-1912).

In the 1870s Japan was certainly a "developing country," although such a description was then entirely unlikely. Japan faced problems similar in nature to those now faced by many nations in Latin America, Africa, and Asia: development of an effective central government as free as possible from outside interference; provision of forces for control of domestic disorders; the study, selection, and adaptive use of the experience of foreign military forces in order to form a national military force capable of national defense; and deciding in an acceptable way what criteria would govern civil-military relations in the state.

Little more than a century ago, Japan was forced onto the world scene by the pressure of European powers and the United States, symbolized by the arrival of Perry's black ships in 1853. Aroused from seven centuries of feudalism and two and one-half centuries of isolation under the decentralized feudal military "dictatorship" of the House of Tokugawa, Japan soon made its mark in international affairs. The Meiji Restoration of 1868 was the beginning of one of the most remarkable social, industrial, and national revolutions in world history. Unlike China (whose experience at the hands of the militarily superior Western powers was well known in Japan), Japan was able to maintain its territorial integrity. The Restoration government destroyed the military class which had governed the country for so long, overcame domestic political and armed military opposition, developed an efficient unitary state, and soon established a reputation for military efficiency.

From a congeries of clan military forces loyal to feudal lords, several of whom were genuinely autonomous, Japan developed national forces which, within a generation, overwhelmingly defeated the armed forces of Ch'ing China in 1894-1895 and in the next decade repeated the feat with Russia. In the Russo-Japanese War of 1904-1905, the Imperial Japanese Navy (IJN) was victorious in the first sea battles using armored cruisers with 12" guns. The combat near Mukden involved the greatest concentration of ground troops yet seen, larger than at Borodino, Waterloo, or Gettysburg. Respected by all and feared by many, Japan's military forces became a dominant factor in East Asian and world politics from the Washington conferences through World War II.

The role of Japan's military forces has been crucial in the past. It is a commonplace to hold the military responsible for Japan's policies in the 1930s which led to the "temporary disaster" of defeat and occupation in 1945. Certainly the militarily aggressive and expansionist policies of the 1930s were a product of many factors, but it is also true that institutional arrangements for civil-military relations were a major part of the problem. The government of Japan could not successfully coordinate the varied functions of state in a pursuit of national goals and eventually came under the control of the military, the result, to some, of a constitutional deficiency. But even this conclusion is partially rebutted by Hideki Tojo who testified, "We should have risen above the system in which we found ourselves, but we did not. It was the men who were at fault."[1] In any event, the institutional arrangements for civil-military relations in Japan which were completed in the early years of the Meiji period generally settled the parameters of military action in government and were essentially fixed until 1945. In the later years of the period, Japan's civil-military relations must be placed in Welch's spectrum on the extreme of military control.

Japan has now built a very modest Self-Defense Force (SDF), although Japan has become the world's third largest national economic unit, has a population three-and-one-half times as large as a century ago, and may well challenge the United States for industrial leadership of the world in the coming decades. Certainly Japan is a leader in the resurgence of the non-Western world. Today civil-military relations lie on the opposite extreme of Welch's spectrum—in the area of almost total civilian control and very little military influence.

Within a couple of generations Japan has experimented with both theoretical extremes in civil-military relations. In the two periods in Japanese history considered here (from 1870 to 1890 and from 1950 to 1970), the essentials of civil-military relations were fixed in a relatively short period of time and stand diametrically opposed to one another. Japan does not seem to fit the generalization argued by Welch and Smith that "strong civilian control over the armed forces emerges gradually through complex historical processes. . . .,"[2] certainly not in the sense of long-term evolutionary development. Vagts holds that "the struggle between civilian and military [in Japan] assumed shapes outside the classifications of the west."[3]

This chapter argues, in part, that the adoption of "military control" in the early period and the adoption of "civilian control" most recently can best be explained in terms of the absolute prerequisite for Japan to adapt quickly and effectively to domestic crisis coupled with external threat; or, in the case of present-day Japan, the specific requirement to obey the dictates of the Occupation authorities. In short, the type of civil-military relations developed in Japan depended mostly on pragmatic reactions to real problems and owed less to ideological preference or to a gradual evolution characterized by diminution of the role of the military.

In both periods of Japanese history, foreign military models and foreign political thought were important, if not decisive, in the selection of institutional arrangements and the adaptation of concepts which gave theoretical support to their concrete organizational expression.

For these reasons, this chapter compares the early Meiji period with the post-World War II period in terms of the need for a structure for civil-military relations and the role of foreign political thought and military models in the structure adopted.

Civil-Military Relations, Early Meiji Period

Direct and sustained military involvement in politics characterized Japan from the 1860s until 1945. Almost from the beginning, military command *(gunrei)* and military administration *(gunsei)* were effectively separated from the control of civil officials and monopolized first by the clan clique *(hanbatsu)* and later by the military clique *(gunbatsu)* which drew its officers from many parts of Japan. The exclusion of civil control from military affairs was in response to domestic crisis and the need to preserve Japan in the face of China's fate at the hands of Western powers. The early military forces relied heavily on the French for guidance in matters of small-unit organization, training, and tactics, and in the adoption of the conscription system, while high-level staff organization and the general principles of civil-military relations reflected the German example, but simultaneously drew heavily on ancient Japanese tradition. The Constitution of 1889 owed much to the Germans, but differed in the theoretical role of the Japanese emperor and the actual political role of the military, which Vagts called "the most political army in the world."[3] Huntington wrote that the "Japanese officer corps [was] the major military body in the world lacking in professional spirit."[4] Japanese servicemen were prohibited from engaging in "politics" by the Imperial Rescript of 1882, and they did not take part in "party politics." The military's politics consisted of pursuing their goals by adept use of the institutional and constitutional arrangements which certified their monopoly in military affairs, supported by the use of a plethora of servicemen's and ex-servicemen's organizations, fascistic and ultranationalist organizations, by propaganda, and by terror and assassination.

In the mid-nineteenth century the feudal military regime of the Tokugawa shogunate (1600-1868) was nearing its demise, threatened by external forces which were little understood and weakened by internal forces demanding change. Perry's visit in 1853 was the initial catalyst for change. The essential objective of change was somehow to preserve Japan from foreign encroachment. The responsibility for military defense lay with the shogunate, but by this time the main institutional role of the *shōgun* and the *daimyō* (feudal lords) "had become primarily political, secondarily military."[5] Individual samurai gave first loyalty to their lords, and while some lords gave loyalty to the shogunate, several of the most powerful lords did not. Historically semiautonomous, the major lords in western Japan soon quarreled with the shogunate, urging greater resistance to the foreigners. After experiencing the might of the West in the British expedition against Kagoshima in 1863 and the combined fleet operation (US, British, Dutch, and French) against the Lord of Choshu in 1864, the western lords reversed their stand, improved their own forces, allied themselves in support of a restoration of the emperor, and ousted the shogunate in the Civil War in 1868-1869.

Even prior to the Restoration of 1868, foreign military forces played a role in the development of the shogunate forces and those of some clans. In 1865 the shogunate began to feel out the French for assistance in building an arsenal and getting French advisors. Negotiations were halting, but a French mission did arrive in Japan in February 1867 with three-year contracts for service, only to be dismissed in twenty months' time, for by then the shogunate had been overthrown. The shogunate's forces, whom the French were to assist, were disbanded in July 1868. The first French mission had not the time to influence the Shogun's forces basically, but it did set a precedent.[6]

If the shogunate had needed military forces to fend off the West—and to fend off opposition clan armies—then the Restoration government had similar need. After the new government was established in 1868, the military forces of Japan continued to reflect the feudal structure of private armies; they were manned by the military class of samurai who gave loyalty to their individual feudal lords. In the civil war of 1868-1869, the new government was unable to develop an integrated military system, although operations against the counterrevolutionary Tokugawa remnants showed clearly the weakness of the forces under direct imperial control. A Military Affairs Department *(Hyōbushō)* was established in 1868,[7] but was ineffective because clan chieftains still had to handle direct operational control in the field.

A national military force began to emerge with the formation of the "Emperor's Own" *(Goshimpei)* on 22 February 1871. Commanded by Takamori Saigo from the Satsuma fief, the Emperor's Own consisted of infantry, artillery, and cavalry units contributed by the fiefs of Satsuma, Chōshū, and Tosa, and numbered 10,000 men. These units were directly subordinate to the War Department and for the first time the central government acquired control of a significant military force which was not subject to the direct influence of feudal lords; it "added quickly to the popularity and influence" of the new government.[8]

Formation of a genuine national military force required further the destruction of the fief system, fief armies, and denial of power to the feudal lords. Those clans which contributed to the *Goshimpei* also led the way, beginning in 1869, in the restoration of clan registers to the central government *(hanseki hokan).* By mid-1871, all but 17 of the 276 feudatories had surrendered their clan registers to the government.[9] Just five months after the formation of the Emperor's Own, an imperial order decreed the abolition of fiefs and the establishment of prefectures. With surprising ease, this "greatest cause of anxiety" was quietly and successfully resolved. The economic situation of many clans certainly contributed to the quiet acceptance of this decree, but the fact that the central government possessed significant military forces "must be counted a powerful factor" in its success.[10]

Although the samurai, as a social class, had been virtually abolished by a series of decrees which pensioned them off, denied them the status symbols of the topknot and the two swords, permitted intermarriage with commoners, and gave them complete freedom in the choice of occupation, the matter of who would man the new military forces was not decided immediately. Former samurai manned the army as specified in orders of 10 February 1870, which required that all volunteers accepted for military duty must be selected from among the military class and its retainers.[11] Yet those who favored conscription and the manning of the army with men from all social classes were in a strong position to oppose those who favored perpetuation of the military class in some form or another, including as a volunteer force. Clearly, those in control of the imperial court saw the need for a new system to enroll military men and in November 1870 issued a proclamation stating that "arms are of urgent necessity for national defense, on which the Imperial prestige rests. It is the intention of the Emperor to study the history of military organizations of the world and thereby institute a new system of conscription."[12]

Certain features of the system adopted were "restorationist" and looked to ancient Japan. As Ogawa aptly summarized it: "The exclusive possession of political power on the part of the military class having been the cause of the decline of Imperial power, the first step toward its restoration was the destruction of the military class and feudalism."[13] What Japan required in 1870 then, was a conscription system like those of Europe, but plainly such a system was, in Japanese eyes, a return to earlier times. The imperial mandate establishing the conscription system (28 November 1872) states:

In ancient times when the prefectural system was in force, the country was protected by the militia enlisted in army corps, and there was no distinction of status between soldiers and farmers. It was in the Middle Ages when the military power was monopolized by the military class that this distinction came into being and formed the basis of the feudal system.[14]

Other experience, more close at hand than ancient Japan, suggested the desirability of a conscription system. The Chōshū clan, which produced Masujirō Ōmura and Aritomo Yamagata (the outstanding political and military figure in Japan from the 1870s until his death in 1922), had earlier experience with conscription. Having faced and lost to the combined forces of France, Britain, the US, and Holland in combat in 1864, the Chōshū formed the *kiheitai,* a conscript group of samurai, townsmen, and peasants. The rationale was simply that experience with Western arms demonstrated that what counted in modern warfare of artillery fire and trained bodies of men was not individual hand-to-hand combat in which the pedigreed samurai took such pride, but rather the selection of outstanding men of good body, spirit, and physical hardiness—from whatever class—and their transformation into Western-style military units. This was the way to withstand the foreigners.[15]

Many reasons have been cited for adoption of a conscription system. These have included the need to defend Japan against Russia, to use the army domestically as a club against dissidents, and more recently, as the first necessary step toward aggression on the continent of Asia. Presseisen believes it was essentially for prestige—to make Japan an equal of the foreign powers—and for Japan conscription was a "sure sign that she [Japan] had become a modern nation."[16] Matsushita maintains the establishment of conscription was "the great accomplishment in Meiji military history"; otherwise, he wrote, "it is unlikely that Japan could have stabilized the nation internally or have developed into a modern state." Its great success lay in its combining the two great aspirations of early Meiji Japan —the need to strengthen the army and to restore imperial rule.[17]

The Conscription Law of 1872 owed much to the French system. French influence was evident primarily in the number of exemptions and in the provisions for substitution of service. These were lessened progressively through several changes in the conscription law after the Satsuma Rebellion (1877), in response to continental conditions in 1883, and again in 1890, by which time Japan's conscription system more closely paralleled that of Germany in terms of rigorous policies concerning exemptions. By 1890 the whole nation was eligible for service and the law was adequate to prepare for emergencies abroad.[18]

That the Japanese conscription law showed such French influence is not surprising. Yamagata had studied the French and Prussian systems in 1870-71 and the second French mission had arrived in Japan just six months prior to the conscription proclamation.

This second French mission, consisting of sixteen officers and men, arrived with three-year contracts, but remained in Japan until July 1880. French advisors founded the Japanese Military Academy *(Shikan gakkō)* and of its first 155 students entering in January 1875, 40 of them knew the French language. Although the greatest French efforts went into the establishment of the military academy, the French mission also taught the Japanese how to organize, train, and command units up to brigade level and demonstrated the use of artillery. For several years, Japan sent ten officers annually to study military matters in France[19] and from 1880 to 1890 France was the only foreign nation with a military attaché in Tokyo. The French taught basic tactics, but did not deal with strategy and command, probably because the French considered Japan a "developing" country and repeatedly insisted that fundamentals must come first. The Japanese resented the idea of a long tutelage and wanted results, particularly after their forces had been shown to be substantially deficient in administrative support and staff functions in the Satsuma Rebellion of 1877. Japan kept the French so long as they were useful, but the next step in the development of Japan's forces, the acquisition of an effective staff system, depended on borrowing from the recent victor over France, the Prussian army.[20]

The General Staff Office *(Rikugun Sambō-kyoku)* of the Imperial Japanese Army (IJA) was initiated as an office of the

Ministry of Military Affairs in 1871; it was patterned after the civil control of the French and subordinate to the ministry. Partly as a result of the Satsuma Rebellion, Yamagata requested an independent General Staff with its own budget and the GSO was established on a separate basis in 1878.

The impetus for this move probably came from Lt. Col. Tarō Katsura, who had just returned from three years study in Germany and service as military attaché in Berlin. Like Yamagata, Katsura was a former member of the Chōshū clan, pro-German, and later a war minister and premier of Japan. The independent GSO was a basic change in Japan's military system. The positions of the war minister and chief of general staff were reversed so that the latter had the higher status. In a sense, he now ranked equal to the premier *(Dajō Daijin)*.[21] The GSO was under the emperor's direct control, and the chief of general staff (who had to be a serving general or lieutenant general) was granted "immediate access" to the emperor *(iaku jōsō)*, a right then denied to the war minister.[22] The General Staff Regulations provided that the GSO "shall be in charge of national defense and strategy *(kokubō oyobi yōhei).*"[23]

By 1879 the three main military functions of operations and strategy, military administration, and training and inspection were allocated to three separate divisions of the IJA. Only the function of military administration (War Ministry) came under civilian control. From this time on, the command prerogative *(tōsuiken)*, exercised by the General Staff directly subordinate to the emperor, was separated from ordinary military administration *(gunseiken)*.[24]

The German army organization was certainly the model for these important changes despite certain differences in the relations among emperor, General Staff, and war minister in the two countries.[25] Although the IJA reorganization proceded major changes in the German system by five years, the pro-German party in the IJA was entirely familiar with military thought in Germany and recognized clearly the advantages of removing control of military affairs from civilian hands so far as possible. When Yamagata proposed the establishment of the independent General Staff, he referred always to "Europe," but it is unlikely that anyone thought he did not mean Prussia specifically. The pro-French party was weakened not only by the relative loss of French military prestige after defeat in 1871, but also by France's adoption of *l'Etat-Major de l'Armée* on the Prussian model in 1871. If the model is clear, the political reasons for its adoption are less so. Presseisen maintains that "the military reforms of 1878 were not motivated by foreign examples; they developed from domestic conditions, specifically the *Goshinsei undo* [emperor's personal rule] sentiment at court."[26] Maxon's reasons include the prestige-laden recommendation (as early as 1871) by the commander of the Emperor's Own, Takamori Saigo, that the emperor ought to have personal command of troops, activity by agitated former samurai, and the new *Aikokusha,* the embryonic "Patriots' Party," the "first feeble civil challenge to the powers of government which had been assured by the loose coalition of western samurai clansmen and Court nobles. This challenge was evidently the decisive factor in the separation of the military functions of administration and command."[27]

The personal role of the emperor in his military command functions was special, and to the Japanese, unique. This relationship was specified in the "Imperial Precepts to the Soldiers and Sailors" *(Gunjin Chokuyu)* of 4 January 1882.[28] The precepts themselves were mainly adjuratory, urging servicemen to cultivate the characteristics of loyalty, propriety, valor, fidelity, and simplicity. The preamble reinforced the ideas and arguments used to justify the adoption of a conscription system less than a decade earlier. It emphasized that 2,500 years ago, during the reign of the founding emperor, Jimmu Tennō, the emperor had controlled the armed forces and that in the earliest days, the emperor never relinquished command to his ministers. Unfortunately, this was altered later by circumstances. In his words, the emperor regretted the mutation of his relation to the soldiers in the Middle Ages and promised never to let it happen again. Such was his reason for becoming the commander-in-chief *(Daigensui)* of the imperial army and navy. Thus would the emperor respond to the benevolence of heaven and fulfill his obligations *(on)* to his ancestors. Together, the emperor and his servicemen would exhaust their power, with one heart, to protect the nation.

This document constituted the wellspring of the military spirit. From its promulgation until demobilization in 1945, these precepts were the "golden rule" by which servicemen lived. It derived from two millenia of mythology; the tradition of *bushi* elaborated over seven centuries of rule by military houses and 250 years of Tokugawa military feudalism was skillfully culled to form a succinct code for the new imperial forces. Memorized and recited by millions of servicemen for three generations, it symbolized the "military spirit" of the new Japan, sanctified the emperor's unique position, focused and reinforced the values of society as a whole, and promoted the utility of the armed forces as a socializing force; in fact, the armed forces became a "postgraduate" school for training conscript civilians in the ethics of society.

The essential elements in civil-military relations—formation of a national military force (1871), enactment of conscription (1872), establishment of an independent General Staff directly subordinate to the emperor with the "right of direct access" (1878), and promulgation of the imperial rescript (1882) proclaiming the emperor's right of supreme command and specifying his unique relationship to the soldiers and sailors of Japan—were in effect prior to Japan's constitutional era, which began in 1890.

For the nine years preceding the promulgation of the Constitution, comprehensive investigations were conducted to ascertain the constitutional arrangements most suitable for Japan. In preparation for the constitutional age, a cabinet was established on 23 December 1885, under provisions of the "Official Powers of the Cabinet" *(Naikaku Shokken).* This *Naikaku Shokken* stipulated in legal terms for the first time the independence of military command. Article VI provided that ". . . although the chief of staff reports directly [to the emperor] on matters of military secrecy, the war minister reports these matters to the premier."[29] The last reorganization of the cabinet prior to promulgation of the Constitution occurred on 24 December 1889. The enabling imperial ordinance charged the premier with coordination of the various branches of the administration, but was indirect in dealing with the "right of direct access" and was not explicit about the independence of the military command. Article VII read: "Matters concerning military secrets and military orders which are reported directly to the emperor shall be reported to the premier by the minister of war and the minister of the navy unless referred to the cabinet by the emperor." The reason for elimination of the words "chief of general staff," was that the navy chief of staff, unlike the army chief of staff, was subordinate to the navy minister. Since the navy minister managed both command and administrative matters, one might look upon the navy minister as a "chief of staff."[30] The effect, according to Maxon, was that the right of direct access by the ministers of war and navy was "implicitly recognized." In practice it meant that service ministers informed the premier of military matters not divulged to other cabinet ministers, and that in many cases the matters reported had already been approved by the emperor and hence, not subject to alteration by the premier or the cabinet.[31]

In the years prior to the promulgation of the Constitution, two German advisors of importance served in Japan, Major Klemens Wilhelm Jakob Meckel and Hermann Roesler.

A Japanese mission visited Germany, Italy, Austria, Russia, and the United States in 1884 and during that trip selected Major Meckel to be hired as a lecturer at the Japanese Staff College. Meckel arrived in March 1885 and immediately undertook his duties in well-attended and highly praised lectures on strategy and staff operations. That fall Meckel introduced the first staff field exercises in the Imperial Japanese Army (IJA). The military academy, which had been a vehicle for French influence from 1875 to 1887, was suddenly reorganized and the French presence was no longer needed. Meckel's most important duty was as advisor to the General Staff of the IJA. One authority states, "As counselor and planner for the high command, he [Meckel] provided it with a military structure that survived until 1945."[32] That assessment is probably overdrawn, but Meckel's influence on the Japanese was such that his bust stood in front of the Japanese Army Staff College from 1909 until 1945.

Hermann Roesler, hired by the government of Japan in October 1878, became a most trusted collaborator of Hakubun

Itō, the man charged with drafting the 1890 Constitution. Roesler served Japan until 1893 and "played a decisive role even among Japanese leaders, except for Itō and Inoue."[33] In fact the Meiji Constitution "bears a very close resemblance to Roesler's draft except for Art. I."[34]

The special position of the military was not explicitly stated in the Constitution because it had already been developed by custom and certain laws and regulations promulgated prior to 1890. However, the emperor's right of supreme command *(tō-suiken)* was explicitly stated. The pertinent articles are:

Article XI.	The emperor has supreme command of the army and navy.
Article XII.	The emperor determines the organization and peace standing of the army and navy.
Article XIII.	The emperor declares war, makes peace, and concludes treaties.

The Constitution reinforced previous enactments and did not in any way reverse the preconstitution principle that the emperor's government and the emperor's military staff *(iaku)* "are separate, that the function of the right of command *(tō-suiken)* belongs to the military staff, and that the government is not assigned this function."[35] Within this framework, it was possible for the decisions of the military to be sanctioned as expressions of the "emperor's direct will,"[36] and this was the case in those unwise policy decisions of the 1930s when the military dominated policy formulation.

In Roesler's conception, the emperor should be above the political division of the parties and should represent the undivided interest of the state.[37] His proposal that the emperor have a personal leadership role was rejected. Instead the Constitution was built on a pluralistic system in which the component organs (cabinet, Diet, Privy Council, and others) were to be part of a single body coordinated by the emperor. This was theory, but in fact, the emperor's coordination role was assumed in the early constitutional period by the *genrō*,[38] an extraconstitutional body composed of a small group of former samurai, who always picked one of their own members as prime minister until 1900.[39]

The problem of coordination was crucial. The constitution sought a synthesis of disparate elements. While Itō believed the new system was simply an outgrowth of traditional Japanese ideas and tried to defend the transcendental nature of the imperial system, Pittau believes the Meiji leadership had achieved an "ambiguous and ambivalent system" which mixed, but could not assimilate, inherently contradictory premises. "The Meiji political rationalization allowed either a liberal interpretation or an absolutist reactionary one."[40]

In the decade from 1890 to 1900, the IJA in particular continued to enhance its position relative to the civil officials in government. An imperial ordinance of 1893 (#52) established the Imperial Headquarters *(Daihonei)* under the direct command of the emperor. It provided that "it shall be the duty of the army chief of staff, with the participation of the staff attached to the Imperial Headquarters, to plan the grand strategy for the imperial army and navy forces."[41] The Imperial Headquarters did "move to the field"—to Hiroshima—during the Sino-Japanese War, but remained in Tokyo during the Russo-Japanese War. The body had a sometimes existence and was reestablished in November 1937, four months after the China Incident began, although it was of little significance as a control or coordinating organization.[42] Other high-ranking military advisory bodies (generally without major influence) included the Board of Marshals and Fleet Admirals *(Gensuifu)* and the Supreme War Council *(Gunji Sangi),* organized in 1898 and 1903 respectively.

A final and extremely important adjustment made in civil-military relations during this period was the enactment in 1900 of the legal requirement that both the war and navy ministers must be active service officers in the top two general or flag-officer ranks. This provision had not been necessary earlier because the clan oligarchy was able to place its active service men in the two ministerial posts. But Yamagata, fearing that the struggle for parliamentary government would lead to civilian control of the services, sought and acquired this limitation.[43] Its effect was that the military could control the formation of any new cabinet by refusing to supply a minister or could force the resignation of any cabinet by having one of its ministers resign.

This chapter is not concerned with those societal factors in Japan which permitted or encouraged the eventual complete dominance of the military in Japan during World War II, but a few generalizations will be useful for later comparison with the current situation. It was no accident that the conscription law and compulsory education were introduced almost simultaneously in the early 1870s. The two systems were complementary. Each reinforced the socialization of the Japanese individual. Respect for the imperial institution, patriotism, loyalty, and filial piety were common objectives. Japanese were enjoined in the Imperial Rescript on Education of 1890 "should emergency arise," to "offer yourselves courageously to the State. . . ."[44] School administrators were cautioned to keep in mind that ". . . what is to be done is done not for the sake of the pupils, but for the sake of the country."[45] During World War II, the Japanese military could claim, "Military instruction directly controls the tendencies of civilian morality . . . . The spiritual nature acquired in the army becomes a model for the civilian spirit."[46]

The philosophical or psychological factors which resulted in the "military control" type of civil-military relations in Japan can not be summarized easily. Maxon's study suggests it resulted mainly from the Confucian tradition and its derivative decision-making group dynamics. Confucian tradition prefers the "government of men" to "government of laws" and condones "government from below" *(gekokujō)*. It lacked the tradition of personal responsibility and made people blindly obedient to authority. Political or bureaucratic leaders look upward to authority and outward for group approval. Leaders tend to make decisions on consensus from below, not on law or principle, but on the political basis of approval from below.[47] This social characteristic is what permitted middle-rank officers to play a decisive role in the military activities in the 1930s.

In contrast to Maxon, Huntington does not even mention Confucianism. Huntington sees the cause in the persistence of feudalism for seven centuries down to 1868, when it was replaced by the national ideology of state Shintō's three basic doctrines: an unbroken divine imperial sovereignty, sacred and inviolable; a divine origin of the Japanese nation itself; and a divine mission to make the boundless virtues of the emperor prevail throughout the world. He sees the national ideology, linked with Bushidō, as a "synthesis of imperial nationalism and feudal militarism." Huntington characterizes it as "authoritarian, ethnocentric, nationalistic, imperially oriented (in the sense of both emperor worship and glorification of the Japanese Empire), expansionist and bellicose with high value assigned to the warrior and warrior virtues."[48]

The outstanding characteristic of prewar civil-military relations in Japan was the ability of the military, especially the General Staff of the Imperial Japanese Army, to monopolize military affairs by a variety of administrative and constitutional devices, and simultaneously to exclude civil officials from matters of military command and military administration. While excluding civil officials from vital military policy formulation, the military were also able to interfere in, and often control, broad areas of both domestic and international policy formulation. This basic asymmetry between military and civil officials highlights the "military control" civil-military relations in Japan from the 1870s until the end of World War II.

Post-World War II Civil-Military Relations

The initial US policy directive to the commander of the military forces charged with the occupation of Japan was issued on the day the occupation began and supreme command passed to General MacArthur with the formal surrender of Japan to the Allied Powers on 2 September 1945. As Supreme Commander for the Allied Powers (SCAP), MacArthur was charged with two "ultimate objectives": to insure that Japan would not become again a menace to the United States or to the peace and security of the world, and to establish eventually a peaceful and responsible government. Subsidiary objectives included the complete disarmament and demilitarization of Japan and the elimination of "the authority of the militarists and the influence of militarism" from Japanese life. These policies were to be carried out with a minimum commitment of US forces and the government of Japan was to exercise its normal powers in matters of domestic administration by the authority of the SCAP. In any case of disagreement among the occupying powers, US policies were to govern.[49]

Measures for the physical confiscation and destruction of military equipment were carried out rapidly, the imperial forces were demobilized, war-related industries suspended operations, the secret police were dissolved, officers of the imperial forces were "purged" (prohibited from holding any public office), state Shinto was disestablished, and the emperor disclaimed, in his New Year's address of 1946, the divinity historically attributed to him. In a relatively short period of time, SCAP had eliminated the tangible and visible trappings of "militarism" and throughout the occupation other more penetrating and time-consuming reforms were undertaken with this same objective—through social, political, and educational change.

From 1945 until after the Korean War began in 1950, the only civil-military relations in Japan were the contacts between Japan's civil government and the military occupation. But provisions were made by the occupation "reformers" to ensure that militarists and militarism remained out of Japan's government structure so that a peaceful, responsible, and democratic government could develop. A new constitution was demanded and in late 1945 the Japanese government was so informed. A cabinet committee established to consider the matter was slow to produce the desired results, so SCAP intervened directly and ordered his Government Section to produce a "model draft" for consideration by Japan. This was done in early 1946. The cabinet committee then adopted the "model draft" as its own. After some minor revisions and lengthy debate the present Constitution was promulgated on 3 November 1946 and took effect on 3 May 1947.

The 1947 Constitution is clearly the work of the occupation authorities. The preamble makes clear that sovereign power rests with the people, that government authority is derived from the people, and that the people "shall secure for ourselves and our posterity the fruits of peaceful cooperation with all nations and the blessings of liberty throughout this land, . . ." The emperor is the "symbol of the State and of the unity of the people, deriving his position from the will of the people with whom resides sovereign power" (Article 1). In contrast, the 1890 Constitution was "granted by the Emperor" (in Japanese, it is so called—*kintei kenpō*) and sovereignty was vested in the "sacred and inviolable" person of the emperor, who also theoretically "exercised the legislative power," had supreme command of the army and navy *(gunseiken),* and had the power to declare war, make peace and to conclude treaties.

One genuinely unique feature of the Constitution is Article 9, whereby the "Japanese people forever renounce war as a sovereign right of the nation and the threat or use of force as means of settling international disputes." The same article seems also to obligate Japan never to maintain "land, sea or air forces, as well as other war potential." At the time of its adoption, this article was not controversial, at least openly, and SCAP, commenting on demilitarization just prior to the effective date of the Constitution claimed: "Japan understands as thoroughly as any nation that war does not pay. Her spiritual revolution has been probably the greatest that the world has ever known. . . ."[50]

Other important new controls were constitutionally imposed to prevent a recurrence of "militarism." The Diet is the highest organ of state (Article 41). The premier and other ministers of state are required to be civilians and the cabinet is now collectively responsible to the Diet (Article 66). Finally, ultimate control of the budget rests with the House of Representatives (Article 85), in contrast to the Meiji Constitution, under which expenditures for a given year were authorized for the succeeding year regardless of Diet action.

Although the constitutional arrangements to encourage democracy and to eliminate militarism from Japan were imposed by the United States, "Japan's defense policy has not, contrary to common belief, been a derivative of United States Far Eastern Security policy."[51] Weinstein has pointed out that as early as 1947, Japanese leaders assessed the international situation and decided that US-Soviet conflict was inevitable, that it was impractical to rely on the UN for security, and that Japan should cooperate with the US side after regaining its sovereignty. In 1947 Foreign Minister Hitoshi Ashida transmitted to the US government a memorandum suggesting a mutual defense agreement between the two countries. Japan should be permitted a centralized paramilitary force for internal security to guard against possible Soviet-instigated insurrections through left-wing elements in Japan, the memorandum argues, and the US would have the mission to deter any direct external Soviet aggression against Japan. For the next few years, neither Japan nor the US seems to have given attention to this memorandum, and it was only after the North Korean aggression against the Republic of Korea in 1950 that SCAP authorized Premier Yoshida to establish the National Police Reserve (NPR).[52]

The 75,000 man NPR was established rapidly in August 1950 to provide internal security forces to replace the US occupation troops which had been dispatched earlier to Korea. Its mission was "to act by order of the Premier in case of special need to maintain public peace." After Japan regained its sovereignty by the Peace Treaty of April 1952, a small maritime force was organized and in August Japan established the National Safety Agency to coordinate the command of the two-service Safety Force. The mission, on land and sea, was "to maintain peace and order in our country and to act whenever necessary for the protection of life and property." On 1 July 1954 the present Japan Defense Agency and the tri-service Ground Self-Defense Force (GSDF), the Maritime Self-Defense Force (MSDF), and the Air Self-Defense Force (ASDF) were established. This new defense structure was given the additional mission to defend Japan against direct external aggression.[53]

Structurally, civil control of the self-defense apparatus is assured. The premier, who must be a civilian and a member of the Lower House of the Diet, possesses the power of "command and control" *(shikikantokuken)* of the Self-Defense Force. The National Defense Council (NDC) was established in July 1956 to assist the premier in the formulation of basic defense policy, the general outline of defense planning, and the general coordination of planning regarding industry in defense-related matters and in matters related to the "call out" of troops. The NDC was originally chaired by the premier and consisted of the following civilian officials: the deputy premier, the foreign minister, the finance minister, the director-general of the JDA, and the director of the Economic Planning Agency. When necessary, the chairman of the Joint Staff Council (uniformed officer) and others may be permitted to attend meetings. Actions of the NDC are, in all cases, subject to final approval by the cabinet.[54]

The National Defense Council formulated the "Basic National Defense Policy" announced in May 1957. The complete text is:

> The purpose of national defense is to prevent direct and indirect aggression, and, once invaded, to repel it in order to preserve the independence and peace of Japan, which takes democracy for its basis.
>
> To achieve this purpose, the government of Japan adopts the following principles:
>
>> To support the activities of the United Nations and its promotion of international cooperation, thereby contributing to the cause of world peace.
>>
>> To promote the national welfare and enhance the spirit of patriotism, thereby laying a sound basis for national security.
>>
>> To develop gradually an effective defensive power within the bounds of national capabilities to the extent necessary for self-defense.
>>
>> To cope with aggression by recourse to the joint security system with the United States of America, pending effective functioning of the United Nations, in preventing and removing aggression.[55]

This policy has been carried out generally in the four "Defense Plans" that have been formulated since 1957; the current

Fourth Five-Year Defense Plan covers the years 1972-76.[56] The NDC's primary continuing function has been to advise the premier in formulation of these plans.

Civilian control of the National Defense Council was strengthened further by cabinet resolutions in October 1972. The membership of the NDC was enlarged by adding the minister of International Trade and Industry, the director-general of the Scientific and Technical Agency, the chief of the cabinet secretariat and the chairman of the National Public Safety Commission. Powers allocated to the NDC under Article 62 of the JDA Establishment Law were broadened to include consideration of (1) changes in the organization and composition of SDF units which require a change in the SDF Law, (2) changes in the authorized strength of the SDF, and (3) matters related to the numbers and types of new equipment for the GSDF (tanks, primary missile weapons, and tactical aircraft), for the MSDF (escort vessels, submarines, and tactical aircraft), and for the ASDF (operational aircraft and primary missile weapons). In addition the NDC is concerned with defense planning which extends over several years or involves large sums of money.[57]

The Japan Defense Agency is an external office of the premier's office. The director-general of the JDA must be a civilian. The agency is one rank below ministry and the director-general ranks as state minister and not as cabinet minister. This provision denies any opportunity for a uniformed officer to serve in the cabinet and to "make and break" cabinets— a power that was all too apparent under the Meiji Constitution. The JDA is charged with the mission "to preserve the peace and independence of Japan, and to protect its security. For this purpose it has the duty to carry out the administration and supervision of the GSDF, MSDF, and ASDF."[58] The director-general receives the right of command and control over the SDF from the premier and provides overall administration.[59]

The director-general is assisted by two vice-ministers, one for parliamentary matters (assistance in the formulation of plans) and the other for internal administration of the agency. To assist in the formulation of basic defense policy, the director-general has several "counselors" *(sanjikan)*. Internally the

JDA is organized into the Secretariat and six bureaus *(naibu kyokubu);* Defense Bureau, Education Bureau, Personnel Bureau, Health and Medical Bureau, Finance Bureau, and Equipment Bureau, which oversee activities at the tri-service level. All bureau chiefs are civilians. Subordinate to the Defense Agency are the Staff Offices of the three services: the chief of each is a uniformed officer. These three officers constitute the Joint Staff Council *(Tōgō Bakuryō Kaigi)* under the chairmanship of another general/flag-rank officer from one of the services. This group is the highest military advisory body to the director-general and is the executive body for carrying out the orders of the director-general.[60]

The Joint Staff Council (JSC) is responsible for coordination of the defense, administrative-support, and training-plan activity of the three services, the collection and analysis of intelligence, and the basic and joint supervision of command and control of the director-general in times of mobilization (JDA Establishment Law, Article 26). The JSC does not have the power, on its own initiative, to issue orders directly to troop units in time of mobilization; rather, its function is limited to advising the director-general, replying to his queries, and assisting in the determination of his intent. When joint forces are organized from two or more services in time of mobilization, the JSC assists the director-general in his exercise of command and control, and command is exercised through the JSC by the director-general. The JSC has operated the Joint Staff College *(Tōgō Bakuryō Gakkō)* in Ichigaya (Tokyo) since August 1961. The college prepares officers for high-level command and staff positions. The student officers are selected in equal numbers from the three services for this nine-month course.[61]

Civilian control is maintained over the two major schools in the SDF—the National War College *(Bōei Kenshūsho)* and the Defense Academy *(Bōei Daigakkō),* respectively the senior service college and the pre-commissioning educational institution of the SDF. The National War College was founded in 1952 and has been located in Meguro (Tokyo) since 1958. Its mission is to develop in senior officers, through theoretical approaches to the broad range of defense-related problems, the requisite powers of synthesis and understanding appropriate to senior-level positions. Essentially its mission differs little from those the US National War College or Britain's Royal College of Defense Studies. The president of the *Kenshūsho* is a civilian who directs the course of study and also supervises the War History Room, an adjunct to the *Kenshūsho* since 1955. The authorized strength of the institution is 127, of whom 94 are civilians. Among the instructional staff of 24, there are 18 civilians.[62]

The Defense Academy is a tri-service, four-year educational institution preparing cadets for commissioning. The first class graduated in 1957 and currently there are 8,000 graduates of the Defense Academy. Now located at Obaradai (Yokosuka), the Defense Academy is staffed by 958 personnel, only 241 of whom are officers of the three services. There are about 400 civilian administrative and technical officials on the staff, and the major portion (321) of the instructional staff is civilian, as are the president and vice-president. The authorized cadet strength is 2,120, with about 530 in each class; they are distributed by service as follows: GSDF—300, MSDF—100, ASDF—130. There is a basic military curriculum for all cadets and a basic military curriculum for those in each service. At the same time, the academy requires about 180 semester hours for graduation, with majors offered in six fields (electrical, mechanical, civil, and aeronautic engineering, and applied physics and applied chemistry). Beginning with the April 1974 semester, majors are now offered in management and international relations.[63]

Two major missions of the SDF are to deter external attack and/or defend Japan against it and to assist in the preservation of public security. These two types of operations are to be undertaken only in emergency. The basic mission of the SDF in time of peace is training to prepare for these eventualities.

Civilian control is mandatory and extensive in its safeguards in both defense operations *(bōei shutsudō)* and public security operations *(chian shutsudō)*. SDF public security operations differ from the normal public peace preservation, which is the mission of the police.

The premier may, with the consent of the Diet, mobilize all or part of the SDF when Japan is attacked from outside or threatened by an external military attack. In this context, "external military attack" *(gaibu kara no buryoku kōgeki)* means the "planned, organized use of military force by another country with the intent of committing aggression against Japan." In such a case, Japan may resort to arms to the degree required for defense of the country, but also "must respect international law and usage." (SDF Law Article 88,2). In the case of a "threat" *(osore)* of the use of military force against Japan, Japan may resort to arms only to the extent that an actual attack occurs. As the single public official with the right to mobilize the SDF for a defense operation, the premier must, prior to mobilization, first consult with the National Defense Council (SDF Law Article 62,2), then with the cabinet, and finally receive the approval of the Diet. If the emergency arises when the Lower House has been dissolved, the premier may convoke the House of Councillors (which is never dissolved, but only "closed" when the House of Representatives is "dissolved") and take action with that body's consent (Constitution, Article 54). Even this action, however, is provisional until approval has been received from the entire Diet.

There are two types of public security missions. The SDF may be mobilized (SDF Law Article 78) to deal with "indirect aggression" *(kansetsu shinryaku)*. The premier, at his own initiative, may mobilize troops when it is determined from the national standpoint that ordinary police capabilities are unequal to the task of public peace preservation in instances of large-scale revolt or public disturbance guided by or caused by an external power. The second type of public security operation results from an initiative taken by the governors of urban and rural prefectures *(to-dō-fu-ken)*. In absolutely unavoidable circumstances, any governor, after conference with his Public Safety Commission, may request the premier to dispatch troops to deal with local public security problems (SDF Law Article 81).

Actions under the initiative of the premier are subject to approval by the Diet. Actions taken at prefectural initiative are subject to, and limited by, the various prefectural Public

Safety Commissions and must not exceed the minimum use of force required.[64]

The SDF is an all-volunteer force and its members are civil servants. SDF members enjoy no special status as did the soldiers and sailors of the imperial forces. The outlook of the serviceman is conditioned first of all by his oath of office which reads:

Realizing the mission of the SDF to maintain the peace and independence of our country, I swear that I shall respect the laws, maintain the solemn regulations with one mind, always cultivate virtue, respect individual dignity, train my mind and body, improve my abilities, not participate in political activity, fulfill my duties with a strong sense of responsibility, think not of danger when faced with difficulty, endeavor to do my duty and thereby *respond to the trust of the people.* (Italics mine)[65]

The intent to make the SDF reflect civilian mores and serve as the people's instrument is quite clear. Perhaps it is not too much to suggest that the current situation is a complete reversal of prewar conditions. In education of SDF members, the basic guidelines of the national policy on education are followed. The first article of the Basic Education Law (1948) reads:

Article I. [The Objectives of Education] Education aims at the perfection of character; as a builder of a peaceful state and society, it loves truth and justice, respects the value of each individual, values highly labor and responsibility, anticipates the nurturing of a healthy people full of the spirit of individuality. In such a manner it must be carried out.[66]

These precepts are not accepted by all Japanese, or by all SDF members, but the guidance has remained unaltered. For SDF members, a minor attempt has been made to provide a postwar "equivalent" to Emperor Meiji's Imperial Precepts to the Soldiers and Sailors of 1882. The "Ethical Principles for SDF Personnel" *(Jieikan no Kokorogamae)* was published in

1961 and its five articles called for awareness of mission, self-improvement, fulfilling one's responsibility, strict observance of discipline, and solidarity. It strikes one as an attempt to inculcate certain mental attitudes necessary for a military force and does not run contrary to general educational or defense policy. In fact, certain portions of it are apparently designed to eliminate some prewar attitudes, for it calls for reason and the "avoidance of ignorance and fanaticism" and emphasizes throughout the absolute requirement of SDF members to have the confidence and trust of the Japanese people.

The SDF mission is limited, and the SDF may not take part in out-of-country offensive operations and no troops have ever been committed to the United Nations for any type of operation. The apparently ambigious constitutional status of the SDF is dealt with by reference to the UN Charter, Article 51, which provides that nothing in the Charter impairs "the inherent right of individual or collective self-defense if an armed attack occurs against a Member Nation, until the Security Council has taken measures to maintain international peace and security." This reference is reinforced by the so-called Sunakawa judgment of Japan's Supreme Court, which states the following concerning the intent of the Japanese Constitution:

> It does not in any way deny the inherent right of self-defense which our country possesses as a sovereign state; the pacificism of Japan's Constitution by no means implies no defense and no resistance. . . . That our country can take measures for self-defense necessary to maintain its peace and security and to insure its survival must be said to be a matter of course, as the exercise of the functions inherent to a state.[67]

The SDF has remained at modest manning levels since the mid-1950s, with an authorized strength of about one-quarter million men and women, in a total population of about 105,000,000.

Table 1. SDF Strength

	GSDF	MSDF	ASDF	Total
First Plan (1957-61)	180,000	34,000	41,586	255,586
Fourth Plan (1972-76)	180,000	37,000	48,000	265,000

Over two decades then, the authorized strengths have increased but 5 percent. And actual strengths have usually fallen short of the authorized strength. For instance, in 1972 the GSDF was manned at 86.2 percent of full strength and the overall average for all services was approximately 90 percent, although the much smaller MSDF and ASDF have averaged about 98 percent manning levels.[68] Very few young people are affected in any way by the SDF, which has maintained a low profile, kept out of politics, and probably is incapable of exerting any undesirable influence on Japanese thinking by internal socialization processes.

If the impact of the SDF on the lives of young Japanese has been minimal, defense expenditures have also been minimal, and many Japanese believe the relatively low level of such expenditures has been a major factor contributing to Japan's economic prosperity. While authorized strengths have remained nearly constant, absolute defense expenditures have steadily risen at an annual rate of 15-20 percent.

Table 2
Japan's Defense Expenditures (in billion yen)

Defense Plans	Defense Expenditures	Defense Expenditure as % of GNP	Defense Expenditure as % of National Budget
First (1957-61)	791.2	1.12	10.1
Second (1962-66)	1,384.2	0.95	8.1
Third (1967-71)	2,527.2 (est.)	0.80	7.2
Fourth (1972-76)	4,630.0 (est.)	0.88	7.0

(Note: The so-called First Five-Year Defense Plan was decided in June 1957 and actually applied to FYs 1958-60, but figures for a full five-year period are used for ease of comparison. Figures are for FY which begin on 1 April of the year indicated. Dollar figures conversions at ¥360 equals $1 are: First Plan— $2.197 billion; Second Plan—$3.845 billion; Third Plan— $7.020 billion, Fourth Plan—$12.777 billion. At ¥300 equals $1, dollar figures for the Fourth Plan are $14.533 billion.)

These data show that the funds allocated to the various Five-Year Plans, considered as a percentage of the GNP or a percentage of the national budget, have decreased, and that the absolute expenditures for defense have nearly doubled with each succeeding plan. While authorized strength of the SDF has risen about 4 percent in the twenty years from 1957 to 1976, defense expenditures have increased about 600 percent. This is in accord with Japan's policy to devote about 1 percent of the GNP to defense (the enormous absolute increase has been made possible by Japan's striking economic productivity) and to assign these resources to qualitative improvement of equipment.

The entire evolution of Japan's defense power has been gradual, limited in comparison to that of other nations with roughly equivalent resources, and almost entirely defensive in nature. This policy has been made possible by Japan's reliance on the United States for deterrence of external attack and the governing instrument has been the United States-Japan Security Treaty of 1952 (revised in 1960).

The US-Japan Security Treaty took effect with the return of sovereignty to Japan. It may be seen as an action forced by the United States to enhance US security in East Asia and to provide for common action in case the peace and security of that area is threatened. Nevertheless, the treaty does, in part,[69] satisfy those objectives sought by Yoshida and Ashida in the late 1940s; namely, the acquisition by Japan of forces adequate to deal with internal security threats and the assumption by the US of the mission to deter external attack. By the 1952 treaty, the US reserved the right to assist in maintaining internal security in Japan, but this provision was dropped in the

1960 revision. The SDF mission has not changed since its inception (1954) and its current mission accords with that envisioned by Yoshida. On the other hand, the SDF was organized on order of SCAP, and its purpose then was to fit in with US strategy. SDF organization, armament, and early training were directed by advisory groups composed of US officers and men. Japan has continued to depend on US advice and support in the purchase of US manufactured weapons and the use of US technology, although the period of reliance on the US is fading fast as Japan emphasizes self-reliance in all of these matters.

Japan's defense policy has been essentially that of the Liberal Democratic Party (LDP) which has formed all governments since 1948. The substance of policy has been articulated and pursued by the LDP without bipartisan support. The LDP is forced to be responsive not only to the political opposition, but also to public opinion. Within the LDP itself, there is not unanimity on important matters related to defense policy; for example, some segments have favored revision of the Constitution to alter the "war renunciation" Article IX. Another proposal is to elevate the JDA to ministry status, and yet another intra-LDP disagreement centers on whether Japan may or may not possess nuclear weapons.

Although the LDP has, and uses, the power to enforce parliamentary discipline on its members in the Diet, it is basically a grouping of factions covering a wide spectrum of more or less conservative thought. The premier (and LDP party president) is not a leader in the sense of being able to enforce his will on the party membership in the Diet; rather, he acts as first among equals and serves the function of referee in intraparty power alignments. Factions tend to act semiautonomously and factional leaders are rivals for his power as premier. Political power is diffused and LDP policies stem from consensus. It is the premier's duty to achieve enough consensus to act. When it is not achieved, he does not act.

The LDP is highly organized concerning policy recommendations, which it seeks from about fifteen subdivisions of the LDP Policy Affairs Research Council. Two of these subdivisions have duties related to defense matters. The

Kokubō Bukai (Subcommittee on National Defense) has about forty members and is responsible to review the defense budget and technical military matters. The *Anzen Hoshō Chōsakai* (Investigative Committee on National Security) has over sixty members and considers broad security policy matters. Membership on both groups includes members of both houses of the Diet and tends to represent the more conservative side of the LDP with a sprinkling of members with military experience. Both enjoy good working relationships with government bureaucracy, but neither is equipped seriously to challenge the work of the JDA. In any event, the committees are large in size and their recommendations must be considered first by the Policy Affairs Research Council, then pass to the Executive Council of the LDP. Factional bargaining and the problems of overlapping responsibilities with other party committees and bureaucracies result in decision only at the highest party level.

Some Tentative Conclusions

Civil control of the military in Japan is comprehensive and institutionally well-guarded. The civil control system resulted directly from the SCAP initiative in the 1947 Constitution. The first postwar paramilitary forces were organized at the order of SCAP. American officers and men equipped, trained, advised the Japanese forces. The SDF has an organization reflecting both the structure of US armed forces and the civilian control concepts of the US, modified to suit the parliamentary custom in Japan.

Japan has not only retained these civil control concepts, but has continued to strengthen them. Several reasons account for this. The 1947 Constitution enjoys broad support among Japanese. Although support for cooperation with the US in defense matters of mutual interest is waning with the perception of alternatives, the Security Treaty still enjoys support and has unquestionably been a major factor in the ability of Japan to develop economically in ways, and to a magnitude, not envisioned twenty, or even ten years ago. Japan has been able to maintain a "low posture" internationally and to avoid risks, military and otherwise. This, in turn, compensates

Japanese for their sense of shame and impropriety about the prewar conduct of the Japanese military. As a matter of fact, Japan has consistently followed a policy of nonengagement or noninvolvement in every international crisis since the end of the occupation.

These observations emphasize that the role of the military in Japan since 1945 has not been of importance in overall policy. Rearmament, the constitutional status of the SDF, and the Japan-US Security Treaty have constantly been election issues, but never have they been decisive issues. The SDF is not regarded as an instrument of diplomacy in Japan; on the contrary, it is difficult to describe its function in terms applicable to other states which have conventional military forces with conventional functions and missions.

One Japanese commentator recently wrote that there is "no Japanese defense policy in the true sense of the word, but only a few outworn principles and a body of unrelated, disconnected programs of individual bureaus in the defense policy." He adds that policy decisions are not made until a matter related to defense is converted into a political or administrative issue by an opposition party or when there is need to reconcile bureaucratic conflicts on a particular defense problem.[70]

One searches unsuccessfully for a statement of Japanese defense policy in terms of traditional concepts of a defense policy or for a role of the SDF as a military component of national strategy. The "Basic National Defense Policy" of 1957 is couched in the most ambiguous terms and the long-awaited *Defense White Paper* of 1970 adds to the confusion. It states the "very foundation for the establishment of defense policies" is a "good conscience" so that trust will be established in the minds of "people throughout the world." Japan is to be thought of as a "non-nuclear middle-class nation" which "will become a great power in an economic sense but never in a military sense."[71]

If one can not discern any traditional strategic role for the SDF by study of Japanese diplomacy and foreign policy, neither can one derive its role from SDF employment over the past twenty-five years. On no occasion has the SDF been mobilized either for its mission of defense against external attack or for preservation of public safety. Judging from the disposition of SDF units, one can only conclude that what Japan has developed is simply a tactical doctrine and not a strategic doctrine.[72]

Although one can describe fairly accurately the unchallenged supremacy of civilian control of the SDF in Japan today, there is little guidance to judge how civil-military relations will develop in the future. Writing eighteen years ago, Huntington noted that Japan then had an "unusual freedom to create new military institutions," but also noted that the "strongly pacifist ideology" of modern Japan was equally as hostile to military professionalism as the "prewar bellicose nationalism." He concluded that "the odds would appear to favor the emergence in Japan of a system of civil-military relations differing in apppearance but not in essentials from that which prevailed prior to 1945."[73]

To date there is no evidence to suggest this state of affairs will come to pass. On the other hand, given Japan's history, it is probably unwise to judge prematurely. If there is any validity to the broad proposition suggested here, namely, that in the past century civil-military relations in Japan have represented both extremes in the spectrum from military control to civil control, and did so mainly as a pragmatic response to external requirements and/or domestic crisis, then it is possible that some future challenge might dictate rapid change in civil-military relationships. One Japanese commentator, whose views are representative of those who believe an emotional overreaction to some shocking future event could cause a dramatic change in Japan's defense policy, suggests "Japan might rush into a dangerous situation even if it knew that it might be dangerous to itself." Examples of such an event might be deployment of "big power" armed forces to cut Japan's lifelines to mideast oil and to southeast Asia, or the harassing and attacking of Japan's ships, or the precipitate conversion of Japan into a communist state. This last event, he suggests, "might provoke an attempted military coup which would be supported by many Japanese people."[74]

On the other hand, Japan seems now to be pursing what

Wakaizumi calls Japan's "grand experiment" of setting the example to "help move the world from almost total dependence on essentially military power politics to a new reliance on economic, political, social, scientific, and cultural cooperation."[75] In this vision of the future, civil-military relations is crucial. For Japan, "Success or failure of civilian control is the key to success or failure of the 'defense policy for peace.' "[76]

Notes to Chapter 6
Buck, *Civilian Control of the Military in Japan.*

1. Yale C. Maxon, *Control of Japanese Foreign Policy* (Berkeley: U. of California Press, 1957), p. 218, quoting "Interrogation of Hideki Tojo" dated 19 March 1946, partly comprised in Exhibit 3336, Transcript pp. 20626-32.

2. Claude E. Welch, Jr. and Arthur K. Smith, *Military Role and Rule* (North Scituate: Duxbury Press, 1974), p. 4.

3. Alfred Vagts, *A History of Militarism* (Elnora, New York: Meridian Press, 1959), p. 418.

4. Samuel P. Huntington, *The Soldier and the State* (Cambridge Mass: Harvard Univ. Press, 1957), p. 126.

5. James B. Crowley, "Formation of the Meiji Military Establishment," in Bernard S. Silberman and Harry D. Harootonian (eds.) *Modern Japanese Leadership* (Tucson: University of Arizona Press, 1965), p. 267.

6. Ernest L. Presseisen, *Before Aggression Europeans Prepare the Japanese Army* (Tucson: University of Arizona Press, 1965), pp. 5-23.

7. Kimio Izu and Yoshio Matsushita, *Nihon Gunji Hattatsu-shi,* (Tokyo: Mikasa Shobō, 1938), pp. 131-133.

8. *Ibid.,* pp. 140-141.

9. George E. Uyehara, *The Political Development of Japan 1867-1909* (London: Constable and Co, Ltd., 1910), p. 60.

10. Izu and Matsushita, *Nihon Gunji,* pp. 141-142.

11. Gotaro Ogawa, *Conscription System in Japan* (New York: Oxford University Press, 1921), p. 9.

12. *Ibid.,* pp. 9-10.

13. *Ibid.,* p. 5.

14. *Ibid.,* p. 6.

15. Izu and Matsushita, *Nihon Gunji,* pp. 143-144.

16. Presseisen, *Before Aggression,* p. 31.

17. Yoshio Matsushita, *Meiji Gunseishi Ron* (Tokyo: Yūhikaku, 1956), Vol. I, p. 251.

18. Ogawa, *Conscription System*, pp. 42-43.

19. Field Marshal Prince Aritomo Yamagata, "The Japanese Army," in Count Shigenobu Ōkuma, ed. *Fifty Years of New Japan* (London: Smith, Elder, 1909), Vol. I, p. 206.

20. Presseisen, *Before Aggression*, pp. 25-67.

21. Seitoku Itō, *Kokubō-shi* (Vol. 4 of *Gendai Nihon Bunmeishi* (Tokyo: Toyō Keizai Shinpōsha, 1941), p. 57.

22. Presseisen, *Before Aggression*, pp. 61-63.

23. Maxon, *Control of Japanese Foreign Policy*, p. 22.

24. *Ibid.*, pp. 22-23.

25. See Gordon A. Craig, *The Politics of the Prussian Army, 1640-1945* (New York: Oxford University Press, 1968), pp. 220, 222-223, 227-229, 230.

26. Presseisen, *Before Aggression*, p. 64.

27. Maxon, *Control of Japanese Foreign Policy*, pp. 22-23.

28. Full text is in Matsushita, *Meiji Gunseishi Ron*, Vol. I, pp. 503-508.

29. Izu and Matsushita, *Nihon Gunji*, pp. 160-161.

30. *Ibid.*, pp. 162-163. In his *Meiji Gunseishi Ron*, Matsushita notes that in early September 1902, one Okuda, director of the Bureau of Legislation, submitted to Prime Minister (General) Katsura a draft revision of the military organization which would have eliminated the "right of direct access." General Katsura ignored the recommendation and by 26 September Okuda resigned voluntarily, suggesting the lesson that those who oppose the military lose their jobs. (Vol. II, pp. 528-529). Matsushita also notes one abuse of the "right of direct access" by War Minister (General) Uehara in late 1912. Uehara demanded two army divisions for garrison duty in Korea, but Yamagata and others felt the frontier was amply guarded and refused. Unable to sway Yamagata to his side, Uehara personally visited the palace, reported the details of his disagreements with Yamagata, and handed in his resignation. This act was judged to violate legal principles *(hōri)*, and Uehara was forced to retract his resignation until it could be submitted along with those of the entire Cabinet (Vol. II, pp. 636, 642).

31. Maxon, *Control of Japanese Foreign Policy*, p. 13.

32. Presseisen, *Before Aggression*, pp. 116-117. Meckel had a successful career after returning to Germany, where he became *Oberquartiermeister* of the GS in 1895. Among students whom he taught at the Kriegsakademie, Meckel included Wilhelm Groener, Erich Ludendorff, and Hans von Seeckt (p. 126). Presseisen notes that Meckel's funeral in 1906 went unnoticed in Berlin, but the memorial service in Tokyo was "enormous" and took place at the auditorium of the Army Staff College (p. 149).

33. Joseph Pittau, *Political Thought in Early Meiji Japan 1868-1889* (Cambridge, Mass: Harvard University Press, 1967), p. 132, quoting Yasuzō Suzuki, "Herman Roesler," in *Monumenta Nipponica*, 4:440.

34. *Ibid.*, pp. 149-150. Roesler recommended unsuccessfully that Article I should read: "The Japanese Empire is one indivisible constitutional monarchy." The adopted version read, "The Empire of Japan shall be ruled over by Emperors of the dynasty, which has reigned in an unbroken line of descent for ages past."

35. Matsushita, *Meiji Gunseishi Ron,* Vol. II, pp. 295-296.

36. Pittau, *Political Thought,* p. 190.

37. *Ibid.,* p. 156.

38. *Ibid.,* p. 200.

39. Maxon, *Control of Japanese Foreign Policy,* p. 56. The original *Genrō kaigi* (Council of Elders) consisted of Yamagata, Ito, Inoue of Chōshū, and Matsukata and Ōyama of Satsuma.

40. Pittau, *Political Thought,* pp. 198-200.

41. Maxon, *Control of Japanese Foreign Policy,* p. 59.

42. Hideki Tojo testified that the Imperial Headquarters was supposed to be a joint IJA-IJN operation, but was in effect really two organizations, one for each service. There were no civil officials involved in it and there was no one official in a position "to hold it all together." It reportedly met once or twice weekly. See Maxon, *Control of Japanese Foreign Policy,* p. 186.

43. Kenneth W. Colegrove, *Militarism in Japan,* (Boston: World Peace Foundation, 1936), p. 22. This provision was eased in 1913 to permit selection of war and navy ministers from among nonserving officers. In 1936 the arrangement returned to the form used from 1900 to 1913.

44. *Kyōiku Chokugo,* 20 October 1890.

45. Speech by Education Minister Arinori Mori at Yokyo University, 28 January 1889, quoted in Herbert Passin, *Society and Education in Japan* (New York: Columbia University Press, 1965), p. 88.

46. Japan War Ministry, *Kyōiku-rei,* revised 10 November 1943, paras. 3, 42.

47. Maxon, *Control of Japanese Foreign Policy,* pp. 2-3.

48. Huntington, *The Soldier and the State,* pp. 124-125.

49. "United States Initial Post-Surrender Policy for Japan," dated 29 August 1945.

50. Supreme Commander for the Allied Powers, *Political Reorientation of Japan* (Washington, DC: GPO, 1948), Vol. 2, p. 765. Unofficial transcript of a press interview of 19 March 1947.

51. Martin Weinstein, "Japan's Defense Policy and the Self-Defense Forces," in Frank B. Horton, Anthony C. Rogerson, and Edward L. Warner (eds.) *Comparative Defense Policy* (Baltimore: The Johns Hopkins University Press, 1974), p. 363-64.

52. For detailed elaboration of the origin and fate of this Memorandum, see Martin Weinstein, *Japan's Postwar Defense Policy, 1947-1968* (New York: Columbia University Press, 1971).

53. Japan Defense Agency, *Defense Strength of Japan* (Tokyo, 1959), pp. 2-3.

54. Bōei Nenkan Hankokai (Defense Yearbook Publishing Society), *Bōei Nenkan 1974* (Defense Yearbook 1974), (Tokyo, 1974), p. 199.

55. *Ibid.*

56. For details, see James H. Buck, "The Japanese Self-Defense Force," in *Navy War College Review* (Jan-Feb 1974): 40-54.

57. *Bōei Nenkan 1974,* p. 200.

58. *Ibid.,* p. 201.

59. *Ibid.,* p. 236.

60. *Ibid.,* pp. 201-202.

61. *Ibid.,* pp. 325-326.

62. *Ibid.,* pp. 326-327.

63. *Ibid.,* pp. 328-331.

64. *Ibid.,* pp. 202-203.

65. "Fukumu Sensei" (Oath of Service), in *Kanpō Gōgai* (Official Gazette), 30 June 1954, p. 29. See also *Bōei Nenkan 1972,* pp. 221-222.

66. Japan Ministry of Education, *Kyōiku Kihonhō* (Basic Education Law) (Tokyo, 1948).

67. Japanese Defense Agency, *The Defense of Japan* (English translation) (Tokyo: 1970), p. 28.

68. *Bōei Nenkan 1974,* p. 213.

69. See Weinstein, *Japan's Postwar Defense Policy,* The Japanese preferred only to maintain US bases in Japan on an emergency basis, not permanent occupancy. Even after the Korean War had begun, the Japanese still saw Japan's role in a security treaty as that of preserving internal order and Yoshida refused to accept Dulles's contention that the National Police Reserve strength should be set at 350,000 rather than at 75,000.

70. "Kazumi Konmi" (pseudonym), "The Future of Japan in Terms of National Security," in *Asian Survey* 14, 4 (April 1974): 365.

71. Japanese Defense Agency, *The Defense of Japan,* pp. ii-iii, introduction by Yasuhiro Nakasone, Director General, JDA.

72. Daizo Kusayanagi, "Eien no Mijukuji Boeicho," in *Bungei Shunju,* (Special issue), Tokyo, July 1974, p. 261. About one-half of the GSDF is disposed in northern Japan for an apparent "defense of the northern frontier" against a conventional small-scale WW II type attack from the USSR.

73. Huntington, *The Soldier and the State,* pp. 138-139.

74. Konmi, "Future of Japan," p. 371.

75. Kei Wakaizumi, "Japan's Role in a New World Order," in *Foreign Affairs* 51, 2 (Jan 1973): 326.

76. Japanese Defense Agency, *The Defense of Japan,* p. iii.

The Development
of Governmental Control
Over the Armed Forces of Finland

William J. Stover

William J. Stover, currently assistant professor of Political Science at the University of Santa Clara, received his B.A. from Nyack College, his M.A. in International Relations from American University, and his Ph.D from the State University of New York at Buffalo. His international experience includes tours of duty in Washington and Southeast Asia for the Department of State Indo-China Working Group. Professor Stover has also taught at The College of Wooster and Findlay College, both in Ohio. He has published articles in the *Naval War College Review* and *Peace Research.*

Introduction

Finland has been neglected by theorists as they generalize about the development of governmental control over the armed forces.Yet Finland is an interesting case for students of civil-military relations for three reasons. First, it is a European state with experiences similar to many newly emerging nations in the Third World. Once held by foreign powers (first Sweden, then Russia), modern Finland was born in civil war and nurtured with economic dependency and persistent social cleavages. Class and ethnic divisions plagued the Finns during the early years of independence, and government instability was chronic.

Second, during the first fifteen years of independence, the Finnish armed forces were a coercive element in national politics. Armed units plunged the country into civil war in 1917 by acting independently from their political authority, and the armed forces continued their politics of coercion after the war, attempting to create a "Greater Finland" in Soviet East Karelia and to crush Marxism and parliamentary democracy at home. In March 1932 one part of the Finnish armed forces, the Civil Guards, attempted a coup d'etat to change Finland's Form of Government (constitution) and introduce a fascist dictatorship.

Third, and most important, Finland succeeded in developing a high degree of governmental control over the armed forces, despite the fact that the military had a tradition of coercion during the first years of independence. After 1932 the military were still active politically, but their activity no longer included coercion. The armed forces subordinated themselves to the government and participated in the political process, attempting to change public policy but not the government itself. The country emerged as a nation in arms where the armed forces used political tactics rather than coercion to accomplish their goals. As such, Finland provides students of civil-military relations with a case study in which to examine theories about the development of governmental control over the armed forces and the successful establishment of civilian supremacy.

An Overview of Civil Military Relations in Finland: 1917-1939

PRAETORIAN MILITARY POLITICS DURING CIVIL WAR: 1917-1918

With the coming of World War I, Finland began to savor the prospect of independence from the Russian empire, which had sought to absorb the grand duchy through a harsh program of Russification. During the war, two political movements—the whites and the reds—emerged, each claiming to speak for the Finnish nation. The whites were a coalition of conservative, liberal, Swedish-speaking, and agrarian parties which believed that independence could be gained only by a Russian military defeat at the hands of Germany.[1] To facilitate this defeat, two thousand white Finns went to Germany where these *jagers* received military training, and white guard armed units were organized clandestinely.[2]

A second political movement, the reds, were a coalition of socialists, unionists, and intellectuals who were also committed to independence from Russia.[3] In response to white military activity, the reds began to organize their own armed units during the late summer of 1917.[4] Trade unions acted as recruiting centers, and the socialist press inspired workers to join the red guards. Following the Soviet model, detachments were established in factories and other places of work, with units named after their union affiliations.

Two armed forces and two political authorities were thus active in Finland immediately prior to the proclamation of independence, the red guards of the socialists and the white guards of the center-right parties. When the whites obtained control over the Finnish Diet in October 1917 through means that the reds considered illegal, the stage was set for civil strife and ultimately civil war.[5]

Both red and white political authorities experienced difficulties in establishing control over their armed units. White guard commanders, specifically General Mannerheim, acted independently from the white political authority, vested in the Finnish Senate. Mannerheim established his headquarters in Vasa, far to the northwest of Helsinki. Communications were often interrupted during the winter of 1917-1918, and it was difficult to relay information about political events in the capital. Moreover, the white Senate was in disarray, Senators were arrested by the red guards, forced to flee the capital, or go into hiding. Indeed, the president of the Senate, P.E. Svinhuvud, made his escape by way of Germany and was unable to provide strong political leadership until the spring of 1918.[6]

As a result, Mannerheim was free to act independently from the white political authority and make his own political decisions. He sought to prevent German intervention in Finland's civil war despite the fact that the Senate believed victory was dependent on the Germans.[7] The general also sought to initiate hostilities, while the white political leaders preferred negotiation with the reds. Mannerheim commanded his white guards to capture Russian troop trains and disarm Soviet troops in northwest Finland despite the fact that the Senate directed him to wait until the negotiations were concluded.[8] Indeed, Mannerheim's military activity began the civil war at a time when white political leaders were still engaged in efforts for peaceful compromise.

The socialists also experienced difficulty in establishing political control over their armed forces. Red guard units, especially in Helsinki, refused to obey the socialist party, and socialist political leaders expressed doubts about the possibility of controlling red guard companies.[9] Leaders of the red guards wanted the socialist party to seize power immediately, and the Helsinki branch of the red guards notified political leaders that if such an order were not forthcoming, the red guards would take power on their own.[10]

The civil war erupted in January 1918, after red guard units in Helsinki adopted a resolution which formally proclaimed independence from the socialist party.[11] Their leaders demanded that the governor of the province resign and seized the former residence of the Russian governor general on 18 January, the same day white guard units initiated hostilities farther north. Both red and white guards thus acted contrary to the will of their respective political authorities. The result was "praetorianism," in which the armed forces acted independently of civilians to direct political activity by means of regular instruction, displacement, or supplantment. Civilian control was absent either in "subjective" or "objective" forms.

FACTIONAL MILITARY POLITICS DURING NATIONAL CONSOLIDATION: 1918-1932

The civil war ended in April 1918. Red armed forces were soundly defeated by Mannerheim's white guards and troops of the German Baltic Division. White guardsmen paraded through Helsinki, and the white Senate returned to the capital to establish itself as Finland's sole government. With political power consolidated in a civilian government, the military were no longer free to act independently. Mannerheim was forced to resign when he refused to accept German assistance in the reorganization of the peasant army. His power was eroded by the new government and the 12,000 German troops camped near Helsinki.

During the period of national consolidation, both the newly

organized army of 30,000 men and the Civil Guards threatened to coerce the Finnish government. They did not act independently but in concert with certain civilian groups of the extreme right.[12] This was a situation of factional military politics which exists when the armed forces are joined by a coalition of civilian groups who share common values with the military. Huntington calls this "subjective civilian control," a condition where the power of certain civilian groups is maximized in relation to the military. He writes:

> The large number, varied character, and conflicting interests of civilian groups . . . make it impossible to maximize their power as a whole with respect to the military. Consequently, the maximizing of civilian power always means the maximizing of the power of some particular civilian group or groups . . . . The general concept of civilian control is identified with the specific interests of one or more civilian groups. Consequently, subjective civilian control involves the power relation among civilian groups. It is advanced by one civilian group as a means to enhance its power at the expense of other civilian groups.[13]

The goals, even the leadership, of the extreme right and the armed forces were often identical, and the military was frequently directed by the extreme right to exert force on behalf of two objectives: the establishment of a "Greater Finland," uniting in one nation all Finnish-speaking peoples and the destruction of Finnish socialism and parliamentary democracy.

Greater Finland, the first goal, was pursued independently during the civil war by Finland's military leaders. Mannerheim drew up plans for the invasion of East Karelia in early 1918. The eastward advance was not successful, but volunteers were recruited both from the white guards and the newly emerging national army to conduct guerrilla-type operations in the east.[14] After the civil war, the rise of German influence in the armed forces complicated plans for Greater Finland. With the Treaty of Brest-Litovsk, Germany sought quiet on the eastern front, and this made it necessary for Finland to prevent her armed forces from attacking.

The defeat of Germany changed Finland's international and domestic politics.[15] In order to disassociate themselves from the central powers, the Finnish white government asked General Mannerheim, a friend of the allies, to become regent. As head of state from December 1918 to July 1919, Mannerheim advocated Greater Finland, but his hands were tied by international considerations. Finland's main policy goal during this period was diplomatic recognition by the allies, who supported the counterrevolutionary white Russians, The latter refused to recognize Finland's independence, let alone the doubling of Finnish territory at Russia's expense.

The goal of Greater Finland received a serious blow during the summer of 1919 from another direction. In July the Finnish Parliament approved a republican constitution by a substantial majority. By rejecting a conservative monarchy, which Mannerheim and the extreme right supported, the parliament set itself against further military adventures in the east and sought to turn its attention inward to recover from the devastation of civil war.

This attitude was confirmed with the defeat of Mannerheim and the election of K.J.Ståhlberg as first president of the Republic by an overwhelming majority.[16] Ståhlberg was a leader of the liberal National Progressive Party and chief architect of the new constitution. In effect, the outcome of this election and the ratification of the new constitution meant that the Finnish government would concentrate on strengthening parliamentary democracy rather than extending Finnish territory.

These goals were in direct contradiction to the aims of the extreme right, and Ståhlberg's presidency was interpreted as a repudiation of military action in East Karelia.[17] To thwart this, the extreme right and the armed forces attempted to delay adoption of the new constitution or throw the election by coercion. Mannerheim declared to conservative party leaders that as regent he could delay ratification of the new constitution; but the conservative parliamentarians refused to go along.[18] Commanders of the Civil Guards and the *jager* officers of the army then announced that they considered the election of Mannerheim essential, They threatened to resign *en masse* if Ståhlberg were elected, but the officers could not stand against the rising republican tide. After the election, Mannerheim's former chief of staff demanded Ståhlberg's resignation; but the armed forces found that they could not prevent the president from making peace between Finland and Russia on 14 October 1920 with the Treaty of Dorpat (Tartu).[19]

The extreme right did not accept this peace, however. Ignoring both the treaty and the policies of the new Finnish government, General Löfström of the Civil Guards called for 30,000 volunteers to fight in East Karelia and sought to procure arms from Great Britain.[20] During the fall and winter of 1921, Civil Guard units and volunteers under the command of Finnish officers crossed the border to assist the East Karelians. These "Forest Partisans" acted without the approval or even the knowledge of the Finnish government. They relied on right-wing organizations in Finland, which supplied money, arms, and material.[21] As the Bolsheviks consolidated their power in northwest Russia, however, Soviet forces were free to counterattack and seal the Russo-Finnish border. The goal of a Greater Finland was thwarted by Soviet armed might.

Despite this, members of the extreme right and the armed forces felt betrayed by the Finnish government.[22] Expansionism was not abandoned, but the extreme right and the armed forces now turned inward to pursue a second goal—the destruction of Marxism and parliamentary democracy, which they believed had prevented the conquest of East Karelia. The extreme right viewed the Civil Guards as the one institution which could crush socialism in Finland. They were "intended to be an internal defense of the Republic against the communist revolutionary attempt";[23] and they provided "the strong internal wall against all unpatriotic, subversive trends corroding the foundations of political and social life."[24]

The power of the Civil Guards was based both on support from the right and on their autonomy from Finland's government and national army. The only connection this organization maintained with the government was through executive orders, not parliamentary legislation.[25] The Guards were also autonomous in their relationship with the Finnish army. General Karl Wilkama, commander of the army, did not cooperate with the Guards since they were "not legalized" and therefore comparable in status to "the Boy Scouts or Salvation Army."[26] This infuriated the Civil Guards, of course, and they called for Wilkama's resignation.

With the election of a new president and the appointment of a new commander of the army, the Civil Guards were strengthened. As a result, parliament legalized the Guards in 1927. They had little choice. One member of the extreme right declared that if parliament did not legalize the Civil Guards, they would "simply refuse to disband."[27] Finland's army and Civil Guards were still separate institutions, since no central command structure existed; nevertheless, a union of purpose was now possible. Both the Guards and the *jager* commanders of the Finnish army agreed that Marxism must be crushed.[28]

The extreme right's struggle with socialism grew acute in 1929, when Finnish communists intensified their activity in the form of strikes, union organization, and propaganda.[29] This culminated with a mass meeting in the southern Ostrobothnian town of Lapua in November 1929. Local residents, many of whom were civil guardsmen, broke up a series of communist youth meetings, stripped the youths of their red shirts, and beat them. This provided the spark which was to set off an explosion of anticommunism in Finland."Farmers, clergymen, academicians, industrialists, military leaders, and territorial expansionists of all occupations united in a movement which formally announced its goal to be the extinction of communism in Finland."[30] It was called the Lapua Movement and was governed by its own law (Lapuan Laki).[31]

In July 1930 the Lapua leaders demanded that the Finnish government close all communist newspapers and arrest communist officials, including members of the parliament.[32] Despite parliamentary opposition, the ultimata were met. The Lapua leaders then demanded changes in Finnish governmental structure, a reduction in the size of parliament, and the abandonment of proportional representation.[33] Rather than meet these demands, Prime Minister Kallio resigned and P.E. Svinhuvud came out of retirement to form a new cabinet sympathetic to the Lapua movement.

To enforce their demands, leaders of the movement pushed forward with the cooperation of the armed forces. A march on

Helsinki, planned for 7 July 1930, was organized by Lapua leaders and five high-ranking military officers.[34] Thirty thousand members of the Lapua movement marched through the capital. Most were armed civil guardsmen organized into regiments, battalions, and companies. Their demands that the parliament approve anticommunist legislation and change the structure of Finnish government were accepted by Svinhuvud, the prime minister, as well as by Mannerheim who took active part at the rally.

Despite this demonstration of armed force and the threat it represented to the parliament, many parliament members were steadfast in their support of the constitutional order. With the Social Democrats voting solidly against the Lapua legislation, a two-thirds majority was lacking, and the bills were defeated. Parliament was dissolved with new elections scheduled for 1-2 October 1930. Organizations of the extreme right began their campaign to insure a new parliament which would approve the Lapua program. This meant the election of at least 134 members who supported the Lapua demands and no more than 66 Social Democrats. The right was successful; 134 center-right members were elected, and the bills were approved with only the Social Democrats in opposition.

The Lapua movement now moved into its final stage, widening the struggle against socialism to all phases of Finnish political, social, and economic life.[35] The means by which this struggle was pursued centered around the presidential election of 1931. Former President Ståhlberg, a liberal, sought reconciliation in Finland. He was opposed by Svinhuvud, who received support from the extreme right and the armed forces.

The election campaign was extremely bitter. The right denounced Ståhlberg for his opposition to the *jager* movement before independence, his policy of reconciliation after the civil war, his signing of the Treaty of Dorpat which thwarted the goal of Greater Finland, and his denunciation of the law of Lapua. Members of the electoral college were warned that the election of Ståhlberg would lead to civil war. Indeed, Ståhlberg had recently been kidnapped by members of the Lapua movement in an operation planned by General K.N.Wallenius, former chief of the Army General Staff and assisted by other high-ranking officers in the army and Civil Guards.[36] Ståhlberg had escaped unharmed, but the Lapua movement again threatened to move against the liberal political leader if he were elected president.

On the first ballot in the electoral college neither Ståhlberg nor Svinhuvud received a majority. Ståhlberg took the lead on the second ballot, but without the majority necessary for victory. Kallio of the Agrarian Party held the balance, and his party had to decide which candidate it would support. The choice was not made freely. Major General Malmberg, commander of the Civil Guard, declared that he could not guarantee the maintenance of order if Ståhlberg were elected.[37] As a result of this threat, conveyed through a leader of the Agrarian Party, every Agrarian elector voted for Svinhuvud. The right emerged victorious and Svinhuvud became president, assisted by coercion from the armed forces.

Svinhuvud was not, however, their tool. In the words of an agrarian leader, he was a "mountain over which no force could pass."[38] This became evident as the Lapua movement prepared for its final assault on Finnish parliamentary democracy, an armed revolt to do away with the parliament once and for all. Leaders of the Lapua movement informed their followers that the cabinet was infected with Marxism and must be cleansed. They declared that a "Finnish Hitler" must "show the working class the road from the errors of Marxism to a sense of nationality."[39] Members of the Civil Guards and the Lapua movement made plans for armed action against the government, to begin in late February, 1932. They threatened:

> Unless the present cabinet immediately resigns and the political course of the country changes, we don't consider that we can preserve peacefulness in the country. In place of the present cabinet, there must come a new cabinet which is free from party aims and which depends in its action upon the support of patriotic elements of the people.[40]

These demands were backed by the mobilization of Civil Guard units in key cities, commanded by Major General Wallenius. Other groups joined the Lapua movement's demands that the cabinet resign. The League of War Veterans declared that it was time to finish the job begun during the civil war. Major General Malmberg, national commander of the Civil Guards, agreed, and the commanding general of the Finnish Army expressed fears that his *jager* officers supported the Lapua movement's demands.[41]

The right expected that Svinhuvud would accede to their demands, but they were mistaken. He now held the reins of Finnish government as the guardian of the Constitution. His whole life had been devoted to constitutional social order and his response to the threats and attempted coup was forceful. He met immediately with the cabinet, the commanding general of the army, the national commander of the Civil Guards, and three other general staff officers. His decision was quick and his order explicit: "Not even one armed man may come . . . to the Capital city," he declared to the officers. "For this you generals will be responsible."[42] The army obeyed. Leaves were cancelled, rail and highway approaches to Helsinki were sealed, and troops, tanks, and artillery stood guard around the capital. President Svinhuvud declared a state of emergency and arrested leaders of the Lapua movement and the rebellious Civil Guards. The Prussian-trained *jager* officers in the small national army obeyed their orders, and the Civil Guards bowed before Svinhuvud's authority. By 4 March 1932 the revolt was over, its leaders were in jail, and its followers had dispersed.

Finland had moved from a period of praetorian military politics during the civil war through a period of factional control where the armed forces subordinated themselves to that part of the polity with which they shared common values, the extreme right wing. By 1933 Finland was on the verge of establishing governmental control over its armed forces.

PRESSURE GROUP MILITARY POLITICS DURING
"EIGHT YEARS RACING THE STORM"[43]: 1932-1939

After 1932 Finland's military leaders no longer used the threat of force to accomplish their goals. Instead, they sought to affect public policy through a three-point pressure-group program designed to increase defense preparedness. One set of efforts was directed toward the government and cabinet through the advice and recommendations of military leaders on the National Defense Council. Created in 1932 and chaired by Mannerheim, this council included the nation's top military officials, who reported to the president, the prime minister, and other cabinet officials.

In the Defense Council Mannerheim and other military leaders pointed out Finland's lack of military preparedness and attempted to get government support for increased expenditures. However, the government did not support Mannerheim's demands. Indeed, upon the recommendations of the Economic Committee, parliament reduced the defense budget in 1932 by 10 percent to the lowest level since 1924. Moreover, parliament refused to consider measures for increasing the productive capacity of the armament factory and defeated supplemental appropriations for weapon procurement. The civilians simply did not believe that war was likely and could see no reasons why public funds should be squandered on defense.

This shocked Finland's military leaders. They began to add another ingredient to their advice and recommendations—ominous forecasts of the future. As each year's budget was prepared, military leaders pointed out Finland's weakness in defense, the deteriorating international situation, and the probable outcome of any attack—sure defeat. But they did not indulge in coercive pressure against the government.

The second point of influence that the military used to affect public policy was directed at the parliament itself.[44] These lobbying efforts were pursued by parliamentary allies of the military and interest groups which consistently supported the military's demands for increased expenditures.[45] Interest groups included the Academic Karelia Society, the Independence League, the League of War Veterans, the Lotta-Svärd Society, and the Civil Defense Organization. Many members of these groups were officers in the reserves or Civil Guards (called Territorial Forces after 1932). Their means of influence included lobbying activities in parliament whenever defense questions were considered as well as demonstrations and propaganda.[46]

The military also had their allies in parliament. Critical questions of defense appropriations were considered in the parliament's Committee for National Defense and Committee for Finance. Here, three small parties never voted against military requests. The Conservative Party, the Swedish Party, and the Fascist Party consistently supported the military in their voting for increased training, weapon procurement, and expenditures. Only the Social Democrats consistently opposed increased military spending.

The third point of influence which military leaders used to achieve their political ends was a vast propaganda program. Universal military training, established in 1932, provided the opportunity to indoctrinate citizens about the dangers inherent in Finland's precarious international situation and the need for unity behind the defense effort.[47] Training manuals, lectures, citizenship courses, indeed military tactics themselves stressed the view that an eastern invasion was not only probable, but imminent.[48]

This effort was supplemented by the Territorial Forces, under the guidance of Mannerheim. Contact with the public was "lively and incessant."[49] Among the forms of propaganda work adopted were festivals arranged by the territorials, publications, films, music, and religious activity organized by the field chaplain and supported by his staff of 250 clergymen.

These activities went far beyond advice and recommendation to the government. Mannerheim and other military leaders sought to change the attitudes of the cabinet, parliament, and the nation toward the questions of military preparedness and to unify the country behind defense requirements. The military's political activities did not include coercion during this period, however, despite the fact that international conflict seemed near. Since even the fear of imminent war was not enough to challenge governmental control in this developing country after 1932, its development merits close analysis.

Factors Affecting Military Politics in Finland and The Development of Governmental Control

One can isolate three sets of factors, of "summary variables,"[50] which affect military politics and governmental control. The first set, termed environmental, relates to the domestic political environment in which government and military power exist. The second, termed organizational, relates to the nature of military institutions. The third is international; it often provides a motive for military politics.

THE FINNISH DOMESTIC ENVIRONMENT: AN EMERGING REPUBLICAN CONSENSUS

After the civil war, the armed forces of Finland existed in a domestic environment filled with political, economic, and social turmoil. The ship of state was adrift. Government was unstable, and political authority was weak and divided. During the first year after the civil war, the Form of Government (constitution) changed from a monarchy under German auspices, to a military regency under Mannerheim, then to a republic based on parliamentary cabinet government. Enacted in July 1919, the republican Form of Government made parliament the seat of governmental power. The president was chief of state as well as peacetime commander in chief of the army; but the prime minister headed the government which "must possess the confidence of the parliament."[51]

Strong support for cabinet government by parliamentary party blocs was wholly lacking in the new republic, however. As a result, government tenure was short, averaging approximately ten months. Only two of the sixteen cabinets represented a majority of the parliament, and the situation deteriorated further during the four years preceding the attempted coup d'état of 1932.[52] These later cabinets were one-party, minority governments with almost no support in the parliament. Short government tenure during the years of the armed forces' threats and intervention may be contrasted with the longer government tenure of 1933-1939 when the armed forces used methods other than coercion to affect governmental policy. Four cabinets were formed, with an average duration of twenty months.

Governmental instability reflected economic problems and social divisions within the Finnish nation. Civil war and its aftermath left Finland with substantial economic difficulties.[53] Loss of trade, food shortage, labor unrest, and foreign debt plagued the government during the early years of independence. When the world depression hit Finland in 1930, the nation was already in a difficult economic situation which especially hurt the small landholders. Crop failures in 1928 and 1929 were compounded by rising interest rates and a scarcity of employment in the lumber camps where many farmers worked during winter. Unemployed, hungry, these farmers were the backbones of the Civil Guards who attempted the coup. It is understandable that their discontent took the form of radical opposition to a government which was not meeting their economic needs.[54]

Economic hardships were multiplied by another element in the domestic environment. Finland inherited a legacy of social cleavage, not unlike that which plagues many newly emerging nations in the twentieth century. Divisions over class, language, and rural-city distinctions were deep and troublesome. Conflict between Swedish-speaking and Finnish-speaking groups were relatively dormant during the civil war, but it broke out anew during the first decades of independence.[55] Social cleavage also resulted from the country-city distinction in Finland. During the interwar years, approximately two-thirds of the Finnish population lived in the countryside, and most farmers experienced hardships.[56] They were hardly able to make the rugged Finnish land support their families at a subsistence level, little money was available to educate their children, and higher education was often denied them.

The deepest and most troublesome social cleavage, however, was based on class, as was demonstrated in the civil war where workers fought farmers and the bourgeoisie. This conflict was not settled by the war and remained to plague Finland long after the guns had ceased firing. Communists as well as left and center socialists maintained their distrust of the Finnish whites. Hatred was fanned by arrest, detention, and political oppression. Even the right wing of the Social Democratic Party found it difficult to reconcile themselves to a Finnish government that approved the excesses of the Civil Guards and the destruction of Marxism and parliamentary democracy by coercive means.[57]

The extreme right constituted another group which aggravated Finnish social problems. Rintala writes: "The first decade of independence was marked by the absence . . . from party activity of both major elements of the extreme right wing. The older generation of conservatives withdrew from party activity, and the war generation refused to enter this activity."[58] Indeed, most of the right wing "opposed parliamentary government *in toto* not merely the parliamentarians and parties in power at a given time."[59]

Social cleavage, economic hardships, and unstable government provided a domestic environment where the armed forces wielded great power in relation to the government. The military used this power on behalf of the extreme right, as they attempted to establish a Greater Finland, crush Marxism, and change the Finnish Form of Government.

After 1932, however, social divisions were moderated by party cooperation in the republican, parliamentary Form of Government. Socialist party leaders disagreed with certain governmental policies, especially national defense; but their commitment to parliamentary cabinet government enabled them to cooperate more closely with other parties in forming cabinets, and governmental stability doubled. As a result, parliamentary republicanism emerged as the legitimate means of transferring power in Finland, and the armed forces were unwilling to challenge the government by force.

THE CHANGING ORGANIZATIONAL CHARACTERISTICS OF MILITARY INSTITUTIONS: COHESION, RECRUITMENT, AND LEADERSHIP

A second summary variable which affects military politics is the organizational nature of the armed forces. The cohesion, leadership, and recruitment patterns of the armed forces concern students of civil-military relations as well as political leaders, for without certain organizational characteristics, the military cannot be directed or controlled by political authority. Indeed, command obedience and discipline are prerequisites to the control and direction of the armed forces.

In a nation like Finland, cohesion, command, and discipline are complicated by the nature of military institutions. A volunteer militia or a citizen army recruited by universal military obligation experiences short periods of training and infrequent service as armed units. This can produce armed forces which are less cohesive than standing units, less disciplined, and less amenable to command.

The cohesion, leadership, and indoctrination of the armed forces were central to the outcome of Finland's civil war and to the praetorian military politics of that period. For the socialists, whose armed forces were relatively well equipped by the soviets, organizational factors made control impossible and spelled sure defeat for red political authority in Finland. The red guard military organization never achieved an effective command structure.[60] Individual units like the Helsinki branch of the red guard remained autonomous. They were free to employ force at their own discretion, undirected by party leaders and undisciplined in command obedience. Indoctrination and selective recruitment were not skillfully employed to produce officers and men who subordinated their own goals to those of the party, and military leadership was wholly lacking.

The whites also experienced military organizational problems, but these were minor compared to the difficulties faced by the reds. Mannerheim's peasant army was relatively cohesive, well led, and indoctrinated to believe that the fight was against Russia, Finland's traditional enemy. In effect, the century-old hostility toward the east was used by the whites to inspire men and make them fight. This effort was directed by well-trained and experienced officers who obeyed their commander in chief. As a result, the direction of this armed force was simplified and the white guards were used to further the goals of General Mannerheim. Despite the fact that Mannerheim frequently usurped political authority during the civil war, however, he never supplanted civilian leadership. Mannerheim's ultimate weapon against the white Senate remained resignation.

During the period of national consolidation (1918-1932), lack of cohesion allowed parts of the armed forces to threaten the government, but it also limited the effectiveness of their attempts. The autonomy of the Civil Guards in relation to the cabinet and president was a formidable problem. The guards refused to be integrated in any national command structure, since this would link "Civil Guard activity to another sphere of military activity."[61] The guards sought to stand alone as protector of white Finland despite the will of the legally constituted government.

Their strength was balanced by the 30,000 man national army. This institution itself was divided, however, by the existence of German-trained *jagers* and Russian-trained former czarist officers.[62] The *jagers* emerged, after 1925, as the top commanders of the Finnish army and maintained that position until the end of World War II. This provided the opportunity for cooperation with the Civil Guards during the second half of the 1920s and enabled both armed forces to exert considerable pressure against the government. The military role in politics conflicted, however, with the indoctrination the *jagers* had received from the Prussian officers who trained them. While the army and the Civil Guards both shared similar goals, the Finnish army was relatively cohesive, disciplined, and under the firm command of Maj. Gen. Aarne Sihvo.

The failure of armed intervention in 1932 illustrated a lack of cohesion among the various branches of the armed forces and the absence of a central command structure. The military was unable to act as a cohesive body. Intervention by the Civil Guards was thwarted by the national army which responded to the orders of General Sihvo, its top commander. Sihvo obeyed President Svinhuvud, his recognized political authority.[63]

After 1932 the Finnish armed forces completed a reorganization which provided greater cohesion and limited the independent role of the Civil Guards.[64] These voluntary units were incorporated into a central command structure, the National Defense Council. Chaired by Marshal Mannerheim, the Council provided disciplined leadership and facilitated cohesion. In addition, changes in recruitment affected the organizational characteristics of the armed forces after 1932.[65] Universal military training produced citizen soldiers from all political parties whose commitment to civilian institutions and the Form of Government superseded their commitment to the army. Officers could not be sure that orders to move against the government would be obeyed by these citizen soldiers. As a result, officers were inhibited from challenging the government through threat of force.

Two international factors were important as a motivating force behind military politics in Finland. First, a contagious effect was present both during the civil war and the period of national consolidation. The Bolshevik coup in Russia bolstered the arguments of Finnish red guard commanders that power could effectively be seized through force and inspired them to back up their arguments with military action.[66] While socialist political leaders disclaimed any Bolshevik-style revolution, the leaders of the red guard were strongly influenced by the Bolsheviks, who maintained direct connections with the red guardsmen in Finland. After the March revolution in Russia, the Bolsheviks sent Adolph Taimi, a Petrograd Finn to Helsinki to organize red guard units. Taimi became a leader of the Helsinki red guard and urged Finnish Socialists to follow the tactics of the Bolsheviks and make a revolution.[67] Red guard commanders were also influenced by Stalin, who personally promised Bolshevik aid and urged the red guards to take power by force.[68] The success of the Bolsheviks was contagious, and the guardsmen believed that it could be easily copied. Inspired by a sense of "primitive internationalism,"[69] they overestimated both the ability of Russian troops to assist them and the willingness of red Finns to accept such assistance from their traditional eastern enemy.[70]

The contagious effect of foreign success was also present in the rise of the extreme right during the period of national consolidation. The boldness of civil guardsmen was bolstered by the success of Fascists in Italy, and the extreme right's program was modeled after the Black Shirts.[71] The chairman of the Military Affairs Committee of the Finnish Parliament recognized this in no uncertain terms:

> People have tried to compare [the Civil Guards] with the Fascists, so that by this comparison, it might be shown how very dangerous the existence of an armed organization like the Civil Guards is to parliamentary life. I must honestly admit that we Civil Guard members are not at all ashamed of that comparison; on

the contrary we recognize willingly and proudly that we are the intellectual comrades of the Italian Fascists.[72]

Civil Guard officers believed that the extreme right could do for Finland what Mussolini did for Italy—establish order out of domestic chaos.

The military leaders' fear of involvement in international conflict formed the second international element which affected military politics in Finland. Mannerheim's decision to initiate civil war by disarming the Russian Soviet troops in Ostrobothnia and preventing their reinforcement was designed to limit Finland's war of liberation to Finland itself, at least until such time as white power could be consolidated.[73] If Soviet troops in Ostrobothnia were allowed to remain armed and receive reinforcement, it would make the Bolsheviks more inclined to interfere in Finland's civil war. This would, in Mannerheim's view, lead to an introduction of German troops in Finland and an international conflict which the general sought to avoid. Mannerheim was not opposed to fighting the Soviets, even to the point of carrying the battle to Petrograd, but not at a time when white armed forces were weak and poorly armed. The general moved therefore to isolate conflict with the Russians by disarming their troops in direct violation of Svinhuvud's orders.

Mannerheim's conditions for accepting command of the white armed forces, a promise of no foreign intervention by Germany, was also designed to limit Finland's civil war to a domestic conflict.[74] When Svinhuvud violated this commitment, Mannerheim entered direct diplomatic negotiations with the Germans to limit their role in Finland. He sought to win a decisive battle before their arrival and prove to the world that Finland was liberated by Finns, not Germans. Mannerheim's opposition to organizing a Finnish national army under German command also reflected his views of the international political situation. To Mannerheim, the British, the French, and the Imperial Russians were the most important, not the Germans. Believing that Germany would ultimately be defeated in World War I, Mannerheim wanted to maintain as great a distance from it as possible. He feared that the allies would believe that Finland was liberated by German forces, rather than by the white army.

The military's assessment of imminent international conflict similarly motivated the armed forces to act politically after 1932. Finland's dependence on the League of Nations, the Neutral Association of Northern States, and an international security agreement with the Soviet Union was an illusion to Mannerheim.[75] Russian and German military planners would soon attempt to secure their northwest border against a possible German attack through Finland, he believed. This meant war, and the military sought to prepare the nation.

Paradoxically, however, fear of imminent conflict both motivated military leaders to achieve greater defense preparedness and inhibited them from using coercion to accomplish their goals. With war dangerously close, the armed forces sought domestic stability and therefore avoided using force, which could split the Finnish nation. Moreover, a military coup or overt coercion might be interpreted by the Soviets as an increase in German influence in Finland, something military leaders sought to avoid. As a result, the armed forces limited their political activity to the pressure-group program.

Summary and Conclusions

Finland succeeded in establishing governmental control over the armed forces through a long and complex process. First, an emerging domestic consensus in support of parliamentary cabinet government provided greater stability for governmental institutions and increased the authority of these institutions as they interacted with the armed forces. Second, changing organizational elements within the armed forces after 1932 facilitated greater cohesion, discipline, and leadership as the Civil Guards were incorporated into the national military establishment under the direction of the National Defense Council. Moreover, universal military obligation after 1932 produced citizen soldiers whose commitment to civilian institutions superseded their commitment to the officers who trained them and thwarted the military's ability to coerce. Third, the threat of imminent international conflict provided a motive for military politics after 1932, but inhibited the armed forces from the use of coercion. Since the military wanted to insure domestic independence from Germany, they did not use force, for it would split the nation and foster suspicions of pro-German sympathies in Finland. All of these factors combined to limit the coercive power of the military after 1932 and to establish governmental control over the armed forces.

Notes to Chapter 7

Stover, *Development of Governmental Control over the Armed Forces of Finland.*

1. John J. Hodgson, "Finland's Position in the Russian Empire," *Journal of Central European Affairs* 20 (1960-61): 158-73; C. J. Smith, *Finland and the Russian Revolution* (Athens, Ga: University of Georgia Press, 1958), pp. 8-12.

2. J.O. Hannula, *Finland's War of Independence* (London: Faber and Faber, 1939), pp. 24-28.

3. John H. Hodgson, *Communism in Finland* (Princeton: Princeton University Press, 1967), pp. 3-19.

4. *Ibid.*, p. 51; Hannula, *Finland's War* pp. 74-75; Henning Söderhjelm, *Det röda upproret i Finland år 1918* (Stockholm: Wahlstrom and Widstrand, 1918), p. 99.

5. J. H. Jackson, *Finland* (New York: Praeger, 1940), pp. 84-86; Smith, *Finland*, pp. 18-19; Erkki Räikkönen, *Svinhuvud, The Builder of Finland: An Adventure in State Craft* (London: Wilmer, 1938), p. 10; Hodgson, *Communism in Finland*, p. 29; Juhani Paasivirta, *Suomen itsenäisyyskysymys 1917* (Porvoo: Söderström, 1949), Vol. II, p. 24.

6. Mannerheim, *The Memoirs of Marshal Mannerheim,* translated by Count Eric Lewenhaupt (London, Cassell, 1954) pp. 140-44; Räikkönen, *Svinhuvud*, pp. 97-105.

7. Mannerheim, *Memoirs*, p. 134.

8. *Ibid.,* p. 139; Räikkönen, *Svinhuvud,* pp. 54-56.

9. Hodgson, *Communism in Finland*, p. 30.

10. *Ibid.*, p. 47.

11. *Ibid.*, p. 49.

12. The extreme right in Finland has been defined by Marvin Rintala in *Three Generations: the Extreme Right Wing in Finnish Politics* (Bloomington: University of Indiana Press, 1962), p. 4:

Before the October Revolution in Russia, it included all those non-socialists who favored armed opposition to Russia, and in 1919 it included all those who favored armed intervention in the Russian civil war. After 1919, the older generation of conservatives and the war generation were joined in the extreme right wing by those members of the educated youth who accepted the world view of the Academic Karelia Society.

Included in the extreme right were the Finnish Defense League, the Civil Guards, the Lotta-Svärd (Women's auxiliary to the Civil Guards), the Lapua Movement, the League of War Veterans and *jager* officers of the national army who had been trained in Germany.

13. Samuel P. Huntington, *The Soldier and the State* (New York: Vintage, 1957), p. 80.

14. Jalmari Jaakkola, *The Finnish Eastern Question* (Helsinki: Söderström, 1942), p. 23; Smith, *Finland* p. 99.

15. Rintala, *Three Generations*, p. 81; Tancred Borenius, *Field-Marshal Mannerheim* (London: Hutchinson, 1940), p. 214; Leonid I. Strankhovsky, *Intervention at Archangel: The Story of Allied Intervention and Russian Counter Revolution in North Russia 1918-1920* (Princeton: Princeton University Press, 1944), pp. 196-212; Mannerheim, *Memoirs*, pp. 192-198.

16. Smith, *Finland*, p. 158; Mannerheim, *Memoirs*, pp. 224-27. An eyewitness commented on this election as follows:

It was no disrespect to Mannerheim . . . to believe that the time had come for another sort of leader. The vital thing in Finland was not so much foreign adventure . . . as the restoration of normal life within Finland itself and the healing of the wounds opened by the revolution. Mannerheim had become a symbol of the white terror. Ståhlberg [was] essentially the civilian-republican instead of the man on horseback. (Arthur Ruhl, *New Masters of the Baltic* [New York: Dutton 1921], p. 45.)

17. Mannerheim, *Memoirs*, pp. 222-25.

18. Rintala, *Three Generations*, p. 99.

19. *Ibid.,* pp. 99-100.

20. Jaakkola, *Finnish Eastern Question*, pp. 29-30.

21. Smith, *Finland*, pp. 196-97; Rintala, *Three Generations*, p. 103.

22. Members of the extreme right saw this as "cruel and such a thing that a people or state which adheres to its honor cannot do." It was "a deed which it is impossible for the Finnish nation to defend before other nations, history, its own self, and its national honor." Rintala, *Three Generations*, p. 99-100 quoting Theodor Homen in Parliament, 1920 *Valtiopäivät Pöytäkirjat* Vol. II, pp. 1481-82 and E. N. Setälä, *Ibid.*, p. 1517.

23. Rintala, *Three Generations,* p. 148, quoting Arne Somersalo, a guard leader.

24. *Ibid,* p. 149.

25. *Finland's Civil Guards,* editied by the staff of the Civil Guards (Hel-

sinki: General Staff, 1923), pp. 13-22; Paavo Virkkunen, *Itsenäisen Suomen alkuvuosikymmeniltä—elettyä ja ajateltua* (Helsinki: Otava, 1954), p. 245.

26. Aarne Sihvo, *Muistelmani,* Vol. II, (Helsinki: Otava, 1954), p. 120.

27. Rintala, *Three Generations,* p. 151, quoting Oskari Heikinheimo in Parliament, 1926 *Valtiopäivät Pöytäkirjat,* Vol. III, p. 2846.

28. Sihvo, *Muistelmani,* Vol. II, pp. 130-33.

29. L. Ingman, *The Lapua Anti-Communist Movement* (Helsinki: Otava, 1930), pp. 3-9.

30. Rintala, *Three Generations,* p. 164.

31. *Ibid.,* p. 165; Jackson, *Finland,* pp. 147-48.

32. Rintala, *Three Generations,* p. 174; Ossian Karsten, *Lapporörelsen och dess motståndare* (Helsinki: Söderström, 1930), pp. 24-24.

33. Rintala, *Three Generations,* pp. 175-80.

34. *Ibid.,* Sihvo, *Muistelmani,* Vol. II, pp. 213-14.

35. Rintala, *Three Generations,* pp. 183-88.

36. *Ibid.,* p. 172; Jackson, *Finland,* p. 161.

37. Sihvo, *Muistelmani,* Vol. II, p. 217.

38. Rintala, *Three Generations,* p. 189, quoting K. A. Lohi in Parliament, 1931, *Valtiopäivät, Pöytäkirjat,* Vol. II, p. 1941.

39. *Ibid.,* p. 191, quoting "Valkoinen oikeus," *Ajan Sana,* 25 February 1932.

40. *Ibid.,* p. 191, quoting *Ajan Sana,* 29 February 1932.

41. Sihvo, *Muistelmani,* Vol. II, pp. 205-06, p. 219.

42. *Ibid.,* pp. 193-94; *ibid.,* p. 219.

43. This is a phrase Mannerheim uses to describe the period from 1932 to 1939. See Mannerheim, *Memoirs,* Chapter 13, pp. 265-322.

44. *Ibid.,*; Mannerheim was less involved in this undertaking. His suspicion of parliamentary politics was inherited from his aristocratic origins and remained to the end of his days. Marvin Rintala, *Four Finns* (Berkeley: University of California Press, 1969), p. 37.

45. No attempt is made to show that Mannerheim personally directed this effort. Right-wing interest groups and parties simply shared the military's views on national defense. Their coincidence of interests led them to lobby for increased military preparedness.

46. Rintala, *Three Generations,* pp. 222-27, p. 237; Erkki Räikkönen, "Isänmaallisen kansanliikkeen syntymähistoriaa," *Kustaa Vaasa* (September 1940): 11-14.

47. Mannerheim, *Memoirs,* p. 269.

48. Citizenship training was an integral part of a conscript's military education. This included lectures on international conditions as well as calls to patriotism. "All conscripts attend(ed) courses in Finnish history, citizenship [and] ethics ...." "The National Defense" in *Finland: Young Republic of the North,* J. Laurila, ed. (Helsinki: Otava 1938), p. 92, and "The Defense Forces of the Republic of Finland" in *The Finland Year Book 1936-37* (Helsinki: Otava 1937), pp. 100-02.

49. "Propaganda Work" in *Finland's Territorial Forces,* published by the Territorial's General Staff (Helsinki: Otava, 1936), pp. 16-17.

50. A. R. Luckham uses the term "summary variable," in "A Comparative Typology of Civil Military Relations," *Government and Opposition*, 6, 1 (Winter 1971), borrowing it from David Easton, *A Systems Analysis of Political Life* (New York: Knopf, 1965).

51. John H. Wuorinen, *A History of Finland* (New York: Columbia, 1965), pp. 231-36, quoting the Republican Form of Government of 1919.

52. Rintala, *Three Generations*, p. 130.

53. Leo Harmaja, *Effects of the War on Economic and Social Life in Finland* (New Haven: Yale University Press, 1933), pp. 4-6, 9-19; J. Jackson, *Finland*, pp. 152-55; Keith Jopson, *Economic Conditions in Finland* (London: Harrison, 1936), pp. 2-5, 36-37, 52-5.

54. This was similar to movement elsewhere in Europe. See F. L. Carsten, *The Rise of Fascism* (Berkeley: University of California Press, 1967).

55. V. Merikoski, "The Realization of the Equality of the National Languages in Finland," in *Democracy in Finland: Studies in Politics and Government* (Helsinki: Otava, 1960), pp. 85-90. See also E. von Wendt, *Svenskt Och Finskt: Finland* (Helsinki: Söderström, 1931).

56. Harmaja, *Effects of the War*, p. 7; Wuorinen, *History of Finland*, p. 269.

57. John H. Hodgson, *Communism in Finland*, pp. 129-39.

58. Rintala, *Three Generations*, p. 122.

59. *Ibid.*, p. 125.

60. Smith, *Finland,* p. 48; Carl Enckell, *Poliittiset muistelmani* (Porvoo: Söderström, 1956), Vol. I, p. 266.

61. Rintala, *Three Generations,* pp. 151-52; Einar Juva, *Rudolph Walden* (Porvoo: Söderström, 1957), p. 150.

62. Rintala, *Three Generations*, p. 143.

63. In General Sihvo's words, "My father's family in its entirety was firmly constitutionalist Young Finn," the same political orientation as President Svinhuvud. Sihvo chose to obey this man who symbolized political authority, and his Prussian-trained officers followed their orders. Sihvo, *Muistelmani*, Vol. I, p. 20.

64. *Finland's Territorial Forces*, pp. 13-14.

65. "The Defense Forces of the Republic," in *The Finland Year Book 1939-40*, pp. 72-76. After 1932 every male citizen was liable for conscription. At age twenty-one, each conscript joined the regular army for a 350-day period of training with reserve and noncommissioned officers serving for 440 days. After compulsory military service, the conscript joined the reserves until age forty. Noncommissioned officers remained in the reserves until age fifty-five and officers until age sixty. These reservists received supplementary training yearly with officers serving sixty days, noncommissioned officers forty days, and men in the ranks twenty days.

66. Smith, *Finland*, pp. 46-48.

67. Hodgson, *Communism in Finland*, p. 62.

68. *Ibid.,* p. 47; courage and daring are necessary, Stalin argued, in an atmosphere of world war, impending revolution in the west and Bolshevik power in Russia. The opportunity must not slip from your hands.

69. Hodgson, *Communism in Finland*, p. 62.

70. The Finnish revolution was not "a Russian wolf in sheep's clothing," as claimed by C. Jay Smith, Jr.,"Russia and the Origins of the Finnish Civil War of 1918," *The American and East European Review* (December 1955): 501. The strength of socialists was no doubt increased by the presence of Russian troops in Finland,but the red guardsmen who counted on Bolshevik aid were disappointed. According to M. S. Svechnikov, who commanded Russian forces in Finland, aid would be severely limited. He indicated later that the Russians may have led the red guards astray: "Voices were raised against the interference in the civil war . . . .It was especially dangerous due to the fact that throughout their stay in Finland, representatives of the Russian Army had emphasized in assemblies, meetings, manifestoes, their solidarity with the Finnish workers and had promised to support them when the critical moment should come." (Quoted in Hodgson, *Communism in Finland*, p. 73.) One socialist political leader warned that "it was one thing to deliver ceremonial speeches about international solidarity, but another to fight and suffer." (Karl Wiik, quoted in Hodgson, *Communism in Finland*, p. 73; also Carl Enckell, *Poliittiset muistelmani*, Vol. I (Porvoo: Söderström, 1956), p. 266.) He was right; by the middle of March, all Russian troops in Finland had been withdrawn, except approximately 1,000 volunteers. Soon even they would leave. News of German intervention drove even those most dedicated to assist Finland in her revolution home to Russia.

71. J. H. Jackson, "Fascism in Finland," *The New Statesman and Nation* 15 (January 1938): 4-6.

72. Rintala, *Three Generations* p. 154, quoting Oskari Heikinheimo in Parliament, 1922 *Valtiopäivät Pöytäkirjat*, Vol. II, p. 888.

73. Smith, *Finland*, p. 86; Erkki Räikkönen, *Svinhuvud*, pp. 246-52; Mannerheim, *Memoirs*, pp. 181-3.

74. Mannerheim, *Memoirs*, pp. 138-9; Rintala, *Four Finns*, pp. 29-30.

75. Mannerheim, *Memoirs*, pp. 268-70.

Civilian Control
and the Mexican Military:
Changing Patterns
of Political Influence

Franklin D. Margiotta

Lt. Col. Franklin D. Margiotta is the Director of Research and Chief of the Division of Staff Communications and Research at Air Command and Staff College. He is an Air Force pilot with extensive B-52 operational experience, has been educated at Georgetown University and MIT, and has been assistant professor of Political Science at the Air Force Academy. His research and publication has focused on future elite cadres within the US military, on the Latin American military, and on methods for comparing military political influence.

In the fall of 1974 forty-three countries had military officers as actual or as de facto heads of government.* Table 1 shows this accounts for 29 percent of the national governments of the

*I am indebted to Professors Wayne A. Cornelius, Douglas A. Hibbs, Jr., Martin C. Needler, David Ronfeldt, and Lucian W. Pye for comments upon an earlier version of this paper; a special contributor to the development of this study has been Professor William H. Brill. Of course, only I am responsible for any errors in this study which represents my analysis and is not the policy or position of the Air Command and Staff College, the Air Force, or any other governmental agency.

world; and it almost triples the number of military regimes found in 1961. As new nations joined the world community, the number of military rulers rose sharply. This trend has not been confined to any one region of the world—Africa had nineteen military rulers, Latin America twelve, Asia ten, and Europe two.

TABLE 1
MILITARY OFFICERS AS HEAD OF GOVERNMENT

Year	Number of States	Military Head of Govt.	Percent Military
1961	125	15	12
1966	135	27	19
1973	150	40	27
1974	150	43	29

Source: *Current World Leaders Almanac,* 1 October 1961; 1 September 1966; Fall, 1973, 1974.

This worldwide increase in military political role is more pervasive than the seizing of power by a few officers. In the early 1960's, the military held few cabinet positions except for some defense ministries in Latin America, Asia, Africa, and the communist bloc. In 1974, besides the striking growth in military rule per se, the military dramatically increased its role in non-military cabinet and bureaucratic positions under both military and civilian regimes.[1]

Of the twenty Latin American countries, twelve had an officer as head of government—Bolivia, Brazil, Chile, Cuba, Ecuador, El Salvador, Guatemala, Honduras, Nicaragua, Panama, Paraguay, and Peru. The military play a crucial role in Argentina, the Dominican Republic, and Uruguay. Generalizations are difficult, however, and variations in the domestic political role of the military are as diverse as the number of political systems. Cuba, with "Major" Fidel Castro as *Jefe Máximo* is obviously different from Peru, where the President and all cabinet members are regular officers. One accurate generalization is that there is a trend toward military participation in domestic political activity in the developing world.

One Latin American political system seems to be reversing this trend. Mexico has had a long history of predatory military intervention into politics. The first ruler of Mexico after independence in 1821, was deposed within ten months. "During independent Mexico's first fifty hectic and catastrophic years, over thirty different individuals served as president, heading more than fifty governments."[2] "Probably no country in Latin America has suffered longer and more deeply than Mexico from the curse of predatory militarism. More than one thousand armed uprisings plagued this unfortunate republic in its first century of nationhood."[3]

Modern Mexico presents a different picture. Since 1920 there has been an institutionalized transfer of presidential power. The last serious threat of a military revolt was beaten back by the loyal central army in 1929. The political role of the military has slowly diminished. A civilian president was elected in 1946 and has been followed by four civilian politicians chosen from PRI, the dominant political party.

The Mexican case study of expanding civilian control helps us understand the military's role in politics. An analysis of the changing political influence patterns is made more interesting by the differing perceptions of the recent political role played by the Mexican military.

There are two general schools of thought. One group of scholars sees the Mexican military as nonpolitical, virtually out of politics, or eliminated from politics. On the other side are those who perceive a diminished, but continuing, political participation by the Mexican military. In fact, some caution that this diminished political role might be only provisional or that an increased political role for the Mexican military is still latent.[4]

These cautions are brought into vivid focus by the reporting and speculation of Needler. President Echeverría of Mexico was reportedly faced with a major crisis in June 1971 when a protest march of students in Mexico City was set upon by a gang called *Los Halcones* ("the hawks"). The organized attackers killed thirteen students and used automatic weapons. Needler reports that the president of Mexico then put down a serious internal challenge from PRI conservative politicians by winning unanimous support from an emergency meeting of senior army commanders. Recent research lends some credence to Needler's speculation that the military was crucial to political stability in Mexico in 1971.[5]

This evidence strongly suggests that the military continues to engage in political activity, but may now be satisfied with different rewards and with lower levels of political influence and political role-holding. Partial explanations for military acceptance of these changed patterns can be provided by testing two hypotheses:

Hypothesis 1—The military in Mexico has been psychologically and materially satisfied and has felt no need to intervene to improve its status or material rewards.

Hypothesis 2—The military in Mexico has been politically involved and has participated in the orderly governing of the country. The potential incentive for ambitious military elites to intervene in the political process has thus been reduced by alternate political rewards.

Civilian Control in Perspective

This chapter focuses upon the observable interactions between the Mexican military and the civilian political elite, since there have been numerous broader descriptions and analyses of the motive forces of the Mexican political system and society. A sample of these studies would include the economic approaches of Vernon, Glade and Anderson, and Wilkie; the cultural and societal analyses of Redfield, Lewis, Iturriaga, Alba, Almond and Verba, and Scott; the revolutionary mystique approaches of Scott, Almond and Verba, Padgett, and Masur; and the emergence of the middle classes as a focus of Johnson and Nun.[6]

Studies of Mexican politics, too, have adopted varying foci. Huntington selects institutionalization as the key variable of

Mexican political stability. Brandenburg opts for an elitist theory that a "revolutionary family" (which includes key military personnel) rules Mexico. Party politics and the role of the semiofficial dominant party, PRI, are discussed by Padgett, Scott, Ezcurdia, Delhumeau, and Needler.[7] Scott, however, selects the executive bureaucracy as perhaps more influential than PRI. Those who stress presidential rule include Tucker, Padgett, and Needler.[8] Needler also suggests that Mexican stability may be understood by the principles of "cooptation, balance, and the pendulum."[9] Hansen summarizes these theories in an excellent eclectic work and selects a modernizing mestizo political elite for his central focus.[10]

Important trends that help explain the decreased military political role can be found in surveying the above authors. These trends include institutionalization and legitimation of the present political system; growth in political and adminis- trative skill among civilian elites; relative political stability; sound and widespread economic growth; professionalization of the military; the history and mystique of the Revolution, which provided unifying symbols and values; and the success of PRI and its cooptative tactics.

Taking as a given the political and societal milieu described in this literature, this study concentrates upon the specific psychological, material, and political rewards received by the Mexican military since the election of a civilian president in 1946, a symbolically important event. This narrow focus pro- vides an admittedly limited view of Mexican political reality, but adds depth and recent data to earlier understanding of the unique military-political patterns of Mexico.[11]

"Military" and "politics" are key terms. The terms "Mexi- can military, armed forces, or army" refer to the officers of Mexico on active duty in the army, the army air force, and the navy—and in particular, to the ranks of captain and above, because these officers have been historically active in politics.[12] The term "politics" includes Easton's broad perception of poli- tics as "the authoritative allocation of values for a society."[13] The Mexican military will be considered political if it is au- thoritatively allocated such "values" as psychological and symbolic status by the president and material and economic "values" by the political system. If members of the military occupy nonmilitary governmental and elective roles in Mexico, this too will qualify them as political.

A major assumption of this study, thus, is that the best way to trace the political role of the Mexican military is to treat the military as political actor. This avoids artificially classifying the military as either political or nonpolitical and follows the methodological perceptions of McAlister and Stepan.[14] This assumption permits the examination of one of the more subtle interactions in Mexican politics—the public relationship between the president of Mexico and his military.

Psychological Assurance to Military Status

The president of Mexico, as chief political actor, seems quite conscious of dispensing psychological "values" or rewards to the military. Finer and Janowitz have suggested that one of the causes of overt military intervention into politics may be the psychological need for self-respect or public recognition of the societal status of the military. Brill theorized that "status deprivation" felt by the military could be an important factor in coups or interventions.[15]

The data indicate a public commitment by the president of Mexico to acknowledging military status and to reassuring the psyche of the officer corps; this is expressed by public speeches and by the amount of presidential time spent on the military. The most complete statement of presidential plans for Mexico is the two-to six-hour oration given to the Congress each September, *Informe que Rinde al H. Congreso de la Unión el C. Presidente de la República.* This is the equivalent of the US State of the Union message, except the Mexican president is assured that his programs will become legislation. Content analysis of Mexican State of the Union messages and presidential inaugural addresses indicates that the chief executive is quite conscious of the military. In eleven of these thirteen major addresses, the military was praised lavishly and equated with the fatherland and the revolution.[16]

TABLE 2
ANALYSIS OF PRESIDENTIAL SPEECHES

President Speech	Effusive Attention to Military?
Alemán (1946-1952)	
Inaugural Address, 1946	Yes
State of the Union Message, 1947	Yes
State of the Union Message, 1952	Yes
Ruiz Cortines (1952-1958)	
State of the Union Message, 1953	Yes
López Mateos (1958-1964)	
State of the Union Message, 1960	Yes
State of the Union Message, 1964	Yes
Díaz Ordaz (1964-1970)	
Inaugural Address, 1964	No
State of the Union Message, 1965	No
State of the Union Message, 1966	Yes
State of the Union Message, 1969	Yes
Echeverría Alvarez (1970-)	
Inaugural Address, 1970	Yes
State of the Union Message, 1971	Yes
State of the Union Message, 1972	Yes

SOURCES: *Informes* published by varying agencies of Mexican government; Mexico City newspapers, *El Nacional* and *Excelsior,* 2 September and 2 December of appropriate years.

An interesting trend developed in the first two major speeches of President Díaz Ordaz (1964 Inaugural and 1965 State of the Union). The president spoke perfunctorily of the military and he merely promised to remember their economic needs and thanked them for their civil service. The *Informe* of 1966, however, displayed the traditional public praise of the military. The 1966 speech *began* (third paragraph) with a tribute:

> We must honor those who guard our Constitution, the most important of our institutions. The Supreme Court guards the laws; for our material preservation we depend upon the armed forces and their deportment has pleased us.

> Our armed forces, the Army, the Navy, and the Air Force, originate from the very heart of our nation; they complete with honor the delicate mission that our country has conferred upon them; to safeguard the sovereignty of our Fatherland, our territorial integrity, and our institutions.

The president then told of specific joint maneuvers that had taken place and the fact that commanders would be rotated periodically to give younger officers more opportunity. He designated the Central Military Hospital to receive 33,580,000 pesos and allocated 26,430,000 pesos to other military construction. *El Presidente* cited the military for their effective cooperation in many areas of civil life and for producing new maps and disaster plans. The speeches from 1969 to 1972 have followed this same pattern; in fact, Echeverría's first *Informe* in 1971 devoted more space to the military, ten long paragraphs, than had any of his predecessors.

The military is usually assured that its welfare will be considered. The presidents have noted they have promoted officers, increased pay, built over 1,600 homes for officers, improved the Central Military Hospital and *El Colegio Militar,* and started a Bank of the Army. The construction of new exchanges, commissaries, and swimming pools has been highlighted. Joint maneuvers, the reorganization of the services, and the building of bazooka shells are some of the trivia that have been presented to the assembled Congress.

A recurring theme in presidential speeches is praise of the military for its civic action projects.[17] The Mexican armed forces have also been praised for their devotion to duty, their preservation of the Constitution, and their influence in training the youth of the nation in citizenship.[18]

The military is given more than public praise by the president, however. His presence is assured at the Army Day in February, Navy Day in June, and at military receptions given for him after his inaugural speech in December and after his State of the Union message each September. Examination of Mexico City newspapers turns up considerable presidential interaction with his military. For instance, the first caller to congratulate President-Elect Díaz Ordaz after his 1964 electoral victory was General Aguirre Benavídes. Three of the next sixteen well-wishers were military officers.[19]

The president often appears personally to dedicate new facilities; Díaz Ordaz went to Tepic, Nayarit to have breakfast with the military, to praise their local work, and to open a magnificent new building.[20] Dozens of officer's wives in many military regions have personally received the keys to their new government homes from the president.[21]

On the occasion of the National Day of the Revolution, President Díaz Ordaz gathered the cabinet to honor seventy-six air force members for their work in aiding civilians during a weather disaster. The major newspapers of Mexico faithfully report presidential attention to the military's status. In fact, they often seem to take their cue from this official concern in their own effusive reporting of military affairs. In a first-page description of the parade on National Revolution Day, the "Extraordinary Military Band" was described as "sensational, emotion-stirring, and valiant."[22] The military in Mexico is appreciative of this favorable attention.

In interviews with Mexican officers during the last three presidential regimes, I received very positive responses about presidential concern for their status. All interviewed officers seemed satisfied that the political system would continue to reward them. Mexican officers often discuss their pay and benefits as though they had received them personally from the president. Deep personal respect, at times approaching reverence, for the individual presidents was expressed. Presidential concern for military status seems to have had a salutary effect upon civil-military relations in Mexico and may have helped insure political stability. The military have also been allocated more prosaic "values" in the form of material resources.

Allocation of Resources to the Military

In recent years the Mexican military has not received an inordinate share of Mexican resources, especially when compared to other Latin American or developing political systems. As we shall see, however, these limited resources have been skillfully managed to provide economic incentives to political loyalty.

SIZE AND RECRUITMENT

The recent strength of the active duty, regular armed forces of Mexico has been estimated at 70,000 to 78,000. The regular forces are completely volunteer and are backed by a minimally trained reserve and a rural militia of ill-equipped *ejido* peasants. Lozoya believes that registration for the reserve serves as an important means of political control and classification of the young male population. He thinks that the peasant militias serve control and information functions in remote rural areas for the military zone commanders.[23]

The size of the Mexican military does not seem to be determined by any logical perception of external threat. As Needler notes, defense against the United States is hardly plausible and defense against Guatemala is hardly necessary.[24] A text used at *El Colegio Militar* formalizes this observation and lists internal order as first priority with territorial defense in third place. The Mexican military serve as a nationwide police and counterinsurgent force which maintains order, enforces the decrees of the central government, socializes and trains peasant youth, and performs significant civic action functions. This internally focused military is one of the smallest, per capita, in the world; in Latin America, only Haiti and Costa Rica have fewer men under arms per thousand population.[25] The recent military budget in Mexico has also been comparatively small.

DEFENSE BUDGETS

Table 3 indicates the trends in Mexican defense spending from 1938 to 1965 and its relationship to the national budget. The most significant feature is the declining portion of governmental expenditure on the military, with a drop to below 10 percent after 1950. Education in Mexico has traditionally received more money than defense. From 1938 to 1965 Mexico consistently spent a smaller portion of budget and of gross national product on the military than any other major Latin American nation.

TABLE 3
MEXICAN DEFENSE EXPENDITURES AVERAGED
BY MAJOR TIME PERIODS, 1938-1965

Time Period	Average Defense Expenditure (millions 1960 $ US)	Average Defense as Percentage Total Govt. Expenditure	As Percentage GNP
1938-1941	61.7	16.6	
1942-1945	70.8	15.1	
1946-1949	54.8	11.4	
1950-1959	62.5	7.8	0.7
1960-1965	140.7	8.7	0.7

SOURCE: Joseph E. Loftus, *Latin American Defense Expenditures, 1938-1965* (Santa Monica: The RAND Corp., 1968), pp. 11, 37, 49.

Two points put defense spending in perspective. First, the federal government in Mexico controls most of the taxing and spending power in the country. State and local budgets do not exist as they do in the United States; in Mexico's centralized system, local governments rely on the federal government for their income.[26] Although the military budget is small percentage-wise, it represents part of nearly all the income available to all levels of Mexican government.

A second important point is that military benefits are often funded in other portions of the federal budget. It appears that 1,600 attractive new homes for officers were funded under the National Bank for Urban Mortgages and Public Works at a total cost of more than 100,000,000 pesos.[27] Military pensions, running at about 20 percent of the defense budget, are paid by the Secretaría de Hacienda y Crédito Público.[28]

Table 4 indicates that the military have received a relatively stable 9 to 11 percent of government expenditure. This share of government expenditure and the portion of gross national product devoted to national defense (0.7 percent) are among the lowest in the world. These expenditures are in the context of a rapidly expanding national budget and national product, however, and Mexico has been increasing its *total* defense expenditure at one of the fastest rates in Latin America.[29] Loftus determined that the Mexican military ranked third in Latin America in the amount of spending per member of the armed forces. Only Venezuela and Colombia spent more per man in their defense budget.[30] Equipment normally accounts for only 5 percent of the Mexican defense budget; most army and navy hardware dates from World War II and the air force equipment is vintage early 1950s.[31]

TABLE 4

MEXICAN DEFENSE EXPENDITURES, 1965-1969

Year	Defense Expenditure (millions $ US)	Defense as Percentage Total Government Expenditure	As Percentage GNP
1965	163.0	10.7	0.8
1966	166.0	10.3	0.8
1967	172.0	9.7	0.7
1968	183.0	9.4	0.7
1969	204.0	9.6	0.7
(1972 estimated — 288.0		not available)	

SOURCES: Mexico, Secretaría de Hacienda Y Crédito Público, *Presupuesto General de Egresos de la Federación* (1963-1969); Interviews, 1972; US Arms Control and Disarmament Agency, *World Military Expenditures* (1967), p. 16; (1969), pp. 11-13.

In summary, the Mexican military has received moderate defense budgets and has not placed undue stress or demands upon the Mexican purse in recent years. The yearly increase in total pesos available has not been spent upon hardware, but instead has gone into a continually expanding program of personal and material benefits.

MILITARY PAY AND SUPPLEMENTAL INCOME

Trends in military pay indicate the president dispenses material as well as psychological benefits to his armed forces. From 1952 to 1958, pay increased 10 percent per year.[32] In December 1958 one of the first things newly inaugurated President Adolfo López Mateos did was to declare a year-end bonus of one month's pay for the armed forces.[33] In each year of his administration (1958-1964), López Mateos raised military salaries by 10 percent.[34] One of President Gustavo Díaz Ordaz's first acts in 1964 was to grant the military "a very nice raise." Ten percent pay raises followed military action during student demonstrations in 1968 and 1971.[35]

Computing officer pay and making the pay scale meaningful in the Mexican context are not easy. Pay varies in different cost-of-living areas; it is supplemented by special distributions for responsibility, position, past offices held, and representation allowances. Base pay may only be a minor portion of total salary. For instance, if a major makes a base pay of approximately $4,800 (US dollars), this would be doubled if he were serving in Baja California, increased by up to 75 percent in the states of the remote Yucatan peninsula and by 25 percent in Guerrero. If this major had ever been a staff officer, he would receive a supplement of $480 a year for the rest of his career. If he was a lower section chief on the General Staff, or a batallion commander, his responsibility pay would add another $480 per year. Officers interviewed have said that they have often drawn up to three times base pay when regional differences and supplements were added in. McAlister has determined that in the general ranks, the supplemental pays alone are often twice base pay.[36] To a certain degree, then, each Mexican officer makes a different salary based upon his past assignments and current location.

This problem is further compounded when trying to determine how officer pay relates to Mexican society. Mexico uses a system of local minimum wage rates and differentiates by types of workers, ownership of the factory, prevailing local economy, etc. In order to provide some comparative context, Mexican officer base pay rates were multiplied by a factor of two, in order to average out differences in locality and supplemental pays. Mexican yearly pay is compared to US officer pay computed for a married officer with typical longevity in grade. Since the US military is the highest paid (in absolute terms) in the world, this will give us a reference point. Both pay structures will be related to 1970 per capita income in each society as a further comparative device.

TABLE 5

MEXICAN AND UNITED STATES OFFICER PAY, 1972
($ US per year)

Rank	Mexico	United States
Captain	$ 8,460	$14,040
Major	9,600	17,916
Lieutenant Colonel	11,520	21,192
Colonel	13,440	25,056
Brigadier General	14,400	30,432
Major General	16,320	34,404

SOURCE: Interviews; United States Air Force *Officer's Pay Guide,* 1972.

Table 5 compares the pay scales of the Mexican and US military in 1972. The rank structures in both countries are similar and are converted to US equivalent ranks for convenience. Mexican general officer pay is probably understated by at least a third. The US officer receives about twice the absolute pay of his Mexican contemporary. This picture is different when we place each pay scale within its societal context. Table 6 shows the ratios of 1972 officer pay to 1970 per capita income in each society and puts the absolute salaries in some perspective. The average officer in Mexico is doing far better than the average Mexican citizen. At all rank levels, the Mexican officer's ratio of earnings to average per capita income is at least three times his North American counterpart's.

TABLE 6
MILITARY PAY AS RATIO OF PER CAPITA INCOME

Rank	Mexican Ratio*	United States Ratio*
Captain	13.7 X	3.3 X
Major	15.2 X	4.2 X
Lieutenant Colonel	18.2 X	5.0 X
Colonel	21.0 X	5.8 X
Brigadier General	22.8 X	7.1 X
Major General	25.9 X	8.0 X

SOURCE: Table 5 and United Nations, *Statistical Yearbook* (1971), p. 395.
*1970 per capita income: Mexico—$632; US—$4,274.

The ability of the Mexican officer to supplement his pay must be added. There are many legally condoned methods for increasing one's income in the Mexican military; they seem to be based upon initiative, energy, skill, and contacts. Some personal experiences related to me by a native of Mexico illustrate these activities.

In the city of Vera Cruz, from 1946 until 1952, a friend held two jobs and was paid two salaries—major in the Mexican army and inspector of road maintenance. Another friend held the extra job of prison superintendent while he was an officer in the army. In 1957 a high school classmate was a captain in the Mexican air force and received permission to dust crops; in return the captain channeled a portion of his extra earnings to his local commanders. A relative is a major in the Mexican army. In 1965 this major was in charge of all purchasing contracts for an army zone. To quote the Mexican interviewee,

"He lives quite well and must report to Mexico City to make payoffs."

To a certain degree, this supplementing of income has become institutionalized in Mexico. The word, "aviadore" (aviator), has been coined to mean a military officer who just "flies in" to collect his military pay while he is working on another job. Both military pilots and farmers were so insistent that the Mexican air force set up a special *licencia* (leave), guaranteeing their pilots two month's leave with pay each year to go out and sell their services as crop dusters. Some air force pilots have been released for up to ten years to take higher paying jobs with Mexican airlines.[37]

No argument can be made that the Mexican military is getting rich. My impressions are that they are satisfied they will be treated well. This attitude is reinforced by the variety of special benefits that have accrued to the military since 1946. Mexican civilians estimated that these benefits add about 40 percent to military income.[38]

BENEFITS

Retirement

A Mexican officer may retire at *full pay* when he has served his country for thirty years. An American officer may retire after twenty year's service with about 40 percent of his total pay and after thirty year's service with about 62 percent of his total pay.

Medical Care

Members of the military and their dependents have traditionally received free medical care in Mexico. The military educates its own doctors, and military hospitals and care are among the best in Mexico. Over 1,200 doctors, or one of every twenty-five doctors in Mexico, have been trained in the Military Medical School.[39] In 1964 President Díaz Ordaz instituted more lenient provisions for the purchase and free supply of drugs and pharmaceuticals.

Military Housing

An extensive program for building houses for military officers began in 1952. From 1953 to 1958, the federal government acquired land for the project. Under the vigorous leadership of President López Mateos (1958-1964), 1,543 homes were completed by 1964. Their cost was over 100,000,000 pesos. A Mexican major living with his family in a small, three-bedroom house pays the government about 5 percent of his base pay, or $25 a month. Repairs are provided by the government, but the officer pays for utilities.

Exchange and Commissary Stores

Since 1960 there has been an increasing emphasis on building exchange and commissary stores at the military installations. In these stores the military families may purchase food, toilet articles, and other items necessary to life at reduced prices.

Technical Training and Schooling

The military officer receives one of the better educations available in his country. About fifty per year are sent overseas to attend advanced schools with their contemporaries in other countries.[40]

Foreign Duty

Officers of the Mexican military may serve overseas as military attachés, instructors in foreign military academies, on regional defense boards, or as students in advanced military schools. These duties are considered choice assignments because the officer is paid a higher wage to meet the living standard of the country in which he resides. He is also able to purchase automobiles, appliances, and other foreign products without paying the normal duty.

Special Schools for Dependents

When General Cárdenas was president, he set up large special schools, called *Hijos del Ejército,* for the dependents of the military. There are other smaller military prep schools for dependents that lead to entrance into *El Colegio Militar,* Mexico's West Point. Military officers consider these schools to be quite good and are happy to send their children to them.

The Military Bank

In 1946 President Alemán set up a National Bank of the Army, funded in the federal budget. This bank is administered by the army and makes low-cost credit available to the Mexican military. By 1952 the bank had lent more than 35,000,000 pesos to its military customers.

Social Security

President Díaz Ordaz began a social security system for the military which now includes life insurance and death and disability benefits. Officers interviewed considered this a very worthwhile benefit.

Other Benefits

President Echeverría has done more than grant pay raises. In 1971-72 a new Organic Law of the Army was passed; a national housing fund was set up to help individuals in the military build or buy private homes; a special "Medal of Loyalty" was created.

Since 1946 the military of Mexico has received an ever-increasing flow of benefits not normally available to the average citizen. Besides attention from the president, a reasonable pay scale, and these many attractive benefits, the Mexican officer can count upon relatively fair and rapid promotion.

PROMOTION OPPORTUNITIES

In Table 7 promotions to the rank of brigadier general in the Mexican army and in the United States army are compared. In 1963 one out of every 6,800 men in the Mexican army was promoted to general; in 1964 one out of every 2,800 was promoted to general. Comparable figures for the US army are: 1963, one out of 21,200; 1964, one out of 19,400. In 1963 the chances of becoming a general in Mexico were five times better than they were in the United States; in 1964 the odds were seven times better in Mexico.

Promotions to the rank of colonel and above in Mexico are considered to be highly political in nature, in the sense that the president directly reviews and decides who shall be promoted. From the rank of second lieutenant to lieutenant colonel, promotions are highly competitive. Those competing for a fixed number of promotions to a particular rank each year are subject to a rigorous medical examination and to a battery of tests which may last for up to two weeks. The highest scorers are promoted.

TABLE 7

MEXICAN PROMOTIONS COMPARED TO UNITED STATES' PROMOTIONS

| | Mexico | | United States | |
Year	Troops In Army	Number New Generals	Troops In Army	Number New Generals
1963	48,000	7	974,070	46
1964	48,000	17	971,384	50

SOURCES: Mexico: *Informe,* 1964; Secretaría de la Defensa Nacional, *Revista de Ejército* (December, 1964); J. Gomez-Quinones, ed., *Statistical Abstract of Latin America 1964* (Los Angeles: Latin American Center, UCLA, 1965), p. 52. United States: *Army Navy Air Force Journal and Register* (9 March 1963; 8 February 1964); Luman H. Long, ed., *The World Almanac and Book of Facts* (New York: Newspaper Enterprise Association, 1967), p. 452.

Table 8 indicates that the Mexican Army promotion cycle is comparable to that of the United States and better than the Spanish in the higher grades. The average Mexican officer will be considered for promotion to lieutenant colonel about fifteen years after he graduated from *El Colegio Militar.*

TABLE 8
PROMOTION PHASE POINTS (1973)
IN MEXICAN, US, SPANISH ARMIES

	Total Years of Commissioned Service		
Promoted to	Mexico	US	Spain
First Lieutenant	2	2	Unknown
Captain (Second)	5	5	4
Captain (First)	8	no equivalent rank	
Major	11	9-10	12
Lieutenant Colonel	15	14-15	18-21
Colonel	19	20-21	25+

SOURCE: Interviews with officers of three countries.

Cross-national comparisons of promotion cycles tell us very little. The US army promotion cycle is in considerable flux because of the Vietnam drawdown and has slipped considerably from the Vietnam buildup years. The US air force and navy are promoting years behind the army in the upper ranks because of differing force structures and personnel policies. Within the US military, there are expedited promotion systems which promote relatively small numbers of officers more quickly than does the Mexican system. The uppermost ranks of the Spanish army have been virtually frozen since the expansion during the Spanish civil war.[41] Our conclusions about the Mexican promotion system must be limited—it is no worse than these comparative army promotion cycles; Mexican officers interviewed were proud of the apparent fairness of their merit-based promotions.

The career military officer in Mexico looks forward to a fair, regularized chance at promotion which will bring him increased pay. He and his family share many benefits not available to the Mexican citizenry. During the turmoil of the revolution, the politically ambitious Mexican officer could also aspire to be president, or governor, or party functionary. Did the election of a civilian in 1946 signal the disappearance of political ambition and political participation in the officer corps? This was the conclusion of some scholars who decided that the Mexican military became "nonpolitical" after 1940-1946. Recent data on political participation by the Mexican military does not support that conclusion.

The Mexican Military in Politics

The election of a civilian politician, Miguel Alemán, as president of Mexico in 1946 was symbolically important as a confirmation of civilizing trends in Mexican politics. What is often overlooked is that Alemán was the son of a famous revolutionary general and local boss, had managed General Avila Camacho's presidential campaign in 1940, and had been secretary of government (the Interior Ministry in many developing systems) from 1940 to 1946. Alemán was followed in office in 1952 by another civilian politician, Adolfo Ruiz Cortines, who had fought in the Revolutionary Army, reaching the rank of major.[42] Both these civilian politicians were thus known to the military and were able to continue the transition to more complete civilian rule. One thing that may have eased this transition was the continuing military presence within *El Partido Revolucionario Institutional* (PRI), the semiofficial and dominant political party of Mexico.

THE MEXICAN MILITARY AND PRI

The only important political party organization in modern Mexico has been PRI. The governing group of PRI is the Central Executive Committee which elects (with the advice of the president of the Republic) the chief executive of the party.[43] When Alemán was installed as president in 1946, General Roldolfo Sánchez Taboada was "elected" president of the party. He was replaced in 1952 by General Gabriel Leyva Valázquez. The post was turned over to General Augustín Olachea, who remained in office until the 1958 election, when General Alfonso Corona del Rosal became president of PRI.[44]

The sequence of generals at the head of the party came to an end with the election of Gustavo Díaz Ordaz. On 7 December 1964 President Díaz chose Carlos Alberto Madrazo to head PRI. Before his selection, Señor Madrazo had been a lawyer, a politician, and a state governor. Madrazo was replaced by another politician in a major shakeup within the party in 1966 and civilians have led PRI since.[45]

Recruitment practices of the party support Needler's thesis that cooptation is one of the keys to understanding the Mexican political system. Talented and ambitious young officers are selected by the military to join the staff of the civilian president of PRI as his assistants. Many of these officers have no important political connections, nor independent income, nor have they articulated any particular desire to get into politics. Those who succeed in their "assignment" may be given the option of continuing their political career within PRI as a governor's aide and eventual PRI functionary or of returning to their suspended military career.

An ostensible reason for recruiting officers into PRI inner circles is their staffing abilities. We speculate that PRI leadership rationally coopts young officers and builds political loyalty patterns early. The political and administrative talents of the military are put to further use by the chief executive.

THE OFFICER IN THE EXECUTIVE BRANCH

Military officers are used in important nonmilitary positions within the federal agencies of the Mexican executive branch. Table 9 shows that there has been little discernible trend in this practice over the years. One significant change is that military officers do not usually serve in cabinet positions other than secretary of national defense and secretary of the navy.[46] These two cabinet posts continue to be filled by active duty officers and their agencies are staffed by the military. Some of the nonmilitary positions held by officers in 1970 were as the "mayor" of Mexico City; the chief of police, director general of roads, and the director general of sports in Mexico City; the federal director of security in the Secretariat of Government (Interior); the ambassador to Ecuador; the chief of aerial services in the Secretariat of Public Works; the director of requirements and qualifications of sanitary inspection and the director of air transport in the Secretariat of Health and Assistance; and the head of the department of press and information in the Attorney General's office.[47]

TABLE 9
MILITARY OFFICERS IN EXECUTIVE BRANCH

Position	1941	1947	1948	1961	1970	1971
Cabinet member	4	2	2	2	3	2
Senior-level bureaucrat	unknown	11	13	8	10	8
Subordinate-level bureaucrat	unknown	5	7	16	7	16

SOURCES: McAlister, *The Military in Latin American Sociopolitical Evolution,* p. 239; Mexico, Secretaría de la Presidencia, Comisión de Administración Pública, *Manual de Organización del Gobierno Federal 1969-1970* (1969); Mexico, Secretaría de la Presidencia, *Directorio del Poder Ejecutivo Federal 1971* (1971); H. Ruiz Sandoval, *Directorio Social* (XVI ed.; Mexico, D.F.: Faser, 1941).

President Echeverría has chosen the military for other nonmilitary positions. In a 1972 move described as replacing "corrupt elements," graduates of the Army General Staff College began taking over Mexican customs posts.[48] In August 1972 two army colonels were selected as ambassadors.

THE OFFICER AS STATE GOVERNOR

Twenty-nine governors are elected in Mexico and two are appointed in the federal territories. Only PRI candidates have won elections to state governor.[49] Table 10 summarizes an important trend in civil-military relations in Mexico. President Alemán (1948) accepted about half of the governors from the military ranks. There has been a significant trend

TABLE 10
MILITARY OFFICERS AS GOVERNORS

Year	President in Office	Number of Officers as Governors (out of 31)
1948	Alemán (1946-1952)	15
1953	Ruiz Cortines (1952-1958)	8
1959	López Mateos (1958-1964)	6
1965	Díaz Ordaz (1964-1970)	3
1972	Echeverría Alvarez (1970-)	1

SOURCES: McAlister *et al., The Military in Latin American Sociopolitical Evolution,* p. 240; Brandenburg, *Making of Modern Mexico,* p. 151; Marvin Alisky, *The Governors of Mexico,* Southwestern Studies, 3, 4, Monograph No. 12 (El Paso, Texas: Texas Western College Press, 1965); Interviews.

toward elimination of the military from this important aspect of electoral politics, with a marked change after the 1964 election. State governors in Mexico hold powerful institutional positions in the Mexican political system. This is not necessarily the case with Mexican senators and federal deputies.

THE OFFICER IN CONGRESS

There is little *institutional* power in the offices of federal senator or deputy. According to students of the Mexican political system, political power in Mexico resides within the presidency, the executive branch, PRI, and a small political elite. The elective positions within the Congress are important, however, because they provide indications of individual political power, are honorific and important symbols of political participation, and may be a steppingstone in career advancement. Lieuwen noted that a statute forbade members of the Mexican armed forces from engaging in political activity.[50] He failed to consider, however, that an officer may legally take a *licencia* (leave) three months before the congressional election. During this political leave the officers are not paid by the military and do not accumulate time toward retirement or promotion. Table 11 indicates that this has not been a major deterrent to the election of officers to the Mexican Congress.

TABLE 11

MILITARY OFFICERS IN CONGRESS

Political Role	1947	1953	1959	1965	1968	1972
Senator (Primary) 60 seats	3	12	12	9	9	7*
Senator (Supplementary) 60 seats	2	0	4	5	5	1*
Deputy (Primary) 162 to 203 seats	5*	10	11	7	4	6*
Deputy (Supplementary) 162 to 203 seats	0	0	3	not found	6	3*
Total Military Legislators	10	22	30	(21)	24	17*

SOURCES: Mexico, Dirrección Técnica de Organización, *Directorio del Gobierno Federal 1948* (1948) and *Directorio del Gobierno Federal Poderes: Legislativo, Ejecutivo, y Ju-*

dicial (1956); Mexico, Cámara de Senadores, *Directorio, XLVI Legislatura, 1964-1967* (Publicaciones Mexicanas, S.C.L. Insurgentes Sur No. 123, 1965); Mexico, Secretaría de la Presidencia, Comisión de Administración Pública, *Manual de Organización del Gobierno Federal 1969-1970* (1969); McAlister *et al., The Military in Latin American Sociopolitical Evolution,* p. 238; electoral lists in *Excelsior* and *El Nacional.*

*Estimates only; based upon number of PRI candidates in electoral lists and electoral experience that PRI-sponsored military candidates end up in the Congress.

The Senate

Mexico elects sixty senators every six years; two from each of the twenty-nine states and two from the federal district. These senators are called *proprietarios,* or primary representatives of their states. In addition, the voters in each state choose two *suplentes,* who function as substitutes and "secondary senators." Only PRI candidates have been elected since 1946. PRI ran and elected twelve military in 1952, sixteen in 1958, and fourteen in 1964 *(proprietarios* and *suplentes).* Eighty-four officers have run for the Mexican Senate since 1946, and fifty-five of them were proposed and elected by PRI (see table 12).

From 1952 to 1958 there were five Senate committees on military matters. In the three on national defense, ten of the twelve positions were occupied by the military-politicians. On both the Military Health Committee (the army plays a large role in public health) and the War Material Committee three of the four senators were military.[51]

This trend continued in the Senate elected in 1964. One of the four senators on the Military Health Committee was a general; all four members were doctors of medicine. The three committees on national defense had eight military members out of twelve positions. An officer-senator also occupied three of the four positions on the Military Justice Committee and the War Material Committee. Military officers have had a major voice in senatorial debate of military matters.[52]

House of Deputies

The voters of Mexico elect federal deputies *(proprietarios and suplentes)* to the lower house of Congress every three years. With the growth of population, the number of each type of deputy increased from 162 in 1946 to 204 in 1973. Other parties win seats or are allocated seats on a proportional basis, but PRI controls about 85 percent of the House of Deputies.

There has been a gradual decrease in the election of military officers to the Mexican Congress since 1946, both in absolute numbers and in percentage of military seats held in the lower house (down from 4 percent military in 1959 to 3 percent in 1968). McAlister suggests that PRI selects military candidates based upon local situations and personalities, rather than by any rational quota system as such.[53] An anecdote related by a Mexican officer supports this thesis—his classmate was approached by PRI functionaries and asked to run for federal deputy. When the major questioned why he was chosen, the PRI officials explained that the local zone commander (general) wanted a military man to run. Under these somewhat strange circumstances, the major was happily elected to Congress! Not all the military candidates for federal office have been lucky enough to find PRI sponsorship, however.

THE OFFICER AS POLITICAL CANDIDATE

Approximately half of the 298 officer candidates in the federal elections have been elected to Congress, with all PRI-sponsored officers winning. Table 12 shows that after a peak of fifty-six officer candidates in 1958, there has been some decline in running for Congress among the officer corps. On the other hand, twice as many officers ran in 1967 and 1970 as did in 1952 and 1955; there is no striking trend. Small numbers of military candidates have been chosen by all of Mexico's parties except PAN (Party of National Action). Since the 1964 election, military candidates have been affiliated only with PRI or PARM, a small coopted party begun by three revolutionary generals in 1958. Since 1958 PARM has attracted 126 military candidates; PRI has sponsored and elected 115 offi-

TABLE 12

MILITARY CANDIDATES FOR THE CONGRESS

Year	Senate	House	Totals
1946	23	22	45
1949	No information found on elections of 1949		
1952	12	5	17
1955	—	15	15
1958	25	31	56
1961	—	27	27
1964	16	31	47
1967	—	38	38
1970	8	24	32
1973	—	21	21
Total military candidates	84	214	298

SOURCES: Mexican electoral lists in *Excelsior, El Nacional, El Universal* for appropriate years.

cers since 1946. The relationships between PRI and PARM are not clear, but under the proportional system, some PARM military candidates become deputies.

Of final interest is the rank structure and age grouping of the military candidates for senator and federal deputy. Expectations that the military-politician would fade from the picture as the active revolutionary generals died off is not borne out in Table 13. While the electoral picture was dominated by generals and colonels over the early years, since 1964 about half the candidates were of the rank of lieutenant colonel or below. With the decline of the revolutionary generals there seems to be an increasing awareness and interest in electoral politics among the younger officers.

TABLE 13

MILITARY RANK OF SENATE AND HOUSE CANDIDATES

Year	Lt.	Capt.	Maj.	L/Col.	Col.	Navy Capt.	Navy Comm.	Navy Adm.	Gen.
1946	0	9	3	0	12	0	1	0	20
1949	\multicolumn{9}{No information found on elections of 1949}								
1952	0	1	1	0	1	0	0	2	12
1955	0	2	1	3	3	0	0	2	4
1958	2	3	5	4	12	2	0	1	27
1961	3	3	1	4	4	0	0	3	9
1964	3	9	4	7	6	2	0	1	15
1967	3	6	5	6	8	2	0	0	8
1970	4	5	2	4	5	0	0	1	11
1973	1	9	0	3	3	0	0	0	5
TOTALS	16	47	22	31	54	6	1	10	111

SOURCES: Mexican electoral lists in *Excelsior*, *El Nacional*, and *El Universal* for appropriate years.

Changing Patterns of Political Influence:
An Analysis

The patterns of political influence of the Mexican military have changed considerably since the days when revolutionary generals dominated the political system. The data indicate that military influence and power has waned since 1946, but that the Mexican military has remained decidedly political.

We are able to describe the changing military political role and to suggest partial explanations for acceptance of these new patterns. By focusing upon changes in the indicators, we may also delineate major historical periods in civil-military relations in Mexico.

MILITARY POLITICAL ROLE SINCE 1946

If the "authoritative allocation of values" and "selection to nonmilitary governmental and political roles" are accepted as reasonable operational definitions of politics, then the evidence makes suspect studies that found the Mexican military nonpolitical. Perhaps the most appropriate conclusion is that the Mexican military is less powerful politically because its influence is wielded at lower levels of the political system and because military officers no longer occupy the key political roles of government.

No longer does a general run for president, although some "political generals" may still have this ambition. The president of the party has been a civilian since 1964. The number of military governors has decreased from fifteen in 1948 to one in 1972. Since 1946 the military has usually held only the defense posts in the cabinet. Even in resource allocations, there are signs of declining military rewards.

The size of the armed forces, relative to other Latin American systems, is small. The percentages of government expenditure and of GNP devoted to the military are limited. Military expenditure fell below 10 percent after 1950 and has remained at that level ever since. Military acceptance of these patterns is of special interest for the study of civil-military relations in other societies.

Why is it that the Mexican armed forces no longer directly intervene in politics as do so many other militaries? Since the scope of this study was limited, generalizations about nonintervention are only partial explanations of Mexican political reality. The data, however, do support the two hypotheses suggested earlier in this chapter.

The transition to increased civilian control has thus been eased by the fact that other rewards to the military have remained rather constant or have increased since 1946. Five civilian presidents have reassured the military with praise in their major speeches to the nation and have found time to attend numerous military functions, parades, and dedications. While the defense budget has stabilized at 9 to 11 percent of government expenditure, it has increased in absolute amounts to well over $200 million. This money has been spent primarily upon personnel. Pay raises of 10 percent or more were granted each year from 1952 to 1964; raises came in 1968 and 1971.

The Mexican officer corps has a relatively secure financial status, is able to supplement military income, and receives a cornucopia of benefits. These include a generous retirement plan; excellent and free medical and pharmaceutical care; low cost, new, good housing; nonprofit exchange and commissary stores; special schools for dependent children; low-cost credit; technical training and schooling; and a social security and insurance system. Promotional phase points in the officer ranks are comparable to other armies, and the potential for promotion to general is better than in the US or Spain.

The Mexican officer has retained his access to many elective and appointive political roles in Mexico, although the possibilities of becoming president, head of the party, or state governor has diminished. PRI still actively recruits able young military officers into party positions, where they develop relationships with the political elite. There has been no detectable decrease in the use of military officers in nonmilitary executive branch positions. The number of officers serving in the Congress ranged from ten in 1947 to a peak of thirty in 1959 and an estimated seventeen in 1972. There is some sign of diminished military interest or success in running for the national legislature. The interest of younger officers in running for Congress has increased since 1946 and foretells a continuing, if lessened, military role in national electoral politics. These indicators highlight major symbolic events which signal deeper trends and patterns within Mexican civil-military relations.

FROM MILITARY TO CIVIL GOVERNMENT IN MEXICO:
A BRIEF HISTORICAL ANALYSIS

The patterns of political influence of the Mexican military might be summarized by using the indicators to define different historical periods of civil-military relations. A useful methodological technique is to view these relations in the political realm on a continuum similar to that presented in chapter 1. Politics has been neither purely civilian, nor purely military, although one or the other group has predominated. On this continuum of relations, four phases or categories of government might be discerned: military government, military-civil government, civil-military government, and civil government. No one of these categories denies an admixture of civilian and military political activity; the difference is one of degree of political influence and political role-holding. While this is a nonrigorous and approximate technique, it does give some structure and order to the trends.[54]

The military government phase began with the overthrow and assassination of President Madero in 1913 by two generals.[55] While there were still some civilians as local political bosses and in the federal cabinet, politics was dominated by force of arms and generals ran the country. In 1929 two events signalled the shifting pattern of relations. General Calles organized the semiofficial party, and the loyal central army beat back the last major revolt from the provinces. Politics became more institutionalized and no longer depended upon raising an army of followers.

Political skills became more important and the system after 1929 might be typified as military-civil government with civilian political power increasing under the General-Presidents Cárdenas and Avila Camacho. The number of officers in the cabinet declined and the budget share to the military decreased slightly despite World War II. The most important signal of the growth of civilian influence was PRI's selection of a civilian to become president in 1946.

The election of Alemán in 1946 may be seen as symbolizing a third phase—civil-military government. Defense expenditures dropped to below 10 percent. The civil-military government included officers as head of the party, in half the governorships, in the executive, and in the House and Senate. The continuing ascendancy of civilian political power in Mexico was symbolized by the selection of both a civilian president and a civilian head of party in 1964.

These selections, along with the decline in military state governors, lead us to classify Mexico as civil government from 1964 to present. The military still retains significant political influence, as civilians did during the military phase of the early revolutionary era. As a group, this residual political power is symbolized by presidential attention to military status and by the expenditure of resources upon substantial material rewards. As individuals, the military officer is still actively recruited into PRI, holds cabinet and subcabinet level executive positions, and is elected to the legislature.

Recent trends are interesting. Mexican political stability was shaken by the student riots of 1968 and 1971, in which the army supported the political establishment. There is no direct confirmation of Needler's speculation that President Echeverría faced down serious conservative opposition after a meeting of army commanders (May 1971) which supported the president. The military has benefitted since that time, however. The 1971 *Informe* contained more passages and praise of the military than usual. A 10 percent pay raise was granted in August 1971. Two ambassadorships and some customs posts were manned by officers. A New Organic Law of the Army has been passed; a national housing fund set up; a new "Medal of Loyalty" created. In part, this treatment of the military may be related to political loyalty. The 1976 elections and the initial speeches of the new president will give us further clues about trends. Until then, it is possible to generalize from the Mexican case study to the broader comparative study of the military in politics.

Implications of the Mexican Case Study

This case study of the Mexican military is informative to the wider study of the military in politics since the Mexican case (1946-1973) may be considered a model of successful cooptation and increasing civilian control.

Many scholars have dealt with the problems of military intervention and military dominance in developing societies. The Mexican model is thus somewhat unique in that it suggests conditions under which the military in a rapidly changing and modernizing society ceases to intervene overtly in the political process.

These conditions may not reflect fully planned, conscious efforts on the part of the Mexican ruling elite; they may have just developed over the years. Since these conditions are at least partially responsible for reducing military intervention, they are worth postulating in broad theoretical fashion. Mexican concepts of nonintervention and their attendant conditions serve two useful purposes: (1) these might be potential tools for consciously managing the *modus vivendi* between the civil and military sectors of a developing society; (2) these concepts might be useful in comparative studies of other developing societies and their militaries.

CONDITIONS OF CIVILIAN CONTROL

1. A primary condition may be the existence of a well-developed, powerful political party which is willing and able to coopt the military elite of the nation. PRI was begun by and flourished under the general-presidents of Mexico. Over a period of many years, other important interest groups developed and were able to balance off the political power of the military bloc in PRI.

2. It took years to decrease direct military participation in the political process. It may be dysfunctional to have a military government one day and a totally civilian government the next. When the military loses its stake in orderly governmental succession, it may sit on the sidelines in judgment until it again feels compelled to step in and "clean up the mess." Mexico made the transition gradually over more than thirty years.

3. One of the keys to nonintervention, then, based upon the Mexican experience, was to keep the army involved in politics. Individual officers ran for political office, participated in party decisions, helped select candidates. Individual ambitions were channeled into formal institutions. The military

elite was given a stake in the future of the government, which made them less likely to take matters into their own hands. PRI did not bargain with the military as a separate overpowering force, but instead successfully integrated the military elite within the party councils. The army actively participated in the decisional processes of the country. As countervailing political forces emerged, the army's political influence was relegated to lower levels of decision-making.

4. Another key condition may be that the Mexican military has not faced a large-scale, viable guerrilla movement. The civilian leadership has not had to use the military against any long-term serious insurrection which could politicize key segments of the military.[56]

5. The material well-being of the military was considered in order to preclude intervention for the purpose of reallocating resources. Military pay and benefits were made adequate, if not substantial. These material signs of the military's status in society have been continually refurbished and additional benefits are announced almost yearly by the president. Most of the defense budget has been spent upon pay and benefits rather than upon military hardware.

6. The military's desires for national prestige and individual status have been satisfied by civilian opinion leaders. In Mexico the armed forces have been psychologically assured of their privileged position in society by an inordinate amount of public praise and attention from the president of the Republic. The press in Mexico aids this process by devoting considerable space to the president and his generals. This psychological reassurance may avoid a "status deprivation complex" which could trigger military intervention.

7. Another observable condition of nonintervention in Mexico has been the military's interaction with other social systems. Military officers have held responsible positions within PRI and within the governmental bureaucracy. This practice extends to lower governmental levels in the states and in the muncipalities. The military actively participates with the civilian community in the training of the youth of the nation. It has also contributed to the modernization of the nation with its civic action projects.

8. Many younger officers may feel gratified in civic action programs which have been traditional with the Mexican military. These programs involve the army in the modernization of the country and may reduce the incentive to change the government in order to speed up progress. Civic action has been made more palatable in Mexico by tying it to increased benefits for the military.[57]

The above conditions for nonintervention may seem to equate civil-military tranquility with pandering to the military and its wishes. In a developing society where the political role of the military has not been circumscribed by long tradition and/or other powerful political forces, consideration and inclusion of the military may be the only partial guarantees against military intervention. The ambitions of the military elite will either be channeled or they may run rampant. For now, Mexico appears to have harnessed the military, and the orderly transfer of governmental power seems to have become firm tradition.

Notes to Chapter 8

Margiotta, *Civilian Control and the Mexican Military.*

1. This study of the Mexican military synthesizes my research attempts to conceptualize and demonstrate comparative indicators of military political influence. The seeds of this case study may be found in my unpublished works: "The Mexican Military: A Case Study in Nonintervention" (M.A. Thesis, Georgetown University, 1968); "Changing Patterns of Political Influence: The Mexican Military and Politics," paper delivered at the Annual Meeting of the American Political Science Association, New Orleans, 4-8 September 1973; "The Military and Politics: Issues in Comparative Study and an Agenda of Research," paper delivered at the Annual Meeting of the Midwest Political Science Association, Chicago, 25-26 April 1974; "Patterns of Civilian Control in Mexico," paper delivered at the Meeting of the Inter-University Seminar on Armed Forces and Society, State University of New York at Buffalo, 18-19 October 1974.

2. Charles C. Cumberland, *Mexico: The Struggle for Modernity* (New York: Oxford University Press, 1968), p. 141.

3. Edwin Lieuwen, *Arms and Politics in Latin America*, rev. ed. (New York: Praeger, 1961), p. 101.

4. Those who argue that the Mexican military is nonpolitical include John J. Johnson, ed., *The Military and Society in Latin America* (Stanford, California: Stanford University Press, 1964), p. 9; Karl M. Schmitt and David D. Burks, *Evolution or Chaos: Dynamics of Latin American Government and Politics* (New York: Praeger, 1963), pp. 142-59; Lieuwen, *Arms and Politics,* p. 101, and in *Mexican Militarism* (Albuquerque: University of New Mexico Press, 1968), p. 148; and Samuel P. Huntington, *Political Order in Changing Societies* (New Haven: Yale University Press, 1968), p. 319. Those who see a continuing role include Lyle N. McAlister, *et al., The Military in Latin American Sociopolitical Evolution: Four Case Studies* (Washington, D.C.: American University Center for Research in Social Systems, 1970), pp. 197-247; Martin C. Needler, *Politics and Society in Mexico* (Albuquerque: University of New Mexico Press, 1971), pp. 65-81; Howard F. Cline, *Mexico: Revolution to Evolution 1940-1960* (New York: Oxford University Press, 1962), p. 177; David F. Ronfeldt, "The Mexican Army and Political Order Since 1940," in *Armies and Politics in Latin America,* ed. by Abraham F. Lowenthal (New York: Holmes and Meier, in preparation). I am especially indebted to David Ronfeldt for discussions about our separate research into the Mexican political process.

5. Martin C. Needler, "A Critical Time for Mexico," *Current History* (February, 1972): 81-85.

6. Economic approaches: Raymond Vernon, *The Dilemma of Mexico's Development: the Roles of the Private and Public Sectors* (Cambridge: Harvard University Press, 1963); William P. Glade and Charles W. Anderson, *The Political Economy of Mexico* (Madison: University of Wisconsin Press, 1963); James W. Wilkie, *The Mexican Revolution: Federal Expenditures and Social Change Since 1910* (Berkeley: University of California Press, 1967).

Cultural and societal analyses: Robert Redfield, *A Village that Chose Progress* (Chicago: University of Chicago Press, 1950); Oscar Lewis, *Life in a Mexican Village: Tepoztlan Revisited* (Urbana: University of Illinois Press, 1951), *Five Families: Mexican Case Studies in the Culture of Poverty* (New York: Basic Books, 1959), *The Children of Sanchez: Autobiography of a Mexican Family* (New York: Random House, 1961); Jose E. Iturriaga, *La estructura social y cultural de México* (Mexico, D.F.: Fondo de Cultura Económica, 1951); Victor Alba, *Las ideas sociales contemporáneas en México* (Mexico, D.F.: Fondo de Cultura Económica, 1960), *The Mexicans: The Making of a Nation* (New York: Praeger, 1967); Gabriel Almond and Sidney Verba, *The Civic Culture* (Boston: Little, Brown, 1965); and Robert E. Scott, "Mexico: The Established Revolution," in *Political Culture and Political Development,* ed. by Lucian W. Pye and Sidney Verba (Princeton: Princeton University Press, 1965).

Revolutionary mystique: Scott, "Mexico," p. 335; Almond and Verba,

Civic Culture, pp. 310-12; L. Vincent Padgett, *The Mexican Political System* (Boston: Houghton Mifflin, 1966), p. 43; Gerhard Masur, *Nationalism in Latin America* (New York: Macmillan, 1966).

Middle Classes: John J. Johnson, *Political Change in Latin America* (Stanford, California: Stanford University Press, 1958); Jose Nun, "The Middle-Class Military Coup," in *The Politics of Conformity in Latin America*, ed. by Claudio Veliz (New York: Oxford University Press, 1967), pp. 66-118.

7. Huntington, *Political Order*, pp. 315-24; Frank Brandenburg, *The Making of Modern Mexico* (Englewood Cliffs, N.J.: Prentice-Hall, 1964); L. Vincent Padgett, "Mexico's One-Party System: A Reevaluation," *American Political Science Review* 51, 4 (December 1957) and *The Mexican Political System;* Robert E Scott, *Mexican Government in Transition*, rev. ed. (Urbana: University of Illinois Press, 1964); Mario Ezcurdia, *Análisis teórico del Partido Revolucionario Institucional* (Mexico, D.F.: Costa-Amic, 1968); Antonio Delhumeau, *et al., México: realidad política de sus partidos* (Mexico: Instituto Mexicano de Estudios Políticos, 1970); Needler, *Politics and Society in Mexico.*

8. William P. Tucker, *The Mexican Government Today* (Minneapolis: University of Minnesota Press, 1957); Padgett, *The Mexican Political System;* and Needler, *Politics and Society in Mexico.*

9. Needler, "A Critical Time for Mexico," pp. 82-83.

10. Roger D. Hansen, *The Politics of Mexican Development* (Baltimore: Johns Hopkins University Press, 1971).

11. Daniel Cosío Villegas, Mexican historian, commented that one can only scratch the surface of Mexican political reality with "empirical indicators" of civil-military relations. Nevertheless, I believe that the data does capture and highlight important trends and that we must strive for measurement if cross-national comparisons are to be meaningful. I must concede the importance of interviewing to this research.

12. If national case studies are to be of any use in cross-national comparisons, then more authors must define which part of the military they are studying. The higher ranks of the Mexican officer corps were selected because this group is politically active and appears in electoral lists and political positions. Professors Lieuwen, Johnson, and McAlister agree that the "military elite" in Latin America is comprised of the higher ranks of the officer corps—reported in U.S. Naval Ordnance Test Station, *A Symposium on Military Elites in Latin America* (China Lake, California: NOTS Technical Publication 3621, 27 July 1964), pp. 33 and 42.

13. David Easton, *The Political System* (New York: Alfred A. Knopf, 1953), p. 130 ff.

14. McAlister *et al., The Military in Latin American Sociopolitical Development*, p. 3 and Alfred Stepan, *The Military in Politics: Changing Patterns in Brazil* (Princeton: Princeton University Press, 1971), p. 8.

15. Samuel E. Finer, *The Man on Horseback: The Role of the Military in Politics* (New York: Praeger, 1962), pp. 61-71; Morris Janowitz, *The Military in the Political Development of New Nations* (Chicago: Chicago Uni-

versity Press, 1964), p. 101; interviews with Professor William H. Brill, Georgetown University, 1966-1968.

16. For summary translations of the military portions of the 1947-1966 speeches, see Margiotta, "The Mexican Military," pp. 92-99 and 107-11.

17. Civic action in Mexico used to mean building economic infrastructure: roads, schools, dams, irrigation ditches. In more recent years, it has focused upon reforestation; curbing plagues, disease, and insects; help during natural disasters; drug control; school repairs; and bringing medical care to rural areas.

18. A comparison with speeches in other systems is interesting. US State of the Union messages deal with defense in terms of policies and programs and not usually in public praise of the military. In Spain almost no mention of the military could be found in the major addresses of Generalissimo Franco. Of fourteen major speeches made 1964-1970, only three had extremely short references to the Spanish armed forces.

19. Described in a newspaper political gossip column written by Rogelio Cárdenas, "Frentes Políticos," *Excelsior,* 7 and 9 July 1964. Primary data sources for reports of Mexican presidential movement are the major Mexico City newspapers, *El Nacional* and *Excelsior,* 1946-1973.

20. *El Nacional,* 29 April 1967.

21. Interviews with Mexican officers; also seven volume, full color, glossy descriptions and pictures by *Banco Nacional Hipotecario Urbano y de Obras Públicas,* which funded and built the housing. These volumes, *Unidad de Habitacion Para Generales, Jefes, y Oficiales del Ejército,* were published from 1961 to 1964 as the housing was completed in the military zones; they include floor plans, pictures of the houses, and pictures of ceremonies between the president and officers and their families.

22. *Excelsior,* 21 November 1967.

23. Estimates of the size of the Mexican armed forces can be found in a yearly series, *World Military Expenditures,* published by U.S. Arms Control and Disarmament Agency, or in McAlister, *et al., The Military in Latin American Sociopolitical Evolution,* pp. 211-213. Interviews with Mexican officers disclosed that the regular forces were volunteer and provided insights into the reserve structure. An adequate description of these forces is contained in Jorge Alberto Lozoya, *El ejército mexicano (1911-1965)* (Mexico: El Colegio de México, 1965), pp. 76-81.

24. Needler, *Politics and Society in Mexico,* p. 66.

25. U.S. Arms Control and Disarmament Agency, *World Military Expenditures,* 1969, pp. 11-17.

26. Scott, *Mexican Government in Transition,* p. 47; and Richard R. Fagen and William S. Tuohy, *Politics and Privilege in a Mexican City* (Stanford, California: Stanford University Press, 1972), Chapter 2.

27. See the 1964 *Informe* and the volumes produced by *Banco Nacional Hipotecario Urbano y de Obras Públicas.*

28. Lozoya, *El ejército mexicano,* p. 125.

29. Joseph E. Loftus, *Latin American Defense Expenditures, 1938-1965*

(Santa Monica, California: The Rand Corporation FM-5310-PR/ISA, 1968), pp. 15-16, 21, 66. There are problems in compiling defense budget figures. Loftus converts his figures to constant 1960 US dollars. The Mexican sources obviously do not. In fact, the reported figures in different Mexican sources often disagree with each other in total amounts and in percentages spent on defense. This is caused by different accounting methods. We selected the figures from Secretaria de Hacienda y Crédito Público because they were basically in line with earlier trends in Loftus and relatively close to those found in US Arms Control and Disarmament Agency compilations.

30. *Ibid.,* pp. 58-62.

31. Needler, *Politics and Society in Mexico,* p. 68; David Wood, *Armed Forces in Central and South America* (London: Institute for Strategic Studies, Adelphi Papers No. 34, 1967).

32. Lozoya, *El ejército mexicano,* p. 124.

33. *Hispanic American Report* (December, 1958): 657.

34. *Informe,* 1964.

35. Interviews with Mexican officers and *El Nacional,* 11 November 1971. Interviews with crucial to understanding the pay scales and the benefits received by the Mexican officer corps. Unless otherwise indicated, my description of benefits came from these series of interviews with knowledgeable Mexican officers and from the presidential speeches (see table 2).

36. McAlister *et al., The Military in Latin American Sociopolitical Evolution,* p. 226.

37. It was reassuring to have a Mexican officer read these words about supplementing income in the military and shake his head and murmur, "Yes, yes." His grin and comments at the use of *"aviador"* to describe this practice confirmed that we had accurately depicted one facet of military income in Mexico.

38. Johnson, *The Military and Society,* p. 132.

39. *Exelsior,* 19 November 1966.

40. Brandenburg, *Making of Modern Mexico,* McAlister *et al., The Military in Latin American Sociopolitical Evolution,* p. 229.

41. In the US military promotion is based primarily upon reports rendered by supervisors. In Spain our understanding is that promotion is based primarily upon a seniority system and that the colonel and general ranks have been monopolized by the civil war generation. This promotion freeze is further compounded by a later retirement age in Spain.

42. Marvin Alisky, ed., *Who's Who in Mexican Government* (Tempe: Arizona State University Press, 1965), pp. 6, 36.

43. Padgett, *The Mexican Political System,* pp. 52-53.

44. Brandenburg, *Making of Modern Mexico,* pp. 102, 108, 113-14.

45. *El Universal,* 8 December 1964; Ruben Salazar, "Mexico Election is Contest Within Party," *The Washington Post* (16 April 1967), p. F9.

46. One notable exception was General Corona del Rosal who moved from the presidency of PRI in 1964 to the head of the National Executive Patrimony until 1966, when he became "mayor" of the Federal District;

both of these are cabinet positions. Corona del Rosal has led an interesting life, mostly as a politician and educator. He continued teaching a few hours a week at the Military College throughout his political career, while asking the press to refer to him by his civilian title of *licenciado* (lawyer), since he was a potential presidential candidate in 1970.

47. Mexico, Secretaría de la Presidencia, *Directorio del Poder Ejecutivo Federal 1971* (1971).

48. *El Día,* 26 January 1972.

49. Needler, *Politics and Society in Mexico,* p. 81.

50. Lieuwen, *Arms and Politics,* p. 118.

51. Mexico, Dirreción General Técnica de Organización, *Directorio del Gobierno Federal Poderes: Legislativo, Ejecutivo, y Judicial,* 1956.

52. Mexico, Cámara de Senadores, *Directorio, XLVI Legislatura, 1964-1967* (Publicaciones Mexicanas, S.C.L. Insurgentes Sur No. 123), 1965.

53. McAlister *et al., The Military in Latin American Sociopolitical Evolution,* p. 241.

54. I must credit communication from David Ronfeldt of the RAND Corporation in which he noted that Latin American regimes are never purely civilian or military. In applying this concept to Mexico, the idea of a continuum of civil-military government with four distinguishable categories was developed.

55. For further discussion of the period before 1946, consult Cumberland; Cline; Brandenburg; Lieuwen, *Mexican Militarism;* and Scott, *Mexican Government in Transition.*

56. I am indebted to Professors Wayne Cornelius and Douglas Hibbs for suggesting that the lack of internal war in Mexico might be a condition of nonintervention; I had neglected this facet in becoming too narrowly focused upon the indicators. Cornelius also suggested that the absence of civilian interference in internal matters of the military such as promotion and discipline, assignments, etc. might be a ninth condition. The absence of major internal war is so obvious and important that I felt free to include it without explicit proof. Further research into internal military personnel matters would be required before I would suggest that internal freedom of action is clear enough to be deemed a condition.

57. While it was not appropriate to discuss Mexican civic action programs in the context of this paper, there is ample evidence of their widespread continued use. *Every one* of the thirteen presidential speeches read praised the military's civic action performance. The military itself is proud of these contributions and the Ministry of Defense's monthly professional journal, *Revista de Ejército,* features news and pictures of civic action programs from the military zones.

Civilian Control
of the Military in Lebanon:
A Legislative Perspective

Abdo I. Baaklini

Abdo I. Baaklini is the associate director of the Comparative Development Studies Center and an assistant professor
at the Department of Public Administration of the Graduate
School of Public Affairs, State University of New York at
Albany. Dr. Baaklini's research interest concerns political
and administrative development in the less developed countries. He has written extensively on the role of legislatures in
developing countries, including *Legislatures and Political
Development: Lebanon 1842-1972.* His degrees are from
The American University of Beirut and The State University
of New York at Albany.

Lebanon's present political institutions limit the military's
role in society, even in times of crisis.*[1] Lebanese society com-
bines a dominant middle class of merchants, businessmen,
middlemen, professionals, and white-collar wage earners,
with a traditional aristocracy, which has found it possible to

*The author would like to thank the Comparative Development Studies
Center and its director, James J. Heaphey, for the financial support to undertake this research, and Miss Alia Abdul-Wahab for her research of the Lebanese Parliamentary debates.

compete politically and economically on an equal basis with the middle class and a free and highly mobile (geographically, socially, and politically) peasantry. Lebanon's political, social, and economic pluralism has confused many scholars into labeling Lebanon a "precarious republic"[2] or "improbable nation,"[3] judgments that seem valid in light of the country's recent turmoil, but of less merit in evaluating the armed forces' role in Lebanese politics. This chapter does not examine the political system as a whole, but seeks more narrowly to show how the political leadership in Lebanon achieves dominance without resorting to the military as an instrument of power.

Lebanon's present class relations originated in political and social events that occurred during the second half of the nineteenth century.[4] The middle class of that time, in collaboration with the Maronite Church (which by the late nineteenth century had become a modern bureaucratic organization displaying characteristics of political parties and military institutions), was able to mobilize the peasants against the aristocracy. The ensuing conflict led to the abolition of feudalism as a system of government. In 1858 a major peasant revolt broke out, preparing the way for a new political order where a governor appointed by the Ottoman Sublime Porte would share authority with a quasi-legislative council, the Central Administrative Council (CAC), which was to be indirectly elected by the various religious and ethnic groups in the country. Under the protection of the European powers (particularly France), the middle class was able to establish its authority at a time when the military as an institution did not yet exist. Between 1864-1915 Lebanon experienced a politically quiet period with a rapidly expanding economy. The newly devised political institutions enabled the aristocracy to continue participating in politics, although it was stripped of its economic and social prerogatives, and the expanding economy allowed it to adjust to and compete with the rising middle class. At the same time, the growing economy and the opportunity for political participation helped placate the peasants and give them a feeling of belonging to the system. Because they had attained some of their demands, they remained satisfied with the church leadership and its protection.[5] Gradually the CAC became a functioning political institution; it trained leaders, arbitrated differences, extracted and allocated resources through the budget, but most important, it became a symbol of nationhood and independence.

With the French mandate of 1920 and the promulgation of the Lebanese Constitution in 1926, this quasi-legislative institution became a full-fledged legislative body at the center of the Lebanese political system. The political leadership after independence was drawn predominantly from the middle class,[6] but due to middle-class divisions along religious, ethnic, cultural and, recently, economic lines, a tacit agreement known as the National Pact was adopted in 1943 between the Christians and the Muslims. It provided a formula for sharing political power without resorting to force.

Since independence in 1943, and in spite of the compelling reasons for a strong military establishment, Lebanon's leadership consistently and deliberately refused to enlarge and strengthen its military establishment. Even after the Six Day War in 1967 and the strong internal and external Arab pressure on Lebanon to strengthen its military establishment, this nation of approximately 3 million maintained a voluntary army that did not exceed 20,000. Only after 1973, with growing internal pressure, did Lebanon agree to a limited selective military draft system. Male students became eligible after completing their high school education; however they could be deferred if they went on to study at the university in a discipline deemed necessary to the country or if they were the principle providers of their families. For all practical purposes this limited draft was an instrument the legislature used to placate the demands of the students and other nationalist groups for full military mobilization against Israeli threats and incursions.

Civilian Control through the Executive

Lebanon's constitution, as well as its political practices and tradition, places the military under strict civilian control. The president of the Republic is the commander-in-chief of the armed forces. He is elected by parliament for one nonrenewable six-year term and is usually a legislator himself. Of the five presidents since independence, three were major political figures and members of parliament when they were elected, the fourth was a journalist, a one-time member of parliament and a cabinet minister, and the fifth was the army chief of staff. All of them, in accordance with the National Pact, have been Christian Maronites. As commander-in-chief of the armed forces the president has the power to declare states of emergency and to act on promotions, salaries, equipment, deployments, budgets, and all other matters pertaining to the military. However, the president cannot exercise his authority directly but must act through the Council of Ministers.

Again in accordance with the National Pact, the cabinet is always headed by a prime minister who is a Sunni Muslim. Since no one political party in the country commands a parliamentary majority, all cabinets are coalitions representing the various religious and political forces in the country. In this sense, the cabinet is more an executive committee of the parliament than the representative of one dominant political group.[7] Since the cabinet has to submit to a vote of confidence, the president's power is ultimately under the supervision and control of the parliament. Moreover the president owes his election to the legislature and his success in forming a cabinet that can enjoy majority support. Furthermore, since he represents only one religious group, with a limited power base, his options as a commander-in-chief are usually limited by the interests of other religious or political groups.

Nonetheless, presidents have come to enjoy strong power over the military. Between 1958-1964 President Shihab was able to forge an alliance between himself, the military, the civil bureaucracy, and the lower-middle-class intellectuals and professionals against the established political parties and politicians, especially those represented in the legislature. He was aided in this task by the fact that he had helped found the armed forces and been chief of staff since independence. Furthermore he came at the heel of a disruptive civil war that discredited many of the political leaders. The country was in a mood for a new "nonpolitical" or "clean" order, which Shihab attempted to create through his anonymous military officers, bureaucrats, and mediocre intellectuals.

Another reason presidents usually enjoy strong influence over the military, despite their political and constitutional limitations, has to do with the nature of the military leadership. When Lebanon was under French mandate between 1920 and 1943, the Maronites, who sought an independent Lebanon, supplied both the military leaders and the rank and file. The Muslim elements, who by and large wanted union with Syria, boycotted all mandate institutions, including the military. Those who opted to join the military went to Syria for their training and remained there, even after the independence of Syria and Lebanon. Although steps have been taken since independence to open the military to other elements of the population, the leadership remains predominantly Maronite.[8] Since the president is also a Maronite, he normally has easy access to the military, particularly in putting down violent political acts that may be interpreted as a threat to national security. Nonetheless, the military leadership, especially under Shihab's command, maintained its aloofness and independence for fear that it might be used politically and therefore lose the respect and support of all elements of the population. Thus in 1952 when President Bishara al Khouri and in 1958 when President Camille Shamun tried to use the military to suppress their internal political opponents, the military leadership refused to cooperate and the armed forces remained neutral.

In terms of class origin, the military in Lebanon was a refuge for the Christian nobility whose economic and social influence were on the decline. Under the French mandate the backbone of the military leadership belonged to remnants of such feudal Christian families as Shihab and Abi Lama'.[9] After independence the military provided an outlet for Christian and some Muslim families of the middle class. Most upper-middle-class families, both Christian and Muslim, were absorbed into the expanding economy as merchants, businessmen, bankers, professionals, and workers in the growing tourist and service sectors.

The composition of the Council of Ministers and its relationship to the legislature is also relevant to the subject of military control. Between 1943-1970, Lebanon had forty-three cabinets with forty-three ministers of defense. Except for a brief transitional period in 1952, the ministers of defense were civilians. In 1952 General Shihab, later the president of the republic, accepted the post of prime minister for two weeks until the parliament elected a president to succeed Bishara al-Khouri, who had been forced to resign for rigging the elections and amending the constitution to perpetuate his own presidency. Not only were the ministers of defense all civilians, but also a high degree of continuity in the post prevailed. In fact, one member of parliament, Deputy Majid Arslan, a Druze by religion, occupied the post nineteen times, as table 1 shows.

TABLE 1

DISTRIBUTION OF MINISTERS OF DEFENSE, 1943-1970

Minister	Number of Times in Defense Post
1	19
1	5
1	3
4	2
8	1

Source: Archives of the Lebanese Chamber of Deputies, compiled by the author.

All but three defense ministers were members of parliament when appointed. The three nonmembers served only one term each as minister and were either former members of parliament or civilian members of professional groups. The preponderance of civilian defense ministers and the high degree of continuity can be viewed as evidence of strong civilian control.

Civilian Control through the Legislature

Civilian control of the military is exercised at the legislative level by two major committees, Foreign Affairs and Defense. Originally the foreign affairs and the defense functions were combined under one committee in the chamber, but in 1961 the two functions were separated. Nonetheless, all defense matters are still discussed in joint sessions of the two committees.

This close association of defense and foreign affairs arises out of the Lebanese desire to subordinate military to foreign policy dictates, especially regarding the other Arab states and the western powers. The importance of these committees, especially the Foreign Affairs Committee, is indicated by the relative continuity of its membership despite such adverse conditions as a 33 percent turnover in parliament every four years and the annual election of all committees by the entire legislature. It should also be remembered that the Lebanese legislature contains no dominant political party. About one-third of the members belong to more than half a dozen political parties; the remaining two-thirds are independents. So the high degree of continuity in the two committees is significant and insures that those serving on the committee become subject matter experts. Tables 2 and 3 show the continuity and change in the Defense Committee and Foreign Affairs Committee respectively.

TABLE 2

CONTINUITY AND CHANGE IN DEFENSE COMMITTEE MEMBERSHIP, 1961-1974

Members	Number of times served in committee
4	7
1	6
3	5
11	4
11	3
4	2
6	1

TABLE 3

CONTINUITY AND CHANGE IN FOREIGN AFFAIRS COMMITTEE MEMBERSHIP, 1961-1974

Members	Number of times served in committee
1	12
1	11
—	10
1	9
1	8
3	7
1	6
5	5
2	4
15	3
16	2
12	1

Source: Archives of the Lebanese Chamber of Deputies. Compiled by the author.

This continuity, by enhancing professionalism and expertise on the part of the committee members, can be utilized to keep the military under control.

Thus far the Lebanese army has resisted the temptation to play a leading political role in the country. With the exception of the Shihabi presidency between 1958-64, when the army was politicized, military institutions have played a role subordinate to the legislature. In 1952 and 1958 the army refused to support an incumbent president against his political opponents. In 1949 and 1961 while some elements of the armed forces joined the Syrian Social National Party in unsuccessful coups d'etat, the majority refused to join and eventually helped the legitimate political leadership to restore order.

This resistance to a major political role can be attributed to the weakness of the military (some Lebanese political parties and groups claim as many members under arms as the army)[10] and to the strength of the middle class vis à vis the other classes. In other words, the middle class had structured its political institutions, particularly the legislature, to give it enough power to rule without military force. This power was enhanced by a rapidly expanding economy and by the difficulties the lower classes had in consolidating their power. While the middle class found in the legislature a mechanism and a forum to resolve its differences, both economic and political, the lower classes thus far have failed to create a political party or a political front capable of resolving differences and of attaining compromises among the various political and religious groups.

The religious composition of the top army leadership has also contributed to a weak military establishment. As officers are predominantly Maronite, the Muslim elements of the population do not care to strengthen an army that could be used to their political disadvantage. The Muslim preconditions for a strong army are that the recruitment process be opened to all segments of the population, that a compulsory draft system be established, and that the top leadership be restructured and reshuffled. A compulsory draft system would assure Muslim youth equal access to the rank and file of the army, while replacing the Christian chief of staff and his Christian aides with a joint military command composed of Muslim and Christian officers would give Muslims access to the top leadership. Christian leaders have opposed such a move on the basis that Lebanon does not have the economic resources to undertake a compulsory draft system. Moreover, the Christian leadership has feared that such a move would politicize the army and open it to elements whose commitment to an independent Lebanon is dubious. Furthermore, a strong Lebanese army would rob the Christian political leadership of a valid excuse for not participating militarily in the Arab-Israeli conflict. So far, it should be remembered, Lebanon has justified its lack of military involvement on account of its weak military.

Having decided against using the military as an instrument of power, middle-class Lebanese leadership built the legislature to further its class ends and to keep the military under control. The Chamber of Deputies contributed and continues to contribute to control of the military in two ways. First, although indirectly, the Chamber maintains the viability of the political institutions and the system by performing certain essential functions, such as conflict resolution and containment, constituency services, allocation of resources, and selection and rotation of leadership (i.e., maintaining orderly succession). It helps defend and maintain essential values such as freedom of religion, press, political parties, education, and economic activities, and it also brings the aristocracy, the middle class, and the peasants under one roof to resolve their problems. In brief, it has maintained a dynamic system.[11]

In addition, the Chamber exercises direct legislative oversight of the military. It is this area we shall explore in detail.

DEFENSE POLICIES

The Lebanese constitution states that the cabinet must secure a vote of confidence from the Chamber of Deputies before assuming power. Thus, any new cabinet has to submit its ministerial program to the Chamber for discussion and approval, and the Chamber is authorized to review all governmental policies, including defense policies. The parliamentary proceedings indicate that the Chamber has in fact played a very important role in the defense policies of the country.

The success of the Lebanese government in maintaining a neutral position vis à vis the superpowers and the Arab states was largely due to the opposing factions represented in the Lebanese house. A tacit agreement between the rightist factions, who insisted on comitting Lebanon to the West, and the more leftist nationalists, who were adamant that Lebanon aid the Arabs in the Arab-Israeli conflict, helped moderate both these tendencies.

One major policy problem the Chamber has continually faced during the past seven years has been the Palestinian commandoes and their status in Lebanese territories. Another has been relations with other Arab countries, especially in regard to the Arab-Israeli conflict. On 23 January 1967 Deputy Sami al-Boustani recognized Lebanon's responsibility in defending Palestine, but he stated that the Lebanese government should follow a clear line of policy in the Arab summit conferences, indicating to other Arab countries that Lebanon's financial situation does not allow it to reserve millions to equip its army for war. He asked the prime minister not to make any huge commitments to the war efforts.

A third important policy question has been Lebanon's commitment to the charter of the Arab League. Article Two indicates that the purpose of the league is to strengthen the ties between the Arab countries and to harmonize their political policies, but many Lebanese deputies have felt that other Arab countries have failed to consult Lebanon about major foreign policy questions. For example, many indicated that Lebanon had never been informed by other Arab countries of their preparation to take defensive military action against Israel in 1967, and so they should not expect Lebanon to contribute to the war effort.[12]

On several occasions the Chamber has also discussed purely defensive policy matters, i.e., policies concerning the purchase of armaments, the kinds of armaments needed, the possibility of compulsory military conscription, etc. After the Israeli raid on Beirut's airport, the Chamber not only questioned Lebanon's defense policy in general, but also considered the kind of armaments Lebanon uses and their purpose for defense. In the parliamentary sessions of 30 January 1969, some deputies indicated that Lebanon needed a new defensive program based on antiaircraft missiles and radar. They expressed their dissatisfaction with the purchase of Mirage jets as being useless and costly for Lebanon.[13] Many of these discussions were eventually embodied in Lebanon's arms and defense policies.

STRUCTURE

Since changes in the structure of the army or the national security force cannot become effective without the Chamber's approval, it can check any changes that might increase the power of the military. Parliament has carefully debated such structural matters as creating supporting units attached to the internal security forces, terminating and later reintroducing military training in the schools, and approving the creation of special army units called the supporters.

A significant proposal was presented by Deputy Raymond Edde on 18 May 1971 to separate the internal security force from army jurisdiction. The original legislation placing the internal security force under the army had been President Shihab's retaliation against the internal security forces for the active role they played in supporting former President Shamun in the 1958 civil war. As integration of the internal security force with the army gave the military a convenient mechanism for interference in internal political matters, Edde and other legislative leaders were determined to separate the two and thereby restrict the role of the military in politics. Edde proposed placing the internal and national security forces under the jurisdiction of the minister of interior once again, and the Chamber passed this proposal by a majority vote,[14] which signified the preponderance of civilian forces under the new leadership of President Franjieh.

JURISDICTION

The Chamber has on several occasions questioned the army's authority and jurisdiction; it has even passed legislation seriously limiting army authority and placing it under direct civilian control. Despite the serious efforts of President Fuad Shihab (1958-1964) and President Charles Helou (1964-1970) to enhance the army's political power, civilian politicians in the Chamber have consistently urged the limitation of military authority, especially that of the intelligence unit. On 26 May 1970 Deputy Saab Salam, a frequent prime minister, clearly indicated that the army, especially the intelligence unit, had overstepped its bounds and that it had been interfering in many areas outside of its jurisdiction. He cited several incidents where men of the intelligence unit were protecting individuals who had physically attacked prominent politicians, but what was more important, he suggested, was the army's direct interference in politics and in the elections.[15]

Questioning army jurisdiction has gone far beyond mere discussions. On 26 May 1970 Deputy Raymond Edde presented a bill, that subsequently passed, which placed the army under civilian control in such a way that the army cannot be deployed internally without civilian authorization and control.[16]

In addition, the bill strengthened the constitutional stipulation that states of emergency can only be declared jointly by the president of the Republic and the prime minister for a maximum period of one week—after which the Chamber's approval becomes necessary.

BUDGET ALLOCATION

Budget review is another major instrument the Chamber uses to contain the military. Lebanese parliamentary proceedings show that review of the defense budget, a routine matter in many legislatures, is often accompanied by long discussions and, in a number of cases, considerable cutbacks. Furthermore, the defense allocations are itemized in detail, and the military budget is subjected to the same close scrutiny as any other departmental budget.

Table 4 shows that in terms of military per capita expenditure between 1963 and 1973, Lebanon remained between $17-19. With the exception of Kuwait, which has a high gross national product compared to its population, Lebanon's military expenditure consumes the lowest percentage of GNP. Calculated at constant dollar value, it has fluctuated within a narrow margin ranging between 2.94 and 2.33 percent of the GNP.

In discussing the budget for 1971, Deputy Raymond Edde expounded on the need for more specificity regarding military allocations. After praising the Ministry of Defense for a 2 percent cut in the budget, he noted that LL 27 million* of the total LL166,177,700 was allocated for the purchase of weapons. When the finance minister noted that this was for buying Mirage jets, Edde quickly responded that no such item was mentioned in the budget proposals and insisted that the Chamber was entitled to know not only how much money was allocated for armaments but also what kinds of armaments were being purchased and why they were essential.[17]

---

*LL stands for Lebanese pound. The approximate 1975 rate of exchange: LL2.25 = US $1.00.

TABLE 4

MILITARY EXPENDITURES, GNP, POPULATION, AND ARMED FORCES OF SELECTED MIDDLE EASTERN COUNTRIES
1963-1972

Country		1963	1964	1965	1966	1967	1968	1969	1970	1971	1972	1973
Lebanon	Population (millions)	2.279	2.340	2.405	2.474	2.546	2.623	2.703	2.787	2.874	2.964	3.057
	Armed Forces (thousands)	16	16	17	19	19	19	19	19	20	20	20
	GNP/Constant $ (millions)	1723.7	1461.7	1581.4	1591.4	1503.6	1684.3	1697.3	1765.2	1936.1	2075.0	2220.2
	Milex/GNP %	2.52	2.33	2.48	2.65	3.08	2.87	2.94	2.75	2.52	2.46	N.A.
	Milex per capita (constant $)	19.02	14.53	16.28	17.05	18.18	18.42	18.47	17.41	16.96	17.23	N.A.
Egypt	Population (millions)	28.000	28.700	29.400	30.100	30.800	31.500	32.200	32.900	33.600	34.300	35.100
	Armed Forces (thousands)	135	160	205	215	220	195	230	255	315	390	390
	GNP/Constant $ (millions)	5615.6	5977.1	6381.0	6420.0	6329.4	6414.1	6834.1	7200.6	7421.1	7773.7	N.A.
	Milex/GNP %	8.61	8.56	9.20	7.13	6.67	8.94	9.59	12.96	13.70	14.62	15.06
	Milex per capita (constant $)	17.28	17.83	19.96	15.20	13.70	18.21	20.36	28.36	30.26	33.12	N.A.
Jordan	Population (millions)	1.813	1.872	1.934	1.998	2.064	2.132	2.204	2.277	2.353	2.432	2.514
	Armed Forces (thousands)	45	45	55	50	60	55	60	70	65	70	70
	GNP/Constant $ (millions)	505.4	600.4	668.8	694.7	745.9	716.6	787.4	702.1	716.9	706.8	680.7
	Milex/GNP %	15.25	13.14	11.86	12.22	13.31	19.46	19.34	16.80	16.77	17.43	16.91
	Milex per capita (constant $)	42.51	42.14	41.00	42.48	48.09	65.42	69.09	51.81	51.10	50.66	N.A.

Israel	Population (millions)	2.385	2.484	2.569	2.630	2.716	2.809	2.880	2.960	3.048	3.144	3.243
	Armed Forces (thousands)	65	65	65	65	75	95	100	105	130	130	130
	GNP/Constant $ (millions)	3330.0	3655.1	3987.1	4030.8	4118.0	4732.9	5319.8	5725.7	6278.2	6894.8	7170.1
	Milex/GNP %	8.58	9.91	8.96	10.64	16.32	17.70	21.35	25.92	23.75	21.62	45.41
	Milex per capita (constant $)	119.74	145.78	139.08	163.12	247.47	298.28	394.42	501.36	489.26	474.22	1003.92
Kuwait	Population (millions)	.397	.436	.478	.524	.573	.627	.686	.743	.770	.799	.828
	Armed Forces (thousands)	2	2	8	8	8	10	10	10	14	14	14
	GNP/Constant $ (millions)	2015.0	2211.8	2304.0	2583.9	2745.5	2881.4	3116.0	3393.0	3634.4	3815.7	4025.6
	Milex/GNP %	1.60	1.94	1.97	1.91	2.93	2.90	2.86	2.54	2.52	2.55	N.A.
	Milex per capita (constant $)	81.21	98.28	94.85	94.00	140.35	133.29	129.78	120.57	118.92	121.77	N.A.
Syria	Population (millions)	4.990	5.150	5.320	5.490	5.670	5.860	6.050	6.254	6.470	6.694	6.922
	Armed Forces (thousands)	75	80	80	80	80	65	75	75	110	115	115
	GNP/Constant $ (millions)	1164.2	1270.1	1304.7	1274.2	1340.0	1403.5	1627.2	1654.6	1881.8	2035.4	2147.4
	Milex/GNP %	8.71	7.28	7.01	6.96	7.07	11.02	9.73	11.77	9.10	12.25	N.A.
	Milex per capita (constant $)	20.31	17.95	17.19	16.15	16.71	26.40	26.16	31.15	26.47	37.24	N.A.

Source: *World Military Expenditures and Arms Trade 1963-73,* (U.S. Arms Control and Disarmament Agency, Washington, DC) 1974.

Probably the most significant and detailed suggestion for a budget reduction was made in 1974 when the budget proposal included LL43,628,600 for equipment and maintenance, twice the amount spent in 1973. The government's justification for such an increase rested on the army's need to replace the Mirage jets lost three years before, to buy three small planes, and to upgrade the maintenance and safeguarding of military equipment. Deputy Chafiq Badr gave a detailed and comprehensive report explaining his recommended cuts. First he argued for the elimination of the LL8,600,000 allocated to buy the Mirages on the grounds that such planes had proven inadequate for Lebanon's defense needs. He also suggested reducing the LL43,628,600 requested for the maintenance and safeguarding of military equipment to LL32,528,600. His detailed, technical justification for this cut, based on his expertise as a major arms dealer, led the Defense Committee and the Chamber to adopt his proposals unanimously.[18]

PROMOTIONS, SALARIES, AND COMPENSATIONS

Legislation dealing with promotions, salaries, and compensations also contains military ambitions. After the 1958 civil war, for instance, the legislature took up the issue of promotion and salary scale within the internal security forces. The major political forces in the legislature generally favored giving the internal security forces a bonus for their supportive role in the 1958 civil war. Some members felt that, had it not been for the internal security forces, Shamun's power would have been seriously weakened and Lebanese national security would have been threatened by local political forces who were openly receiving Syrian military aid. The House initiated legislation that called for the promotion in two grades of all internal and national security men regardless of rank, a suggestion which would rectify the previous government's acts of 1951 and 1955 that promoted only those security officers who were already in the upper rank. Despite the government's insistence that only some men be promoted, the House voted unanimously on to promote all internal and general security men who had been appointed before January 1954 and had not benefited from any previous general promotions. The Chamber's act can also be viewed as an attempt to reward the internal security forces for their part as a counterbalance to the armed forces.[19]

PARLIAMENTARY INVESTIGATION

The House can also investigate the military and hold it accountable for any action that it undertakes. Perhaps the most important incident during which the Chamber not only practiced its investigatory powers but also took definite action was the Croutal scandal of 1972.

In accordance with its military commitment as a member of the Joint Arab Military Command, Lebanon reluctantly agreed after 1967 to strengthen its antiaircraft defenses against the Israeli air force. Part of the funds for this increased defense capacity were to come from the JAMC budget and part from the regular Lebanese budget. However all expenditures were to be incurred in accordance with the regular accounting procedure for the purchase of military equipment and hardware, which is specified by law. This meant that expenditures could only take place after the legislature had authorized funds for specific purposes and only under close supervision by the Court of Accountants which oversees all government spending.

On 28 August 1968 Chief of Staff Colonel Emile Boustani signed a contract to purchase Croutal missiles at a price of F66,400,000. The French company, however, failed to deliver the missiles by the time designated, so the Lebanese cabinet terminated the contract but agreed to pay the French company a total of F9,500,000. The Chamber was furious and decided to investigate the matter. Although the deal was conducted in full compliance with the legal and procedural requirement, it was learned that hush money had been paid to those who arranged the deal, and several officers and civilians were accused of embezzling public funds.

In August 1972 an extraordinary parliamentary session was convened to discuss the Croutal missile scandal and to elect a parliamentary committee to investigate it.[20] It is important to note that the Parliamentary Committee of Investigation was granted the same judicial and investigatory powers as those of investigatory judges (including the right to subpoena), thought it did not receive the power to pass sentence.[21]

The Parliamentary Committee dealt with all aspects of the scandal, such as the relationship of the officers to the French company, the involvement of the chief of staff, and the role of the Court of Accountants. After the committee submitted its report, the Croutal issue was turned over to the regular courts. Indictments were handed down to several high officers including the commander-in-chief of the army. The *An Nahar* daily newspaper hailed the action of the parliamentary committee as a victory for democracy.[22] In addition, the Chamber passed a law on 14 September 1972 which gave the High Judicial Council, a civilian body, power to try all crimes related to armaments and ammunition agreements. By transferring this power from the military to the High Judicial Council, the Chamber sought to prevent recurrence of such crimes because the membership of the Council, unlike that of the military courts, would be less likely to cover up those crimes.[23]

IMMUNITY TO THE PRESS AND DEPUTIES

An important legislative proposal of 9 March 1974, which passed in July 1974, sought to seriously limit the army's control of the press and to give the press total immunity from military jurisdiction. The issue dated back to 1973, when *An Nahar* published the proceedings of the secret summit conference session of 1973. This action was considered a breach of the national security of Lebanon and the Arab countries, and the case was turned over to the military courts. The decree of 9 March 1974 proposed that press crimes would not be dealt with in the military courts but would be under the jurisdiction of the Courts of Appeal. Another important provision forbade precautionary arraignment of journalists, even under emergency conditions.

CONTROL OF THE MILITARY THROUGH THE PRESS

The Chamber also contains the military through declarations and articles which individual deputies publish in the press. The relationship of the press to civilian politicians is a unique and interesting one, for unlike most countries, this relationship in Lebanon is very amiable and cordial. Many of the deputies represent major party blocs whose own newspapers provide an effective vehicle for their opinions regarding the government and the army. Those deputies who are not affiliated with a paper have ample opportunity to express their views in a number of other daily newspapers. One can safely say that all ninety-nine deputies have unlimited access to the press. The press, for example, played a significant role in unraveling the Croutal scandal, for *An Nahar* cooperated closely with the parliamentary investigation committee by supplying it with the necessary documents and official letters which it was able to locate.

The Military in the Lebanese Political System[24]

In the past few years, violent civil strife between those who support the Palestinian presence in Lebanon and their right to struggle for the liberation of their land and those who oppose this presence has underlined the precarious position of the military in Lebanon. Those who have opposed the Palestinian presence, represented by some Christian political parties like the Phalange and the National Liberals parties, have felt that the military should prevent the Palestine Liberation Organization (PLO) from undertaking military activities from Lebanese soil against Israel. Such activities, they claimed, were being used by Israel as a pretext to retaliate against Lebanese civilian targets, creating an atmosphere detrimental to the political and economic development of Lebanon. It was also feared that Israel might use the existence of the PLO in South Lebanon as an excuse to occupy that part of the country. Christian and rightist leaders feared that the PLO's armed presence in Lebanon was tipping the balance of power in favor of the Muslim and leftist leadership. A strong and decisive military action against the PLO was deemed necessary. Between 1969 and 1973 a number of clashes between the army and some elements of the PLO took place. However, through the vigilance of the legislature, these incidents were contained and tension was temporarily alleviated. After the Jordanian army liquidated the PLO military presence in Jordan in 1970 and 1971, Lebanon became the main staging area for PLO military operations against Israel. Once again tension between the Lebanese Christian right and the PLO and their supporters began to build up, culminating in the bloody incidents of May 1973 where the Lebanese army (under the direct order of President Suleiman Franjieh) used all its might to deal a heavy blow to the PLO forces in Lebanon.

The lesson of 1973 was not lost on the Muslims and PLO supporters. Nor did the cabinet and legislature miss its implications. Muslim leaders and many legislative leaders (both Christian and Muslim) charged that President Franjieh had tricked the then Prime Minister Amin al-Hafiz into approving a state of emergency declaration. Once it was declared, the president as commander-in-chief ordered the army, through its Christian leadership, against the PLO and its supporters. Clearly the president could not be trusted to use the military. States of emergency should be declared by the legislature and once declared, the army should be placed under the direct control of the cabinet where all elements of the population are properly represented. The legislature and the cabinet insisted that the president should not unilaterally control and direct the use of the military.

Muslim and leftist leaders both inside and outside the legislature also clearly saw that the Lebanese army was an obedient instrument of the Christian rightist element and that in time of crisis the army was likely to be used against them. If the army was to be used in internal affairs, its leadership structure and composition must be changed and it must be placed under cabinet control where most political positions are represented.

Between 1973 and 1975 the position of the Muslim left with regard to the army prevailed and became undeclared cabinet and legislative policy. For the Christian rightist elements, this meant that in future confrontations with the PLO and its supporters, they could not be sure of the army's active support. They, therefore, hastened their own military preparedness, stocked arms and ammunition, and upgraded their military training programs. In April 1975 when the Phalange party ambushed a bus carrying some PLO supporters and killed over thirty persons, violence broke out in Beirut and Tripoli. The Phalangists still hoped that the army would come to their rescue, but if not, they were militarily prepared to fend for themselves, boasting that they commanded a first-rate militia of several thousand men and that an unspecified number of armed supporters could be mobilized in a short time. Prime Minister Rasheed al-Solh, fearing a recurrence of 1973, refused to declare a state of emergency or to call the army into action. Instead he chose to resign, accusing the Phalange party and its supporters in Parliament of fomenting violence in the country and serving the interests of Lebanon's enemies.

The resignation of al-Solh's cabinet put President Franjieh on the spot, for to use the military, he needed cabinet approval. For more than a month, while violence in several Lebanese cities continued and unabated, Franjieh failed to put together a cabinet that could secure a vote of confidence. Muslim leaders in the legislature, under pressure from their constituencies, dared not join a cabinet that Franjieh could use to call out the army against the PLO. No one wanted to serve as prime minister and share the fate of Amin al-Hafiz, who had to resign in 1973 in political disgrace for allowing Franjieh to use him. In a desperate move, Franjieh put together an extraparliamentary cabinet composed of military officers and some civilians as a way of taming the recalcitrant legislature. No sooner was this military cabinet announced than violent street demonstrations broke out in the main cities denouncing the move.[25] Demonstrators even prevented some members of the proposed military cabinet from reaching their offices. In less than three days, President Franjieh, under popular and parliamentary pressure, withdrew his nominations and started new consultations to formulate a parliamentary cabinet. Meanwhile, the level of violence had escalated between the Phalangists and the Lebanese supporters of the PLO, who saw in Franjieh's military cabinet an explicit threat to use the army to protect Christian rightist interests. Franjieh saw no way out except to form a parliamentary cabinet representative of the main legislative groups. Rasheed Karami, Franjieh's arch political opponent, became prime minister. The Phalangists, under the veto of Kamal Jumblat and his leftist and nationalist supporters, were precluded from joining the cabinet, but in return, neither Jumblat nor his supporters were represented either.

Between mid-July and the end of September 1975, Karami's cabinet succeeded, without using the army, in partially restoring order between the warring factions.[26] However, October brought more dramatic and violent fighting, which threatened to become a full-scale civil war. Nonetheless, the legislature, under Karami's cabinet, refused to call in the army. Instead steps were taken to strengthen and equip the internal security force, which is under the minister of the interior, and to put it in charge of maintaining some semblance of law and order in the country.

At the time of writing, fighting has continued and escalated. It is difficult to predict what the future will bring. It is safe to conclude, however, that the following developments, which became pronounced during the crisis, are likely to continue.

The presidency has been weakened perhaps beyond repair. President Franjieh, because he used the army unilaterally in 1973, has forfeited the traditional presidential role of arbitrator among the various religious and political groups. By his action he not only weakened the presidency but also impaired the ability of the army to be used in future internal crises.

The cabinet and consequently the legislature have emerged as the main arena for political action as well as political compromise. Between mid-July and the end of October 1975 the focus of the political activities was in the cabinet. The president was overshadowed by the prime minister. When the last ceasefire was arranged, the credit went to Karami who, with his ministers, spent eight continuous days in their offices and refused to leave the building until a ceasefire took hold. President Franjieh was enjoying his summer retreat at his presidential palace.

One characteristic of the recent fighting has been that none of the combatants has articulated a new vision of a new political order. Muslim leftists have demanded a more equitable political representation and economic distribution within the present political and economic orders. Undoubtedly the recent fighting will eventually lead to some changes in the composition and leadership of the military, to a more active socioeconomic governmental role, and perhaps to more equitable representation of hitherto underrepresented political groups.

These groups will doubtless try to amend the electoral law to allow for a stronger representation of the Muslim left. Nonetheless, the constitutional set-up is likely to continue as it is, with the core of the system—its sectarian-parliamentary proportional representation—unchanged.[27]

The recent incidents have confirmed the centrality of the legislature in the political system. The presidency, the army, traditional and modern political parties have all been discredited. It is now clearer than ever that Lebanon can only exist if it has a functioning legislature representing the full spectrum of its religious and political groups. Political integration in the Lebanese context requires the opportunity for each group to maintain its traditions and values and for each to gain proper representation in the structure of power. The 1973 incidents were due to the president's attempt to bypass the legislature and act "decisively" on his own. Time and again whenever a president attempts to weaken the legislature, violent street clashes break out.

Finally, the recent fighting in Lebanon has made apparent that the fate of Lebanon is intimately connected with the fate of the Palestinians. Peace in Lebanon depends on the establishment of peace for the Palestinians. The PLO in Lebanon has emerged as the main force without which no ceasefire can hold. From a participant in the fighting, the PLO has become the main instrument of scaling it down. Elements of the PLO roam the streets of Beirut in joint patrols with the Lebanese Internal Security Forces to insure implementation of the ceasefire agreements.

Conclusions

It is rather precarious to build generalizations based on the consideration of one case. Yet one cannot help abstracting some variables that seem to be relevant in determining the civil-military relationship in Lebanon, with the hope that they may prove relevant to other contexts. Civil-military relations in Lebanon appear to have been shaped by the following factors.

The emergence of political institutions, such as the Central Administrative Council of 1864 and the Chamber of Deputies of 1926, preceded the existence of a strong military establishment. This forced the various contending political forces to negotiate and compromise rather than use violence. Unfortunately, many developing countries upon attaining independence have contained strong military establishments and nonexistent or weak political institutions.

The existence of a legislature helped to bring the different classes, religious, and ethnic groups in Lebanese society into a working relationship, where each group developed a realistic assessment of the needs and legitimate interests of the others. The existence of a legislature provided a mechanism for social and political mobility to some (especially the middle class) and an opportunity for undertaking socioeconomic transformation for others (especially the aristocracy). The existence of a legislature also provided a mechanism for selection of political leadership and the smooth transference of power from one president to another. In time, the political need to maintain national unity became the primary criterion for choosing among alternatives. Thus, to preserve the compromise formula of the National Pact, the leadership opted against creating a strong army, although the internal conditions of the country and the external threat against Lebanese independence would have justified a strong military establishment. Instead we find that Lebanon dispersed power, both political and military, among the various political groups in the country. It is no surprise, therefore, that some of the political parties in Lebanon were able to muster military strength comparable to that of the military institutions.

During the past century the Lebanese economy has been expanding. It is a service-oriented economy where banking, tourism, trade, and exchange account for more than two-thirds of the national income. The expansion of the economy plus its tertiary nature have combined to produce a fluid class structure. In due time, the Lebanese aristocracy and peasantry adjusted to new economic institutions and means of production, and so increased the ranks of the middle class.

With a strong dominant middle class possessing a modernizing outlook, the need for the military as a source of power became unnecessary. The necessity to eliminate a "reactionary" aristocracy or a "revolutionary" peasantry, which modernizing middle classes often face in other developing countries, did not arise. Since military power was not centralized in one single institution, and since not all segments of the middle class have equal access to the military institutions, the use of the military as an instrument for settling disagreements was very risky. Other groups besides the military could resist and retaliate against any possible military action and the middle class was always conscious that using the military in settling disputes would fracture the middle class along sectarian lines. Consequently, regardless of how acute, political disputes usually had to be resolved through compromise and discussion within the confines of the legislature.

The Lebanese leadership, because of the country's structural, geographic, and demographic characteristics, was able to avoid getting involved in the Cold War. This hands-off policy of the superpowers helped in keeping the military weak and outside the realm of political activities. Because of its weakness, none of the superpowers found it advantageous to use the military to attain its foreign policy objectives in Lebanon or in the Middle East. In this Lebanon's military weakness has proved a blessing.

The ability of the legislature to air grievances, debate alternate strategies, and coordinate conflicting demands kept the military content and under political oversight and control. This control was achieved through budget review, promotions, salaries and compensations, determining the structure, defining jurisdictions and defense policy, and providing the legislature and the press with certain immunities to perform their oversight functions without fear of being dismissed.

Finally, contrary to Huntington's assertion that the military is the best institution to build political order and stability which may lead to political institutionalization in developing countries,[28] the Lebanese experience shows that political institutions can be built by other forces provided the military remains a weak institution.

While the Lebanese case may be atypical of most developing countries, nonetheless it is relevant from a research perspective. By identifying variables that have led to one pattern of civil-military relationships, we can focus in our future research on the presence or absence of these variables. The Lebanese case provides insights into what political organizations help insure civilian control over the military.

Notes to Chapter 9
Baaklini, *Civilian Control of the Military in Lebanon.*

1. For a review of the literature on the military see the following: Welch, Claude E. Jr., and Arthur K. Smith, *Military Role and Rule* (North Scituate: Duxbury Press, 1974).

Van Doorn, Jacques (ed.), *Military Professions and Military Regimes: Commitments and Conflicts,* (The Hague: Mouton Press, 1969).

Janowitz, Morris, *The Military in the Political Development of New Nations* (Chicago: University of Chicago Press, 1964).

Nordlinger, Eric A., "Soldiers in Mufti: The Impact of Military Rule Upon Economic and Social Change in the Non-Western States." *The American Political Science Review,* 64 (September 1970): 1131-48.

2. Hudson, Michael, *The Precarious Republic: Political Modernization in Lebanon* (New York: Random House, 1968).

3. Meo, Leila, *Lebanon: Improbable Nation* (Bloomington, Indiana: Indiana University Press, 1965).

4. Baaklini, Abdo I., *Legislatures and Political Development: Lebanon 1842-1972* (Durham, NC: Duke University Press, 1975).

5. This applies only to the Maronite peasants who were the majority in Mount Lebanon. The Druze peasants maintained their allegiance to their Druze aristocracy.

6. For example, in the legislature elected in 1972, less than 11 percent of the elected deputies could claim an aristocratic background. The rest were all recruited from the middle class.

7. Lebanon has more than half a dozen political parties represented in the parliament with a combined power of less than one-third of the members. The remaining two-thirds are independents who belong to no political party but have their power base in their constituency. See Baaklini, *Legislatures and Political Development,* chapter 5.

8. *New York Times* of 12 March 1975 reported that after a recent incident where the army was ordered by the president, through his cabinet, to put down a violent protest in the city of Saidon where several civilian and

military were killed, the Muslim leadership and members of the legislature were demanding that the army be placed under the command of a committee composed of various representatives of the political and religious forces in the country to replace the existing situation where the commander is a Maronite general.

9. Riyashi, Iskandar, *Qabl wa-ba'd (Before and After)* (Beirut: Maktabat al Arfan, 1953).

10. See *New York Times,* 19 September 1974.

11. Baaklini, *Legislatures and Political Development.*

12. Lebanese Parliamentary Proceedings, 1969, pp. 576-77.

13. Lebanese Parliamentary Proceedings, 1969, p. 600.

14. Lebanese Parliamentary Proceedings, 1971, p. 1952.

15. Lebanese Parliamentary Proceedings, 1970, pp. 312-14.

16. Edde's proposal dealt with the following issues:

*Excluding states of emergency, the army is not allowed to interfere in keeping order or in maintaining internal security in the country, unless a formal authorization is given to it by the civilian authorities who alone can decide under what conditions the army should take over.

*The right to authorize the army to keep the internal security is reserved to the following civilian authorities: prime minister, minister of the interior, prefects, during emergency conditions. The authorization coming from a prefect can be given to the military commander of the region and the Ministry of the Interior should be informed about that authorization immediately.

*The authorization to the army should be official (written, signed, and dated) and should indicate its purpose. In emergency conditions, the authorization could be given through a telegram or telephone call.

*The military authorities should remain in close contact with the civilian authorities, and they should always seek the advice of the latter regarding any steps that the army wants to take.

*The army is not allowed to be in control during the election time except by a special authorization from the minister of interior. It is not permitted, under any condition, to interfere in the election procedures.

*Authorization will be annulled by a decree issued by the civilian authority that issued the order.

17. Lebanese Parliamentary Proceedings, 1971, pp. 1670-71.

18. An interview with Deputy Badr in the summer of 1974.

19. Lebanese Parliamentary Proceedings, 1959, pp. 459-464.

20. Lebanese Parliamentary Proceedings, 1972, p. 290.

21. *Parliamentary Life,* 2 (1973): 106. This is a journal published by the Lebanese Chamber of Deputies in Lebanon.

22. *An Nahar,* 25 December 1971. This is the leading Lebanese newspaper published in Arabic in Beirut.

23. Lebanese Parliamentary Proceedings, 1972, pp. 512-3.

24. This part is based on information gathered during a visit to Lebanon in July and August 1975 when the author was able to meet and talk to many of the principal participants in the recent civil strife.

25. The legislative leadership against a military cabinet included all Muslim leaders such as Karami, Salam, Solh, and Ass'ad. It also included Jumblat, who represented the national and leftist forces in the country and some Christian leaders such as Edde. Only the Phalangists and the National Liberals were willing to support a military cabinet.

26. Karami's first act as prime minister was to remove the army chief of staff, Major Ghanem, who was responsible for the 1973 incident, and appoint an obscure neutral officer as his replacement.

27. One of the major demands of the leftist-national forces under the leadership of Kamal Jumblat is the abolition of the sectarian system of representation. However the recently elected president came from the Maronite sect as the National Pact requires.

28. Huntington, Samuel P., *Political Order in Changing Societies* (New Haven: Yale University Press, 1968), pp. 240-61.

Background to a Coup:
Civil-Military Relations
in Twentieth-Century Chile
and the Overthrow
of Salvador Allende

Albert L. Michaels

Introduction

Associate professor of History and director of the Council
on International Studies at the State University of New York
at Buffalo, Dr. Michaels received his degrees from the University of Pennsylvania. His publications include several articles on Mexican history; he has coedited *Insurgent Mexico*
(1969) and *Revolution in Mexico* (1969).

On 11 September 1973 the Chilean armed forces overthrew
the government of Salvador Allende. In the course of the coup
President Allende and many hundreds of his supporters died.
The victorious military did not, as many expected, prepare the

country for a return to a Christian Democratic government, but established a junta which has shown no signs of relinquishing power to any civilians. In this chapter, I will seek to explore the nature of civil-military relations preceding this coup and the reasons for the coup itself. Although many important sources are not yet available on this subject, this investigation may prove interesting to students of civil-military relations and those interested in Salvador Allende's attempt to peacefully and democratically prepare the path to a socialist Chile.

Many experts have described the twentieth-century Chilean military as highly professional and noninterventionist.[1] The reality is somewhat more complicated. It is true that the Chilean military had intervened less often and less forcefully than their Brazilian and Argentine neighbors, but its officers had always taken an active interest in national politics. Their interventions took three basic forms: direct intervention, i.e., overthrowing governments in 1924 and 1932; organizing military lodges with political goals, such as PUMA (Por Una Mañana Auspiciosa) and Linea Recta in the 1950s; and taking an active role in strike-breaking and riot control both in rural and urban areas. These interventions, although not as spectacular as those of the military in neighboring countries, have been nonetheless constant. What makes Chile different, however, is that after 1932 the military did not openly try to take over the offices of state.

Several specialists have tried to explain the Chilean military's apparent lack of political ambitions. One explanation for the apparent passivity of Chile's military is the social-base analysis of José Nun, an Argentine sociologist. In his well-known essay[2] on Latin American military intervention, Nun argues that the frequent military coups in Latin America stem from the failure of the Latin American middle classes to achieve the hegemony which would enable them to become a bourgeoisie. The disruptions of urbanization, industrialization, and inflation forced the military, officered by the children of middle-class families, to seize power in order to dislodge the oligarchy or to prevent social revolutions, destructive to both class and institutional privileges. Nun's analysis of Chilean civil-military relations is based on his perception of a growing middle-class influence in the military after the War of the Pacific in 1879. In the 1920s, he sees the Chilean military frequently intervening in politics in order to achieve middle-class financial security. By the end of the 1930s they had succeeded; the middle-class Radical party dominated Chilean politics. The Radicals created new government jobs and ruled through an increasingly powerful state bureaucracy. Chile was the "only country in the world to have a minimum salary before a minimum wage."[3]

Allain Joxe has elaborated Nun's basic conceptual framework in his interesting 1970 study of the Chilean military. Joxe also regards the Chilean military as the traditional protector of a middle class locked in a hegemonic struggle with a decaying oligarchy and a rising proletariat. The struggle grew in the twentieth century with urbanization, United States domination of the copper industry, and increasing state intervention in the economy. The army, part of the new bureaucratic middle class, kept intervening in politics, until its class privileges were relatively safe under a strong presidential system in the 1930s. After this, the military's political participation remained "permanent and latent" and its "non-intervention" after 1933 only defined the "effectiveness" with which it had achieved its political goals.[4]

A contemporary Chilean observer, Rene Balart, agrees with Nun and Joxe's view of the military as a powerful influence on Chile's political life.[5] Unlike the others, Balart stresses the army's frequent post-1930 interventions. Military lodges worked for increased budgets and a more powerful executive. The military itself intervened frequently to quell riots, strikes, or land seizures, leaving many dead, the victims almost always from the lower class.[6]

Jorge Nef, a Chilean political scientist, rejects the label of "professionalism" that others have placed on the military. Although he views the 1920s, early 1930s, the military lodges, riot control, and strike-breaking as definitive examples of an ambitious, politically active officer corps, he believes that "military adventurism" was not deterred by professionalism; rather he sees the military's power constrained by competition between the various services for funds, fear of armed opposition from the *carabiñeros* (federal police), lack of an organized civilian group to articulate a militaristic ideology, and the "avoidance of risk taking and status deprivation so common to the Chilean middle class."[7]

In my view, the Chilean army has often intervened in twentieth-century Chilean politics. It can be argued that the Chilean military had good reason to play politics, especially after Alessandri's election in 1958, when the military ran into increasing difficulty in maintaining its customary share of the budget. Although Chile had the second largest military establishment in Latin America in relation to its population,[8] the Chilean military did not obtain a commensurate share of national resources. In the late 1950s the military budget began to decline, and it never returned to the high figures of the mid-1950s. In the 1930s the military's share of the budget had risen to as high as 23 percent, by 1955 it had fallen to 11.9 percent and in 1965 it consumed only 5.8 percent.[9] Between 1967 and 1969, the military's share of Chile's gross domestic product fell from 3.3 to 2.4 percent, although it rose again in the election year of 1970.[10] By 1970 the military received a smaller budget allocation than either education or social welfare.[11] All ranks suffered from low pay; a junior lieutenant received no more than a worker, and his wife often had to work to maintain the family's middle-class status.[12] The air force budget tended to rise at the expense of the army,[13] but its officer corps had grown only 9 percent since its foundation in 1921.[14] The navy and air force received priority in the purchase of modern equipment and technology. Most army officers understood this and bitterly resented it.[15] The army also faced budgetary competition from Chile's militarized police, the *carabiñeros*. Founded in 1929 (when President Ibáñez reorganized all the nation's police into one unit under the Interior Ministry) the police enjoyed fire power almost equal to that of the army. They later came to have a larger share of the budget and a larger share of United States aid.[16] The size of both forces was about equal.[17] The army did, however, draw its officer corps from a higher social status. The *carabiñero* officer generally came from the lower classes, the police officer corps being one of the principle vehicles of social mobility in Chilean society.[18]

In 1967 a North American scholar, Roy Allen Hansen, completed an interesting study of the decline of the Chilean military career and the attitudes which the decline had engendered.[19] Through intensive interviewing, mostly of retired officers, he ascertained that most of Chile's officers came from a lower-middle-class background. The lower classes had little chance of becoming officers due to the high cost of military education and the competitive examinations for the military school, which required three years of good secondary school training. The upper or upper middle classes did not join the army for somewhat different reasons. The low level of external threat, slow promotion opportunities because of lack of expansion, low salaries, and low technological capabilities all effectively lowered military prestige, making it highly unlikely that status-conscious elite youth would choose a military career. By 1967 the officer corps recruited most of its ranks from the lower middle classes.[20]

Hansen also made some interesting observations concerning the career trajectories of the Chilean officers; after five years of military education, the young officer would be sent to a small provincial town as a garrison instructor. His social relationships were both with his troops and, more importantly, with the rural upper classes. The rural elite accepted the young officers as members of their "set," included them in their social functions, and courted them as potential husbands for their daughters.[21] The young officer next became a captain, and the most talented either went into the War Academy (general staff officer) or the Polytechnical School (military engineering). The next step would be twelve to fifteen years spent as a major or colonel commanding troops in his field of specialization. After this, he either retired or became a general. The higher the rank an officer reached, the more time he would spend either in travel (frequently to the United States or Panama) or near the capital.[22] The latter part of the officer's career was characterized by general staff contacts, travel, and close contacts with the urban middle classes.[23] He had no contact with the working class except for his own troops.

Thus one may say that by 1970 the military (and particularly the army) had steadily declined in prestige. This decline made the military career less attractive to elite youth, and it meant bitterness in the officer corps. Most evidence suggests that the officers were middle class, and as such, suffered from all the insecurities of that class—they were victims of foreign domination of the economy, inflation, stagnant economic conditions, and militant working class organizations demanding a greater share of the national surplus. The officers wanted better pay, better weapons, and higher status. The problem facing the Chilean governments was how to meet these demands while at the same time making concessions to the workers and peasants and pacifying the worried upper and middle classes. The situation was further complicated by intraclass contradictions. The military, as part of the public bureaucracy, was competing with sectors of the middle class for influence, status, and social security. There was also competition between various elements of the public sector for control and use of public funds, which were unfortunately limited by a regressive system of taxation and the stagnating economy. This intraclass competition may well have limited serious military plotting in the 1958 to 1973 period. It took the socialist government of Allende to provide the middle class with the cohesiveness necessary to bring about serious structural changes in the Chilean political and economic system, changes which they hoped would firmly secure the status and financial gains won by the middle classes after the military interventions of the 1920s and 1930s.

The Government of Eduardo Frei

The roots of the 1973 coup go back to the early twentieth century. At this time, Chilean officers resented their falling behind Argentina and Brazil in military technology and the government's frequent use of troops as strike-breakers, especially in the nitrate fields. By 1920 fear of communism became another source of military discontent.[24] The frequent military interventions and plots between 1914 and 1933 represented attempts both to head off popular mobilization and modernize the military itself.[25] In the early 1950s, after a twenty-year interval of middle-class Radical party rule, the military again began to organize. The PUMA (Por Una Mañana Auspiciosa) and Linea Recta lodges comprised groups of officers who hoped that Carlos Ibáñez would emulate Juan Perón and establish a strong military populist regime in Chile. Mostly younger officers, they hoped that Ibáñez, himself a former officer, would disperse the politicians and solve Chile's problems through dramatic authoritarian reforms.[26] These lodges failed in their aims, and many of their members were forced to retire, but they clearly showed the impatience of many young officers with the inefficiency of the Chilean political system. Some officers may have been associated with Linea Recta,[27] notably Roberto Viaux and Augusto Pinochet, who played important roles in the 1960s and 1970s.

Military disillusionment with politics greatly increased between 1952 and 1970. Although Ibáñez tended to increase military spending,[28] he did not solve Chile's political or economic problems. His successor, rightist Jorge Alessandri (1958-1964), reduced the military budget throughout his administration. In 1964 military expenditures dropped to $83,800,000 (in constant dollars of 1960). They had reached a high of $135,000,000 in 1953.[29]

The Christian Democratic government of Eduardo Frei (1964-1970) continued to downgrade the needs of Chile's already embittered military. Salaries did not rise and army equipment was not modernized.[30] The United States provided some support, but mostly for civic action projects or for elite groups like the "Grupo Movil," or the Black Berets; the army base at Peldehue became "one of the best known and most active centers of counter-insurgency in Latin America."[31] The military, discontented and angry, responded in various ways: retired officers often conspired with active officers and right-wing politicians to overthrow the government,[32] others opened relationships with the left; in May 1970 President Frei dismissed several Black Berets for maintaining contacts with the Revolutionary Movimiento Izquierda Revolucionario.[33] The government also retired its naval commander, Rear Admiral Porta Angulo, for unauthorized contacts with the Socialist Senator Salvador Allende.[34] Other officers applied direct pressure on the government. In February 1969 the army forced the Frei government to cancel a meeting with President Ongania of Argentina because of the Argentinian purchases of tanks and supersonic jets; the Chilean generals hoped to force Frei to make similar purchases.[35] In late 1969 certain officers either felt strong enough or desperate enough to take direct action. On 21 October General Robert Viaux led a tank regiment to seize the barracks of the Tacna regiment in Santiago. The rebels demanded higher pay, modern equipment, and the resignation of the unpopular Christian Democratic minister of defense. Later in an interview given after his retirement, Viaux gave vent to the disillusionment and the frustration affecting so many Chilean officers:

> Chile lacks the means to defend itself against threats from its neighbors. The past two governments of Presidents Alessandri and Frei neglected national defense. The services are undermanned, discipline is slowly deteriorating and pay rates are too low. Using the regular channels, I personally brought these things to my superiors several times but my complaints were ignored . . . . President Frei had already packed his bags, but I agreed to a compromise in the hope that our legitimate demands would be met. We were betrayed; all we got was a pay adjustment.[36]

Viaux's "Tacnazo" accomplished very little. The government dismissed the minister of defense, gave the army a small pay raise, and promised to consider buying new weapons.[37] The commander-in-chief of the army and the minister of defense retired, as did Viaux and his supporters. General Rene Schneider, a noninterventionist, became the new army commander.

As the 1970 election approached, Schneider and Viaux became politically involved. In May 1970 General Schneider told the newspaper *El Mercurio* that the army would respect parliament's constitutional right to choose freely between the two candidates receiving the greatest number of votes in the presidential election.[38] Schneider's statement was probably helpful to the left as it encouraged those voters who might hesitate to vote for Allende for fear of a military coup. Viaux, already the center of rightist plotting, responded "that General Schneider was speaking for himself . . . . Neither the Navy nor the Air Force supports his position."[39]

The 1970 election which gave the leftist Allende a small plurality over the conservative Alessandri and the Christian Democrat Tomic, split the military; Schneider declared that the army would remain neutral.[40] "The army, he promised, would only act to guarantee the Constitutional verdict."[41]

At this time President Richard Nixon gave the United States Central Intelligence Agency instructions to launch an all-out effort to prevent Allende from becoming president of Chile. The CIA became involved in the plotting of two military coups—planning that included proposals to kidnap General Schneider, thus giving the military a justification for declaring martial law and assuming the powers of government. One group, around General Viaux, inspired very little confidence in Washington and attempts were made to halt his plot. Another group, around General Camilo Valenzuela, the commander of the Santiago garrison, won United States' approval and on 24 October they received three machine guns and tear-gas grenades for use in a coup attempt. These were later returned because the plotters could not marshall enough political support, but the Viaux group had already acted and mistakenly killed Schneider when he resisted.[42] The resulting public outrage helped Allende win the backing of many who had hestitated to support his taking office. The plot's failure also helped to remove a key group of officers from positions where they later could have caused serious problems.

The danger of a rightist coup having been overcome, Chilean politicians began to debate ways to prevent the left from using the presidency to "politicize" the military. The Christian Democratic solution was to incorporate a clause into Chile's Constitution designating the army as the watchdog, "the Guarantor," of the Constitution.[43] Allende at first refused:

> We can't allow the army to be cast in the role of arbiter and guardian of democratic guarantees.

> Such an arrangement would run counter to the
> democratic and civilian tradition in Chile. I do not
> think this solution would be acceptable in any coun-
> try in the world.[44]

After much negotiation, Allende backed down. Moreover,
he promised not to interfere in the military's command structure; all appointments would follow the tradition of seniority
and professionalization. The final Allende-Christian Democratic pact, the "Estatuto de Garantias," which preceded
Allende's taking office, amounted to giving the military de jure
autonomy.[45] The government became almost helpless in dealing with the military; it could neither promote its supporters,
nor could it easily remove plotters from military command.

President Salvador Allende inherited a restive military from
his predecessor, Eduardo Frei. Frei's government had used
the military and police against strikers, urban rioters, and
squatters. The military had killed and wounded workers at
Puerto Mont and at the Salvador mine. (These incidents further harmed the military's reputation with militant workers
and squatters.) Furthermore, Carlos Altamirano, the new head
of Allende's Socialist Party, was an outspoken antimilitarist
who had been jailed for insulting the military. The military
profession had suffered both under the conservative Alessandri and the Christian Democrat Frei; it could hardly enthusiastically support Allende. The Allende coalition included
a militant working class, which not only had been traditionally
oppressed by the military, but also was prepared to challenge
the class structure which separated the poorly paid officers
from the lower classes. Allende and his advisors must have
realized how difficult it would be to coopt the officer corps,
nonetheless, they made a strong attempt that almost succeeded
in winning over the army.

The Allende Government

NOVEMBER 1970 TO OCTOBER 1972

Salvador Allende's government had some opportunity to
win over large numbers of military men to its leftist program.
Between 1958 and 1970 the Christian Democratic and Con-

servative parties had failed to markedly improve either salaries or equipment. In 1970 a *carabiñero* captain complained to a British journalist, "Opposition politicians never showed any interest in the armed forces in the past, so why should we bail them out now?"[46] Allende could win military support by raising the military budget. But the danger lay in the government's provoking class conflicts, as the middle-class officers might be faced with serious peer group and family pressure to put an end to a regime that threatened the status and privileges of the classes with which officer corps identified.

Allende started by openly recognizing the justice of the "professional demands" which had led to Viaux's 1969 revolt.[47] Throughout his term, Allende constantly sought to meet many of these demands: his government raised military salaries at every rank.[48] These increases were generally more favorable than those applied to equivalent civilian salary grades.[49] Special home construction credit was given to officers along with housing allowances, automobiles, and scholarships for military children. Travel opportunities were also increased.[50] After Allende came to power, officers in uniform could be seen in the better Santiago restaurants and hotels for the first time in years.[51] Faced with falling copper prices and food shortages, the Allende government confronted a chronic foreign exchange crisis, yet funds were always produced for new military equipment. The navy received new ships.[52] In September 1972 the government allowed the air force to investigate purchasing new airplanes, although it had placed a moratorium on the importation of many categories of capital goods.[53] Between 1970 and 1973 the defense budget rose dramatically despite inflation.[54]

Previous Chilean governments had tended to take the armed forces for granted. The military believed itself to be left out of the decision-making process on most major issues. Allende sought to give the military, "plagued with self-doubt about their role in a country where foreign wars seemed a distant probability," a new ideal of their role in a new society.[55] The government believed that the military should not remain on the fringes of society, but should integrate with Chile's developmental process directly.[56] In order to accomplish this aim the government appointed senior officers (both retired and active) to the boards of some forty corporations including the National Development Corporation (CORFO), the copper mines, and the Nuclear Energy Commission. General Orlando Urbina, the commander of the Second Division, organized the UNCTAD III conference in April 1972. Another general, Pedro Palacios, became minister of mines. Important officers were also assigned as administrators in the mines and as political "intendentes" in unruly provinces. In attempting to pacify the military, Allende was literally "riding a tiger." He hoped that by stressing his government's legality, its respect for the middle sectors, and its defense of national economic sovereignty, he could win over enough officers to enable him to serve out his term. The president constantly visited barracks on national holidays and gave out medals to show his high regard for Chile's soldiers; he usually referred to himself as "generalissimo of the armed forces," a position to which he was only entitled in time of war.[57] These tactics succeeded for a time despite Chile's increasing class conflict. The credit for their success was in part due to Allende's tactics and in part due to the presence of a sympathetic military commander-in-chief.

General Carlos Prats González became commander-in-chief of the Chilean military following Schneider's death in October 1970. Prats and his wife died on 30 September 1975 in Argentina when a bomb exploded in their car. A friend of both Schneider and Allende, and a firm constitutionalist, he tried to discourage military plotting and insure the holding of regularly scheduled elections. Prats was not a Marxist, nor was he hostile to the United States; he had graduated from the United States Army Command and General Staff College at Fort Leavenworth in 1951. In 1971 he insisted that the United States military mission remain and that joint military maneuvers continue despite opposition from the extreme left.[58] Yet while Prats remained in power, the military right was virtually helpless. Prats constantly repeated that the nation had chosen Allende's program and that he hoped that it would be completed. He praised the government's stand against monopolies and imperialism as well as the "social discipline" of the workers during the October 1972 strike. In January 1973 Prats attacked the opposition for deliberately disrupting the action of the state.[59] The anti-Allende forces heartily detested Prats; the conservative newspaper, *El Mercurio,* frequently attacked him.[60] Renan Fuentealba, the president of the Christian Democratic party, reviled Prats for his political ambition and his failure to prevent opposition civil servants from being dismissed for their role in the October strike. The Supreme Court criticized Prats because, while serving as interior minister, he had not used the police to resist illegal seizures of small farms.[61] The opposition had good reason to suspect Prats. Yet the enigmatic soldier, by agreeing to military participation in the Chilean cabinet in October 1972, unwittingly played a major role in the further politicization of the military. At the time, he rationalized the military's new role as "coparticipation between the political parties and the armed forces."[62] The "coparticipation" was, however, a distinct departure from the nonintervention of Schneider. Prats's motives were unclear; he may have been telling the truth when he said that he feared a coup, after which the "people would become Tupemaros."[63] On the other hand, he was reputed to "enjoy power" and to have political ambitions.[64] Whatever his motivation, Prats legitimized the military's more open role in Chilean politics.

Allende's tactics worked until October 1972. A minor crisis did occur when Alejandros Ríos Valdivia, Allende's first minister of defense, tactlessly stated that the military would have to support the "reforms which lead towards the crystalizing of a program, whose final goal is the socialist state." After a political uproar, Ríos backed down and promised not to politicize the military and he kept his word.[65]

The government-military coparticipation reached a new peak during Fidel Castro's visit in November 1971. Military leaders openly conferred with Castro and in January 1972, Army General Carlos Araya and Air Force General Humberto Magliochetti led a delegation to Cuba to confer with their Cuban counterparts.[66] In these months, the military often came to the government's defense. In early December 1971 rioting between left- and right-wing extremists caused Allende to declare a state of emergency in Santiago province. The provincial commander, General Augusto Pinochet, took a hard line, using police to arrest unruly demonstrators, at the same time temporarily shutting down three opposition radio stations and the rightist paper, *La Tribuna,* for inflamatory statements. In the midst of the crisis Pinochet warned "I hope the army doesn't have to come out because if they do, it will be to kill" and stated his determination to maintain order against all unruly elements "blue, yellow or green."[67] Allende seemed to be making progress by treating the military with more deference than either Frei or Alessandri.[68] The military controlled at various times the Ministry of Mines, several provinces, the armaments industry, and social and colonial development in the frontier zones. Yet serious problems in civil-military relations still remained.

The most important issue concerned the future of United States-Chilean relations. The Pentagon had enjoyed close relations with the Chilean military since the mid-1950s. The United States government supplied a significant share (9 percent) of Chile's military budget and trained many Chilean officers in the United States and Panama. Allende's election presented both countries with a dilemma. The United States did not want to aid the socialist Allende, but it feared that a Chilean military deprived of arms might turn to the Soviet Union for assistance. This would both strengthen Allende and cement Chilean-Cuban military ties. On the other hand, if Allende cut off all North American military aid, Chile would be forced to buy much new equipment whenever her US surplus broke down. There was also a danger that a break would alienate many Chilean officers who shared a fierce anti-communism with their North American counterparts. The problem was resolved by compromise. The United States continued to supply the Chilean military with weapons and training. Rather than being cut off, the Chileans received privileged treatment. The United States Embassy placed three military attachés in Santiago and thirty officers throughout the country. The United States gave the Chileans $45.6 million in military aid in 1970-1973, twice the total sent in the 1960-1964 period.[69] President Nixon exercised his waiver authority to permit Chile, along with other Latin American countries, to purchase F-5E military fighters, explaining that such action was critical to United States national security.[70] This increased aid, given despite Allende's socialism and his expropriation of American-owned copper mines did not signify United States friendship for Chile, but the determination of the United States government to prevent Russian penetration of Chile and a desire to maintain contact with the one Chilean institution capable of checking Allende's radical reforms. Allende, on his part, tried to handle United States-Chilean military relations as a professional, not a political problem. Therefore, he took no steps to disrupt military collaboration. Immediately after Allende's inauguration, General Mather, the head of the United States Southern Command, visited Chile. Other United States officers frequently traveled to and from Chile; at the same time, 200 Chilean officers and NCO's traveled to the United States or Panama for training. The United States military mission remained; joint Naval Maneuvers (UNITAS) took place with the Chilean government moving to prevent violent protests. Despite rumors to the contrary, the Chileans even allowed the United States Air Force observation stations off the Chilean coast to remain open.[71]

Given Allende's objective of maintaining Chile's independence from the United States, it was natural that his government attempt to obtain modern Soviet equipment. In December 1972 it was rumored that the Russians had offered the Chileans low-interest, long-term (1 percent, fifty-year) credits to buy Soviet military hardware, including MIG 21s. The Chilean military, led by the air force, refused, but the offer did facilitate increased military aid from the United States.[72] In May 1973 Chilean officers also rejected the attempts of General Prats to purchase Soviet tanks.[73] In the end, despite Allende's socialist and nationalist program, the Chilean military remained firmly linked to the United States. Yet the Chilean officers seemed to be gaining the best of several worlds: higher salaries, fringe benefits, and status under a socialist government combined with greater aid and modern weapons from the capitalist United States.

Many Chilean officers did not support Prats's doctrine of military "coparticipation." The failure of the rightist military plot in October 1970 discouraged many, especially in the middle ranks; it also removed the most highly placed rightist officers. After Allende's inauguration, the opposition plotting continued. Both the National and Christian Democratic parties cultivated military contacts. At the same time many officers maintained links with "Patria y Libertad," a paramilitary organization.[74] Under these provocations Allende showed remarkable patience. He did remove two outspoken conservatives, Rear Admiral Victor Bunster del Solar and Colonel Alberto Labbe, for antigovernment activities. Labbe, the director of the Chilean Military Academy, had taken the cadets on maneuvers to avoid having them receive Fidel Castro.[75] A more serious incident occurred in September 1972, after the discovery of an abortive right-wing coup, the so-called "Plan September." A naval officer reported General Alfredo Canales Marquez for making antigovernment statements. The influential fifty-four-year-old director of military education retired and the opposition press accused the government of "political" meddling.[76] Canales in retirement launched a series of antigovernment attacks. The government, he argued, was bringing "ruin" to Chile by allowing armed groups of extremists and by its propagation of class struggle; under these conditions the army's "duty" was to pressure the government into taking firmer measures against the extremists. The armed forces, he wrote, have the moral responsibility of preventing civil conflicts and civil war. In an *El Mercurio* editorial Canales stated that the high command could judge the government's constitutionality. If the Constitution was violated, the military had the duty to intervene to restore constitutionality.[77] Canales's doctrine was a dramatic rejection of Schneider's professionalism but was remarkably close to Prats's doctrine of "coparticipation" in its justification of the military's political role as a preventive of civil war.

The ultraleftist Movimiento Izquierda Revolucionario (MIR) created another serious problem for civil-military relations. MIR supported Allende but feared that his vacillations would lead to disaster for the left. The young radicals did not enter the government but concentrated their energies in activities that would force the government to accelerate radical reforms.

They had somehow obtained primitive arms and threatened to meet a coup with armed resistance. Allende, although he disagreed with MIR tactics, did nothing to discourage its activities. He maintained miristas in his personal bodyguard and in January 1971, as part of a general amnesty, he released forty-three persons jailed for terrorism under the Frei government.[78] Understandably, the military hated and feared MIR because it challenged the military monopoly of force. A further cause of tension was frequent reports that MIR and other government supporters were smuggling weapons to arm leftist paramilitary groups.[79] The military also feared that the young radicals would infiltrate its lower ranks and seriously disrupt discipline. *Punto Final,* a radical socialist journal, often carried articles demanding voting rights and better living conditions for the military rank and file.

THE DECLINE: ALLENDE AND THE CHILEAN MILITARY, OCTOBER 1972 TO SEPTEMBER 1973.

On 10 October 1972, Chile's 50,000 truck drivers launched an indefinite strike in demand of higher pay, more spare parts for their vehicles, and other concessions. Government efforts to achieve a compromise failed and soon small farmers, lawyers, pilots, businessmen, and white-collar workers joined the truck drivers. There was much violence as government supporters and opposition engaged in heavy streetfighting. On 31 October the military joined Allende's cabinet; General Prats González became minister of interior and vice president, Admiral Ismael Huerta took over public works, and Air Marshall Claudio Sepúlveda Donoso became minister of mines. (Although earlier General Pedro Palacios had been mining minister, he had served as a technocrat rather than as a military man.) The entrance of these three US-trained senior officers into the cabinet marked a new turn in the politicization of Chilean civil-military relations. Admiral Huerta soon became critical of the government's food distribution policy and resigned, to be rapidly replaced by another navy man.[80] The strike ended in a compromise, but the military decided to stay on until the March elections. On 27 March the military left the cabinet to allow Allende to form a new government on the basis of the election results.

The military's entrance into the cabinet in late 1972 made the coup of September 1973 probable. The officers could not function amid the squabbling, petty jealousies, and inefficiencies of the Unidad Popular government. Their frustration was increased by their inability to appoint military men to the lower echelons of the ministries assigned to them. In practice, the ministers were often ignored by their Allende-appointed assistants.[81] The military's entrance into politics angered the extreme left, who believed that the soldiers were trying to slow social change,[82] the right accused the military men of betraying their professional obligations by supporting the government. The effect was to isolate Prats from the majority of the military, who were basically antigovernment. Most important, the military was now playing the "moderating role" that the Christian Democrats had demanded in October 1970. The soldiers also tended to act as the middle classes' spokesmen within the government. All major political parties seemed to agree that the military had a duty to take an active part in politics in order to prevent civil war and economic chaos.

On 23 January 1973 the government increased the military's political role by appointing two army colonels, one admiral, one air force general, and one *carabiñero* general to the ministry of economy to work on solving the nation's serious food crisis. The next day Allende appointed Air Force General Alberto Bachelet to direct the "national secretariat of distribution and commercialization," which had recently been established by presidential decree. Bachelet continued in this position throughout the Allende government; his presence increased the fears of some small businessmen that the military was cooperating in a state takeover of the entire economy.[83]

The election in March solved nothing. The minority government, bitterly opposed by the upper and middle classes, could not solve Chile's long-standing inflationary problem. In the midst of rising tension there was an increasing "feeling that something decisive was about to happen."[84] Serious rioting broke out in May, leaving several dead and reopening the possibility that the military would reenter the cabinet to prevent civil war. In June military men openly opposed the government's mild plan to reorganize Chile's educational system. Admiral Huerta was especially active as an opposition spokesman. General Prats called a special meeting to explain the reform to the armed forces but was shouted down.[85] Later in the month a council of generals, by a vote of eighteen to six, rejected Prats's suggestion that the military reenter the cabinet.[86] Prats's humiliation was compounded by an incident on 27 June, when he fired his gun into the air after being insulted by a middle-class woman in a passing Renault.[87]

The military was obviously becoming restive. There were reports of plots and counterplots. The noncommissioned officers in two air force units went on strike for higher wages, the first strike movement in the military under Allende.[88] The military's uneasiness in this period becomes clear in an open letter five retired officers sent to Allende in June 1973; the import of the letter was that Chile's social situation had seriously deteriorated, both in the urban areas and the countryside. More serious still, legal authorities had lost their legitimacy, the laws were not being impartially applied, and the Constitution had been violated. The government, the officers wrote, had "wrecked the economy," impeded unarmed public meetings, made requisitions without respect to private property, and tried to deny freedom of education. Finally, these errors might lead to a split between the armed forces and the government.[89] Allende believed this letter to be important enough to answer it publicly.

On 24 June a Santiago regiment revolted; Colonel Roberto Souper, the commander of the Second Armored Regiment, led 400 of his men and four tanks against the National Palace and the Defense Ministry. General Prats led the counterattack; heavy fighting resulted in the death of twenty-four persons and the wounding of many more. The rebels rapidly surrendered, even before their allies in other units could act.[90] The rebellion, an effort of troops supposedly linked to "Patria y Libertad," had little chance of success, but it had serious repercussions. As soon as the fighting began, workers' brigades rushed to their plants and set up defense zones. Many of these plants remained under worker control, thus increasing fears in the surviving private sector.[91] The government asked for a ninety-day "state of siege," with limitation of constitutional guarantees; the Christian Democratic deputies refused to support the government's request unless the military reentered the cabinet. Allende did not yet concur, and the government motion was defeated. A grateful Allende praised Prats's loyalty, and on 5 July the armed forces commanders pledged their loyalty to Allende.[92] These measures did not help. "Patria y Libertad" planned and carried out sabotage.[93] Unidentified terrorists assassinated Allende's chief military aide, Captain Arturo Araya. And on 26 July the powerful truckers launched a second "indefinite walkout." Strike-related violence again began to increase throughout Chile.

In March 1973 the Allende government won 44 percent of the vote in congressional elections. This result dismayed the opposition, which had hoped to impeach him by winning a two-thirds majority. The upper- and middle-class opposition, concentrated largely in the National and Christian Democratic parties, then bent all its efforts to bringing about a military coup. In late August 1973 the Chilean opposition deputies voted a resolution accusing Allende of overstepping the Constitution and the law. The Constitution, they claimed, had suffered a "grave collapse." The armed forces were urged to establish order throughout the nation. Eduardo Frei, the Christian Democratic leader, asked for sufficient military force to guarantee the Constitution and the law. This declaration had followed a long series of bitter disputes in which the Chilean courts and the controller general disputed the legality of many government acts. They were supported by many officers ready and anxious to seize power for their own ends. The importance of the March elections was verified by Air Force General Gústavo Leigh, who told an Italian journalist, "We began preparations to overthrow Allende in March, 1973, immediately after the legislative elections."[94]

The military plotters had a valuable weapon in the "Ley de Control de Armas"; this law, allowing searches for and seizures of illegal weaponry, was passed immediately after the October strike; Allende did not veto it. For nine months the law was not applied; then between July and September 1973 the military carried out twenty-four operations mainly against leftist groups and factories controlled by militant workers.[95] The operations proved immensely successful. The military found arms, intimidated many workers, identified government supporters within the military who did not enthusiastically take part in the searches, and most important, the officers could be reassured that their rank and file would rapidly go into action against the workers.

The abortive coups (October 1970 and June 1973) had shown the conspirators the importance of getting rid of Prats and the other officers who persisted in their support of the legal government. On 9 August Prats, Admiral Raul Montero, General César Ruiz Danyau (air force), and General José Marío Sepúlveda entered a cabinet of "national security." The military, before joining the government, made Allende promise to restore "order," to appoint military men to lower echelon ministerial positions, and to outlaw parallel armed organizations.[96] Prats again had relieved the government, but the military presence enraged both the right and much of the left, including MIR, the Social Christians (MAPU), and the Altamirano wing of the Socialist party. The loyal military themselves were in a terrible dilemma. Their presence in the government obligated them to use force against the strikers,[97] with whose cause many of their officers sympathized. Although such actions tended to drive a wedge between the military and the opposition parties, it also increased the determination and desperation of the opposition within the military. This contradiction led to increasing cohesion in the anti-Prats faction in the military and finally to Prats's resignation on 22 August 1973. His resignation followed on the heels of an antigovernment demonstration outside Prats's house by military wives (including those of six generals). The police broke up the women's demonstration with tear gas, enraging their husbands and other commanders. Prats explained his departure as an effort to avoid a serious crisis over this particular incident.

> The protest demonstrations outside my house were attended by the wives of a number of generals. I could not be the cause of a split in the army. I would have had to send them all into retirement and that would have precipitated a coup.[98]

Prats's resignation had certainly been preceded by military unrest, including the resignation of Air Force General Ruiz Danyau from the cabinet. Yet according to Juan Garces, a close Allende advisor, Prats resigned not because of military opposition but because Allende refused to allow him to force the dissidents into retirement from the army.[99] Generals Marío Sepúlveda (Santiago garrison commander) and Guilermo Pickering (director of military institutes), both constitutionalists, departed with Prats. Orlando Letelier, a former international banker and diplomat, became minister of war and Augusto Pinochet became commander-in-chief of the army. Pinochet had commanded the troops who had forcibly put down the mining strike at El Salvador in 1966. In the Allende period he had loyally supported Prats and appeared to be a firm constitutionalist.

In September Chile polarized into two camps. The arms raids, arrests of leftist sympathizers in the navy,[100] and Prats's resignation had placed the military in the opposition ranks. Many leftists became more and more convinced of the necessity of a "dictatorship of the people." One socialist deputy called General Torres de la Cruz, the leader of frequent arms raids in the south, "a satrap, meglomaniac and a madman." Even Luis Corvalán, the moderate Communist party leader, engaged in violent rhetoric in a late August speech.

> If the reactionaries resort to armed struggle let no one doubt the people will rise up as one man and smash them immediately. In such a situation which we do not seek, which we wish to avoid, but which we may have to confront, we will use everything at our disposal even the very stones as weapons of combat.[101]

On 5 September serious violence again took place. Air force troops machine-gunned the Sumar nylon factory, wounding three workers and damaging the building. Twenty-three civilians were arrested but not before a large civilian crowd of 1,000 surrounded the building, preventing the troops' departure. At this time the leftist leader, Jaime Faivovich, warned that "the armed forces are provoking the workers; they want to give the impression that they are the supreme authority of this country . . . . The military coup is already under way in Chile."[102] Less than a week after the Sumar raid, the military seized power, ending forty years of democratic government.

Conclusion

The events of September 1973 showed that the Chilean officer corps could act with impressive speed and cohesion. The departure of Prats, Pickering, and Sepúlveda prepared the way for the majority of the army, navy, air force, and *carabiñero* officers to put an end to a democratic tradition which many had long abhorred. The coup itself was not the result of a changed attitude towards democratic institutions among the officers but the result of an institutional crisis which enabled the military to seize power with the support of probably half the population, including most of the upper and middle classes. The political and economic crisis of August-September 1973 gave the military the excuse to seize power, but behind that seizure lay a number of other complex motivations.

AN INTERVENTIONIST TRADITION

The military had often intervened before 1933, occasionally ruling through juntas. The motivations of these early militarists were often obscure. Some wanted the establishment of a middle-class hegemony, others claimed to desire "socialism" or any other clear alternative to Chile's inefficient political institutions. What is important is that the military had intervened and had done so successfully less than fifty years before Allende fell. The PUMA and Linea Recta lodges (1951-1955) continued this tradition. Their members, mostly younger officers, wanted to help President Ibáñez establish a strong executive system which would be able to override the squabbling of Chile's diverse (1950s) political parties. There were frequent plots and conspiracies during the Alessandri and Frei periods, but none were of a serious nature until Viaux's Tacnazo. Again in October 1970 important senior officers joined a dangerous antidemocratic plot. Prats and Allende did manage to hold this conspiratorial tendency in check for almost two years, but the Labbe and Canales incidents, the reduction of

Viaux's sentence by a military court,[103] and the June 1973 uprising showed the fragility of their control. It seems obvious that many, if not a majority, of Chile's military officers believed they could run the country more efficiently than the politicians;[104] all that was needed was for the opportunity to present itself.

PROFESSIONAL GRIEVANCES

The Alessandri and Frei governments had largely ignored the military. Salaries remained low and equipment dated. Although Chile had received much United States military aid, the Viaux incident suggests that this aid did not go nearly far enough to satisfy the Chilean military's perceived needs. Allende went a long way towards remedying these problems, raising salaries and appropriating scarce foreign exchange for new weapons, yet his government created a new set of problems. Most officers had been indoctrinated in ideological anticommunism, but communists played an integral part in Allende's government. Leftist groups such as MIR and MAPU had new freedom to organize among the military rank and file for better living conditions and political rights, thus threatening traditional discipline and chains of command. The self-arming of MIR and other government supporters also served to alienate the officers of all services who feared the loss of their weapons monopoly.

THE OPPOSITION OF THE MIDDLE CLASS

Although United Nations statistics show that the middle classes did relatively well economically under Allende, most of this sector turned bitterly against the government. Chile's world record 238 percent inflation partially explains this, as does the 5.7 percent drop in Chile's gross national product.[105] More important, however, was the growing militancy of Chile's working class. The struggles of the Allende years had changed the working class's economic perspective to a desire for socialism.[106] An excellent definition of middle-class hostility to Allende came from a small shopkeeper who told a French correspondent:

It's because when popular unity was in power I felt crushed, I felt I was being victimised for my life style. People who used to respect me actually insulted me.[107]

Most officers (except in the *carabiñeros*) originated in the middle and lower middle classes.[108] Allende sought to keep military salaries above the rate of inflation, yet this did not suffice. On 11 September the Chilean officer corps proved the importance of class loyalties, which transcended all efforts of the government to win them over with economic concessions.

Notes to Chapter 10
Michaels, *Background to a Coup.*

1. Roy Allen Hansen, "Military Culture and Organizational Decline" (Ph.D. dis., University of California/Los Angeles, 1967), p. 65; Alfred Stepan, *The Military in Politics: Changing Patterns in Brazil* (Princeton: Princeton University Press, 1971), p. 55; John Johnson, *The Military and Society in Latin America* (Stanford: Stanford University Press, 1964), pp 69-71, 169-170; Edwin Lieuwin, *Arms and Politics in Latin America* (New York: Frederick A. Praeger, 1961), p. 168.

2. José Nun, "The Middle Class Military Coup", in Claudio Veliz, ed., *The Politics of Conformity in Latin America* (London, New York, and Toronto: Oxford University Press, 1967).

3. *Ibid.,* p. 105.

4. Allain Joxe, *Las Fuerzas Armadas en el Sistema Político Chileno* (Santiago: Editorial Universitaria, S.A., 1970), pp. 30-45.

5. Rene Balart, "Las Fuerzas Armadas y la historia política Chilena," *Punto Final,* 3 July 1973, pp. 1-8.

6. *Ibid.*

7. Jorge Nef, "The Politics of Repression: the Social Pathology of the Chilean Military," *Latin American Perspectives* 1, 2 (Summer 1974): 58-78.

8. Stepan, *The Military in Politics,* p. 24.

9. Joxe, *Las Fuerzas Armadas,* p. 89.

10. Gertrude E. Hare, *Latin American Military Expenditures* (Washington: Office of External Research, Bureau of Intelligence and Research, Department of State Publication 8720, 1973), p. 24.

11. Hansen, "Military Culture," p. 24, *New York Times,* 20 September 1970.

12. Hansen, "Military Culture," p. 200.

13. *Ibid.*

14. Cristan Zegers Ariztia, "The Armed Forces, Support of a Democratic Institutionality" in Tomas P. Machale *et al., Chile: A Critical Survey* (Santiago: Institute of General Studies, 1972), p. 312.

15. Hansen, "Military Culture," pp. 200-201.

16. Hansen, "Military Culture," p. 111. *New York Times,* 20 September 1970; Joxe, *Las Fuerzas Armadas,* p. 98.

17. Hansen, "Military Culture," p. 196 puts army at 21-22,000; *New York Times,* 20 September 1970 puts *carabiñeros* at 26,000; Joxe *Las Fuerzas Armadas,* p. 46 puts *carabiñeros* at 24,000; a later work by Laurence Birns (ed.) *The End of Chilean Democracy* (New York: The Seabury Press, 1974), pp. 33-34, in a section on Chile's armed forces, puts the army at 32,000 and the *carabiñeros* at 32,000.

18. Joxe, *Las Fuerzas Armadas,* p. 61; *Times of the Americas,* 14 November 1969.

19. Hansen, "Military Culture."

20. *Ibid.,* pp. 200-203.

21. *Ibid.,* pp. 163-180.

22. *Ibid.,* pp. 178-180.

23. *Ibid.,* p. 181.

24. Joxe, *Las Fuerzas Armadas,* p. 54.

25. Nef, "The Politics of Repression," p. 67.

26. Joxe, *Las Fuerzas Armadas,* pp. 54, 74-82; Johnson, *The Military and Society,* p. 125; H.E. Bicheno, "Anti Parliamentary Themes in Chilean History" in Kenneth Medhurst, ed., *Allende's Chile* (London: Hart Davis Macgibbon, 1973), p. 104; Raul Ampuero, "El poder Político y las Fuerzas Armadas," *Punto Final,* Suplemento, 10 April 1973, p. 8.

27. Nef, "The Politics of Repression," p. 62; Kyle Steenland, "The Coup in Chile," *Latin American Perspectives* 1, 2 (Summer, 1974): 4-30.

28. Joxe, *Las Fuerzas Armadas,* p. 89.

29. *Ibid.,* pp. 84-96.

30. Edward Martin "Coup in Chile," *Wall Street Journal,* 12 September 1973, pp. 1, 7; John D. Habron "About Face for Chile's Generals," *Christian Science Monitor,* 16 October 1973. Marcio Moreira Alves "The Coup that Never Was," *Commonweal,* 28 November 1968, pp. 277-278; *Times of the Americas,* 16 November 1969.

31. *Le Monde,* 29 October 1969; Joxe, *Las Fuerzas Armadas* estimates that the United States supplied Chile with 9 percent of her military budget (108).

32. *Le Monde,* 20 May 1970; *Times of the Americas,* 17 December 1969; *New York Times,* 26 March 1970.

33. *Le Monde,* 20 May 1970.

34. Robert Moss, *Chile's Marxist Experiment* (New York, Toronto: John Wiley and Sons, 1973), p. 161.

35. Marcel Niedergang, "Chile: Candidate for the Officers Club," *Le Monde,* 8 July 1970, p. 6.

36. *Ibid.*

37. Moreira Alves, "The Coup that Never Was," p. 278.

38. Niedergang, "Chile: Candidate for the Officers Club," p. 6.

39. *Ibid.*

40. Interview with *El Mercurio,* 7 May 1970, quoted in Niedgergang, "Chile: Candidate for the Officers Club," p. 6.

41. Ampuero, "El Poder Político," p. 9.

42. *New York Times,* 24 July 1975.

43. *Le Monde,* 14 October 1973; Stepan, *The Military in Politics,* p. 79.

44. Quoted in *Le Monde* 14 October 1970.

45. Nef, "The Politics of Repression," p. 67, *New York Times,* 1 November 1974.

46. Alistair Horne, *Small Earthquake in Chile* (New York: Viking Press, 1972), p. 142.

47. Phillipe Labreveux, "The Chilean Army: Behind the Facade of Unity," *The Manchester Guardian,* 12 January 1974, p. 15.

48. Richard Gott, "Allende Rides a Tiger," *The Manchester Guardian,* 18 November 1972, p. 7; *Latin America,* 8 December 1972.

49. Allain Joxe, "Is the Chilean Road to Socialism Blocked?" in J. Ann Zammit, ed., *The Chilean Road to Socialism* (Austin and Sussex: University of Texas Press and Institute of Development Studies at the University of Sussex, 1973), p. 234.

50. *Latin America,* 8 December 1972; Joxe, "Is the Chilean Road to Socialism Blocked?" pp. 234-235; Labreveux, "The Chilean Army," p. 15; William F. Buckley, "Chile's Communist Experiment Could be Drawing Near its End," *Miami Herald,* 7 December 1972; Gott, "Allende Rides a Tiger," p. 7.

51. Moss, *Chile's Marxist Experiment,* p. 155.

52. *Ibid.,* p. 160; Buckley, "Chile's Marxist Experiment Could be Drawing Near its End"; Labreveux, "The Chilean Army," p. 15.

53. *Latin America,* 15 September 1972.

54. Labreveux, "The Chilean Army," p. 15; Hare, *Latin American Military Expenditures,* p. 22.

55. Gott, "Allende Rides a Tiger," p. 7.

56. Salvador Allende, "Interview with the Foreign Press, May 5, 1971", in Juan Garces, ed., *Chile's Road to Socialism: Salvador Allende* (Middlesex, England: Penguin Books, 1973), pp. 135-137.

57. Ariztia, "The Armed Forces," p. 315.

58. *Washington Post,* 24 October 1972; *The Manchester Guardian,* 30 December 1972.

59. *Chile Hoy,* 7 January 1973; *Latin America,* 8 December 1972, 18 January 1973.

60. *The Times of the Americas,* 31 January 1973.

61. *Latin America,* 22 December 1972; Moss, *Chile's Marxist Experiment,* p. 191.

62. *Ibid.,* p. 167.

63. *Latin America,* 8 December 1973.

64. Habron, "About Face for Chile's Generals"; *Latin America,* 8 December 1972.

65. Ariztia, "The Armed Forces," p. 313.

66. *Manchester Guardian,* 8 January 1971; *Granma* (Havana) 30 January 1972.

67. *Manchester Guardian,* 11 December 1971; *New York Times,* 3, 4, 10, 12 December 1971; *Latin America,* 10 December 1971.

68. *Manchester Guardian,* 24 June 1972.

69. Labreveux, "The Chilean Army," p. 15; Richard E. Feinberg, "Dependency and the Defeat of Allende," *Latin American Perspectives,* 1, 2 (Summer, 1974): 41.

70. US Department of State, *Department of State Bulletin,* 16 July 1973, p. 90; Labreveux, "The Chilean Armed Forces," p. 15.

71. *New York Times,* 30 June 1971, 12 December 1972; Robinson Rojas, "The Military," in Dale Johnson, ed., *The Chilean Road to Socialism* (Garden City, New York: Anchor Books, 1973) p. 320.

72. *New York Times,* 4 December 1972; *Miami Herald,* 12 October 1972; *Christian Science Monitor,* 28 December 1972; *Washington Post,* 24 October 1972, 19 August 1973.

73. Labreveux, "The Chilean Army," p. 15.

74. *Chile Hoy,* 7-13 September 1973.

75. Moss, *Chile's Marxist Experiment,* p. 162; Ampuero, "El Poder Político," p. 10; Ariztia, "The Armed Forces," p. 315.

76. *The Times of the Americas,* 11 October 1972; *Miami Herald,* 24 September 1972; *New York Times,* 24 September 1972; *Latin America,* 6 October 1972; Moss, *Chile's Marxist Experiment,* pp. 162-163.

77. Ampuero, "El Poder Político," p. 10; Moss, *Chile's Marxist Experiment,* pp. 162-164.

78. *Granma* (Havana), 20 June 1971.

79. *New York Times,* 30 July 1972; *Los Angeles Times,* 12 April 1972.

80. *Chile Hoy,* 24-30 August 1972; Moss, *Chile's Marxist Experiment,* p. 172; *Latin America,* 9 February 1972.

81. *Washington Post,* 10 August 1973; *Latin America,* 24 August 1972.

82. Moss, *Chile's Marxist Experiment,* p. 157.

83. *Miami Herald,* 23, 24 January 1973; *Latin America,* 26 January 1973.

84. *Los Angeles Times,* 11 May 1973.

85. *Chile Hoy,* 24-30 August 1973; Edward Martin, *Coup in Chile,* pp. 1, 7.

86. Moss, *Chile's Marxist Experiment,* p. 141.

87. *New York Times,* 28 June 1973.

88. *Latin America,* 22 June 1973.

89. *Ercilla,* 13-14 June, p. 73. *Latin America,* 8 June 1973.

90. *Washington Post,* 30 June 1973; *New York Times,* 30 June 1973; *Chile Hoy;* 31 August-7 September 1973; 24-30 August 1973.

91. Barbara Stallings and Andy Zimbalist, "Showdown in Chile," *Monthly Review* 25, 5 (October, 1973): 17.

92. *New York Times,* 1 July 1973; *Miami Herald,* 1, 13 July 1973.

93. *Chile Hoy,* 7-13 September 1973.

94. Ralph Miliband, "The Coup in Chile," in Ralph Miliband and Ralph Saville, ed. *The Socialist Register* (London: The Merlin Press, 1973), p. 454. Admiral José Toribio Merino claims that he and other naval officers did not begin plotting until mid-August 1973. See *Miami Herald,* 9 September 1974. General Pinochet claims that military plotting began in April 1972. See James Petras, "Reflections on the Chilean Experience: The Petite Bourgeoisie and Working Class," *Socialist Revolution* 4, 1 (January through March, 1974): 49.

95. Laurence Whitehead, "The Generals Trim Allende's Power," *The Manchester Guardian,* 8 September 1973; Zimbalist and Stallings, "Showdown in Chile," p. 20; *Miami Herald,* 12, 18 July 1973; *New York Times,* 8, 10 August, 2 September 1973; *Punto Final,* 11 September 1973.

96. *New York Times,* 9, 10 August 1973; *Latin America,* 24 August 1973.

97. *New York Times,* 16 August 1973; *Miami Herald,* 17 August 1973; *Latin America,* 10 August 1973.

98. *The Manchester Guardian,* 8 September 1973.

99. Juan Garces, "How They Killed a Democratic Revolution," p. 15; Steenland, "Coup in Chile," p. 146.

100. *Chile Hoy,* 24-30 August 1973.

101. Laurence Whitehead, "Allende's Legacy of Bitterness," *The Manchester Guardian,* 11 August 1973, p. 8.

102. *Washington Post,* 9 September 1973; Steenland, "The Coup in Chile," p. 13.

103. *The Times of the Americas,* 20 October 1972; *Latin America,* 22 December 1972.

104. Hansen, "Military Culture," pp. 264-305. He discusses military attitudes in 1967.

105. *Ercilla,* 12 June 1973; Pierre Kalfon, "Chile's Ailing Revolution," *The Manchester Guardian,* 14 July 1973, p. 6; William Montealbano, "Inflation Tightens the Squeeze on Chile's Middle Class," *Miami Herald,* 27 May 1973; Comision Economica para America Latina, *Notas Sobre la Economia y el Desarollo de la America Latina,* 160 (June 1974): 11, puts the inflation at 500 percent between December 1972 and December 1973. Danielle Hunebelle's "Chile," *International Letter* 6 (1 March 1974) claims that 1973 inflation reached 753 percent.

106. James Petras, "Reflections on the Chilean Experience," p. 53.

107. Jean-Pierre Clerc, "A Year of Law and Order," *The Manchester Guardian,* 28 September 1975.

108. *The Manchester Guardian,* 5 January 1975.

Two Strategies
of Civilian Control:
Some Concluding Observations

Claude E. Welch, Jr.

The preceding chapters have raised varied arguments point-
ing to a single conclusion: civilian control can be achieved
and maintained in developing countries, but only with skill,
patience, leadership, and a not inconsiderable amount of good
luck. Barring extensive external pressures or the impact of violent political revolution, political leaders must work, within
the constraints of limited time, resources, and political flexi-
bility, toward the subordination of the armed forces.

No single prescription for civilian control can be devised to
apply to the scores of developing countries. Political systems
are unique in their combinations of circumstances. The precise ingredients—the political strength of the military, the
political strength of civilian institutions, the resources available—vary from state to state. It is possible to offer modest
and tentative generalizations, however, about strategies for
civilian control. In essence, these strategies encourage movement across the continuum of civil-military interactions presented in chapter 1, away from military *control* of politics or
military *participation* in politics that smacks of blackmail,
toward military *influence* in politics. This chapter, as a closing
commentary on the ten case studies, suggests two approaches
to enhancing civilian control of the armed forces, one concentrating on the mutual restraint of officers and politicians, the

second concentrating on enhanced governmental legitimacy and effectiveness.

We should initially distinguish, albeit roughly, between factors that are essentially unalterable by government action, and factors potentially changeable by government action; the latter category should be further differentiated into short- and long-term factors.

Short of engaging in wholescale, successful war, or in annexations unopposed by affected states, no country today can realistically aspire to a major redrawing of frontiers. Secession and decolonization have been far more characteristic of the twentieth century than political amalgamation. Efforts at regional integration, despite their success in harmonizing economic policies, have yet to result in totally new political systems with centralized control of force. The geographic settings mentioned in chapter 1 should accordingly be regarded as givens.

In the short term, barring discovery and exploitation of valuable natural resources, or wholesale capital transfers from another country, no state can significantly alter its economic situation. Thus, if civilian control of the military is causally linked to relatively high levels of affluence, the prospects for political subordination of the armed forces in most of the Third World appear dim for the foreseeable future. To the extent that competition for a slice of a small economic pie encourages overt military involvement in politics, the ineluctable fact of underdevelopment will weaken civilian control.

Each generation of historians may revise the views of their predecessors; they cannot remove the weight of the past. Of particular importance is the extent to which a pattern of extensive military involvement in politics persists over time.[1] Once the cycle of coup and countercoup has been started,[2] no simple steps can reverse it. As Finer has written, "The most likely outcome of one military coup and one military regime in the Third World is a second coup and a second military regime, separated by bouts of indirect military rule, mono-partism, and feebly functioning competitive party politics . . . ."[3] Where political legitimacy is weak, or lacking—or, in Finer's terminology, with "minimal" or "low" political culture[4]—civilian governors may rule on the sufferance of those who control the armed forces. In other words, a heritage of military intervention or extensive involvement in politics cannot be undone.

The final given is the extent of latent social differentiations. Heterogeneous or plural societies, one can suggest, may be particularly susceptible to military intervention. The reasons lie in social fragmentation, which presents a grave potential for domestic strife in the absence of widely accepted values. Deutsch, in differentiating between assimilation and social mobilization, has pointed to the intractability of issues faced by a state like Guyana.[5] Political disputes become increasingly polarized and linked to race, as "primordial sentiments"[6] become more salient. These sentiments can cut across the institutional boundaries of the armed forces, resulting in their politicization and embroilment in domestic disputes. Although it is possible to avoid exacerbating social cleavages in the short term,[7] the potential for conflict cannot be denied. The explosion of conflict may well incite a more marked military role in politics.

But there exist numerous ways in which astute political leaders can counteract the effects or consequences of what have been identified as givens. Although geographically open or indefensible frontiers may delimit an individual state, its diplomats can negotiate pacts that will reduce susceptibility to outside military pressure. Geographic vulnerability can be reduced by negotiating alliances—although it is by no means axiomatic that alliances diminish the political involvement of the armed forces; alliances may in fact enhance such involvement.

Despite the fact that the general level of economic development may shift with glacial torpor, the collection of government revenues and patterns of their distribution can be dramatically altered in a short period of time and used to abet civilian control. The "pay-off" tactic can be employed, for example, although the contrary examples of Mexico and Chile suggest that pesos alone cannot preclude intervention where profound social and political strains exist. In fact, an increase in military expenditures designed to ensure obedience may have a converse effect, whetting the armed forces' appetite for more. In the 1963-72 period, probably the most rapid escalation of defense costs came in Uganda: nearly 34 percent per annum, with a leap from $1.16 million in 1963 to $78.4 million in 1972.[8] Admittedly Uganda fell under the sway of General Idi Amin in January 1971, but even at that point military expenditures had reached nearly twenty times the 1963 level. President Milton Obote tried to purchase loyalty; he may only have intensified the desire for more, attainable only by overt intervention.[9]

Leaving aside long-term issues of political legitimacy for the moment, can latent social differentiations be counteracted to buttress civilian control of the military? In a plural society, the fragmentation of the boundaries between the armed forces and social institutions has deleterious consequences already noted in this study. These consequences seem unescapable for two reasons. First, in states recently under colonial administration, pressures for indigenization of the officer corps will be (or have been) intense. Newly promoted or commissioned officers are far more likely than their expatriate predecessors to be aware of, and affected by, local political issues, and accordingly are more likely to become directly involved in them. Second, what Huntington deemed a "praetorian society" pits various social forces against each other; in this quasi-Hobbesian condition, "The wealthy bribe; students riot; workers strike; mobs demonstrate; and the military coup."[10] Under such conditions of conflict, given the weakness of mediating institutions, social divisions will spill over into the armed forces. Rare indeed are national militaries, as in India, that have deliberately remained aloof from political disputes based on "primordial sentiments." So long as a national community is weak, as Deutsch has emphasized,[11] polarizing tendencies exist. These tendencies might buttress civilian control in the short run, so long as the armed forces and government share the basic givens of race, ethnicity, or class; Guyana provides a case in point. Where either or both embody different social foundations, however, a tremendous potential for civil-military conflict exists.

Relatively simple to alter quickly are the constitutional

constraints officially set down for civilian control. As would be expected, however, such official prescriptions are translated into actual behavior only with time and difficulty, barring the absence (as in Japan) of significant external pressure or (as in China) of revolutionary political change. The problem for the scholar arises in distinguishing between shifts that are largely cosmetic in nature (does naming the president as commander-in-chief in fact give him respect and authority?) and shifts that betoken fundamental alterations in civil-military relations.

Possibly the best measure of the strength and extent of civilian control of the military is governmental ability to alter the armed forces' responsibilities. Some government decisions raise fundamental issues: for example, budget diminution, demobilization, or use of troops domestically. Are these decisions readily accepted by the armed forces? accepted with grumbling? accepted in form, but not implemented in practice? never considered by the government for fear of reaction? announced, then used as a pretext for military intervention? Where civilian control is tenuous, governments should avoid rapid, wholesale restructuring of the military responsibilities, prerogatives, and perquisites, unless the cohesion, structure, and values of the armed forces have been severely shaken. Where abrupt changes have come about, as in Japan or China, they have been linked to profound political transformations (war, revolution, intense international pressure) that have led members of the armed forces to accept the need for dramatic revision.

Chapter 1 of this book identified two bases of civilian control: a mutual sense of political restraint on the part of officers and politicians alike, keeping the armed forces within a relatively narrow, circumscribed set of responsibilities; and the existence of a legitimate, widely supported political institution able to ensure military compliance. Each is linked to a particular emphasis on means of control. The first approach concentrates on the *military* establishment: its boundaries, mission, values, organization, recruitment, and socialization. The second approach focuses more on the civilian *political* establishment, giving paramount attention to its legitimacy. The former emphasizes the military's political strengths, the latter civilian political strengths. I shall denote them respectively as Strategy 1 and Strategy 2.

In the near future, civilian control in developing countries is more likely to be achieved and maintained through Strategy 1 than Strategy 2. The generally low level of economic development, latent social cleavages and a low level of national integration, the short period of independence in many instances, the weakness of political institutions, and the profound changes in military values resulting from decolonization interact to create a low level of political legitimacy. In this situation the analyst should not ask the question, "Why does the military intervene?," but pose the more timely question, "Why does the military *not* intervene?" The answer, I suggest, is quite simple: leading members of the armed forces do not wish to seize power, even though various groups (both civilian and military) may be pressing for an expanded political role for the armed forces.

Finer has developed a similar argument, worth quoting at length:

> Now it is possible to conceive of states where the conditions are favourable to intervention: a latent chronic crisis of legitimacy exists, and all governments are abnormally dependent upon the support of the military, *but* the military lack volition. This is quite a different situation from one where, whether the military lack volition or not, a consensus exists, civilian counterforces are strongly organized, and the conditions for the success of a military takeover are highly unfavourable.
>
> In the first case cited, the military will be *disengaged* from active politics; in the second they will be *neutral*. In the first, the reason for the absence of military intervention is to be found in the mentality of military leaders. In the second, irrespective of this mentality, it is to be found in the nature of the society itself. In the first, the situation may change with a change of military mentality. Not so in the second, where a profound cleavage of society

would be necessary before any intervention could succeed. In the latter, the attitude of the military is a neutral one: to serve alternating sets of leaders with impartiality. In the first it is not neutral: it is temporarily uninterested.

In the Third World, military disengagement is not only possible, it is quite common. But military neutrality—that is another matter.[12]

Recognizing Finer's distinction between disengagement and neutrality, and the difficulties of achieving the latter in any political system, what steps might be taken to enhance disengagement? How can civilian and military leaders mutually avoid the desire to increase their power at the expense of the other?

One step can be taken with regard to the "boundaries" of the military and political institutions.[13] The "praetorian" conditions noted above testify to the erosion of distinctions among military, political, and social roles. Where government authority is exercised by a minority, buttressed by subjective civilian control over the military, institutional boundaries are fragmented. Ethnically fragmented states such as Burundi, Guyana, or Rhodesia illustrate both how (in the short term) one sector of society can wield power over a majority—and how steps toward majority rule inevitably will affect civil-military relations, including (should civil war break out) the possible destruction of the existing armed forces. Fragmented boundaries appear an effective means of civilian control only in relatively homogeneous societies, in which a nation-in-arms might couple military effectiveness with civilian oversight, or in societies ruled over by a dominant, widely supported political party. The Chinese Communist Party or the Tanganyika African National Union stand out as examples of civilian control abetted by boundary fragmentation. As implicitly suggested in chapter 1, however, integral boundaries should be maintained where they exist. The ouster of Nkrumah stemmed in large measure from his tampering with what Ghanaian officers perceived to be their political neutrality and professional prerogatives. Where the armed forces exercise and enjoy institutional autonomy largely isolated from fissiparous social tendencies, domestic conflicts may not spill over into the military, and the government can more readily exercise its control.

The mission of the armed forces provides a second set of steps. Where possible, the orientation and responsibilities of the military should be directed internationally. Extensive involvement of troops in internal disputes risks the possibility that they will turn against their purported masters. Domestic violence tries the loyalty of the military to the government—and if pacification can remain in the hands of police or gendarmes, the armed forces may remain politically disengaged.

Such disengagement from active political roles should be encouraged by civilian leaders. Many forms are possible, illustrated in preceding chapters: symbolic references and praise for officers who accept civilian control; astute use of promotions to weed out the politically ambitious; exchange of spheres of policy autonomy for acceptance of overall civilian policy guidance.[14] Service to the government, not service to "the nation," might be emphasized.

The organization of the military can, fourthly, reinforce what has already been suggested regarding mission and values. Functional specialization should be achieved, especially through the maintenance of police or paramilitary units able to maintain domestic order. Mounting a successful seizure of power becomes more complicated in a structurally differentiated military, due to the problems of building a coup coalition.[15] To be certain, policies perceived as "divide and rule" may backfire on civilian political leaders, as shown by Ghana. The Finnish example suggests that absorption of civil guards or similar groups into the regular military might ease the achievement of civilian control.

Finally, recruitment and socialization can be utilized to foster military disengagement from politics. The wisdom of Solomon may be necessary—for integral boundaries may result in armed forces becoming, in effect, separate social estates, with minimal psychological support for the political system as a whole. Intense professional training, many scholars have indicated, inculcates a sharp sense of distinctiveness and identification not necessarily directly amenable to civilian control.[16]

The usual tendency, it appears, is recruitment on the basis of values shared with the governing elite (hence the ubiquity of subjective civilian control), leading to the problems already noted. 'Twixt this particular Scylla and Charybdis, my inclination would be toward universalistic recruitment coupled with socialization in military values.

These steps must be taken together with steps designed to foster restraint on the part of civilian leaders. Such restraint frequently has been tied to areas of professional responsibility. Huntington, for example, sees "autonomous military professionalism" making the armed forces "politically sterile and neutral."[17] Give the military a sphere in which it can regulate its own affairs, the argument runs, encourage the appropriate forms of training, and officers should accept subordination to government officials. France under the Third Republic appeared to exemplify the success of such policies; as Ralston has written, "the primary desire [of French officers] was for independence in their own special sphere. This did not necessarily preclude governmental intervention in, or surveillance over, military affairs."[18]

Appropriate symbolic recognition should be furnished the military. As in Mexico, where presidential proclamations regularly refer in glowing terms to the armed forces, civilian leaders can abet the political disengagement of the military by praising and rewarding behavior that upholds civilian control. Distribution of perquisites and privileges can be utilized; promotions policies can be so designed as to favor supporters of civilian control. Actions thus exist that political leaders can take that, while recognizing areas of military autonomy, nonetheless incorporate these areas under the overall umbrella of civilian control.

Civilian politicians should follow policies of restraint in periods of domestic crisis. Risks are involved: politically aware officers, concerned by domestic violence, may step up their involvement to the point of takeover, claiming that only they can rescue the society from anarchic chaos. With situations like that of Allende's last days, military intervention becomes likely; the trick is to avoid escalation of conflict to such a level that it can be used as a pretext for intervention.

Nonetheless, political leaders should eschew the temptation to call on the armed forces for direct support at times of dispute or crisis. Even a modest step, such as Allende's invitation in late 1972 to join the cabinet, brings further politicization of the military and undercuts the "autonomous military professionalism" central to Huntington.

To describe the obligations of civilian leaders, no better summation exists than that of Janowitz:

> In a pluralistic society, the future of the military profession is not a military responsibility exclusively, but rests on the vitality of civilian political leadership. . . . the following requirements must be met by authorities: one, to limit military goals to feasible and attainable objectives; two, to assist in the formulation of military doctrine, so that it becomes a more unified expression of national political objectives; three, to maintain a sense of professional self-esteem in the military; and four, to develop new devices for the exercise of democratic political control.[19]

Taken together, the steps just sketched belong to Strategy 1. Intended to encourage a sense of military disengagement without denying the central responsibility of civilian leaders, Strategy 1 fosters military disengagement from politics. The strategy seeks thus to reduce the political strength and involvement of the armed forces. It depends largely on manipulating the military: its powers of decision-making, its symbolic significance, its values and mission as affected by government policies.

Strategy 1 seeks to curb the political strength of the military. It achieves civilian control by relying on military disengagement from a direct political role. Strategy 2, more important in long-range terms, achieves civilian control by enhancing the authority of the controllers themselves. In other words, Strategy 2 necessitates recognition that civilians exercising power do so rightfully, as a consequence of their position within government. Legitimacy, as Lipset stressed, concerns values: "Groups regard a political system as legitimate or illegitimate according to the way in which its values fit with theirs."[20] Huntington has asserted that only conservatism permits a combination of high military power with objective civilian control.[21] Yet political legitimacy, and the corresponding type of civilian control, can take many ideological guises: "traditional," as medieval monarchies; class- or party-oriented, as in communist systems; nationalistic, as in nations-in-arms.

To formulate a schema for political legitimacy would take this volume beyond its appropriate bounds. I can only echo the observations of others: encourage governmental efficiency; try to insulate political institutions from the corrosive effects of social strife; develop national symbols transcending parochial differences; ensure that individual citizens sense satisfaction in their personal political involvement. These homilies will tax the ingenuity of the wisest leaders. Implementation of these points is of crucial importance. If they are put into practice, greater military involvement in politics may be viewed as usurpation. The power to seize control should not be confused with the power to exercise control, as Rapoport has stressed; members of the armed forces cannot successfully usurp control, over an extended period, from a government considered legitimate by the populace.[22] The most effective barrier against coups d'etat is thus not the *absence* of military desire to exercise power, but the recognition such power cannot be seized and exercised effectively over a long period. As has been suggested elsewhere,

> Political legitimacy is the most crucial factor affecting the likelihood of military intervention. Where public support for civilian institutions is strong, military participation in politics is unlikely to extend to the overthrow and outright supplantment of civil authorities. Where public support is weak, expansion of the military's political role seems probable. Military intervention is primarily a characteristic of a certain kind of political system, rather than an outgrowth of the personnel, ethics, or organizational imperatives of the military institution itself. For this reason, strategies for establishing civilian control

that focus on reforming the armed forces are likely
to fail unless they are accompanied by effective
measures to strengthen civilian political institutions.[23]

To conclude on a somewhat melodramatic note, however,
the time for establishing civilian control is short, the task itself
long.

The first overt seizure of power by the armed forces constitutes the most important shift in civil-military relations. This
coup d'etat shatters the facade of civilian supremacy and may
bring a profound politicization of the armed forces. It is a step
not readily reversed. The establishment of governmental control may extend over several decades or be hastened only by
domestic or international pressures.

Of the eleven states examined in detail earlier in this book,
four—China, Finland, Japan, and Mexico—moved from military control of politics to civilian control of the military. Finland and Mexico experienced civil war and factional military
politics late in World War I. Military disengagement from active political roles in both cases did not come until the late
1930s, with the presidency of a respected general (Cárdenas
and Mannerheim) who sought to professionalize the armed
forces through their withdrawal from politics. The strength
of a mighty neighbor led Finnish politicians toward a nation-
in-arms, providing for a small standing army supported by
readily mobilizable reserves; despite the looming presence of
the United States, Mexican politicians steadily reduced the
size of the armed forces, considerably raising salaries and
benefits in the process. Japan was shocked into a dramatic
transformation of civil-military relations, marked by the stig-
mata of defeat and occupation, and by the drafting of strong
constitutional constraints on the armed forces. The economic
miracle made possible an escalation of military expenditures
without their hindering economic development. The Japanese
experience of transformed civil-military relations resulted
from unique circumstances, although one can generalize that
defeat in war makes more likely both a change in government
policies toward the military and a change in the government
itself. Finally, the conditions prevalent in China appear distinc-

tive. The PLA and the CCP grew hand in hand from 1927 through the civil war. Guerrilla military and political roles were intertwined. As shown earlier in this book, the extent and nature of PLA involvement in politics changed at times of domestic stress. Although communist control over the armed forces cannot be doubted, civil-military relations in China have ranged widely across the continuum presented in chapter 1, with military participation in, or even military control of, politics being characteristic during the Cultural Revolution.

Latin American states are heirs to long traditions of extensive political involvement by members of the armed forces. For Chile, one can confidently assert, there has been no prolonged period of unquestioned civilian supremacy. Since World War II, the strength of the military relative to the civilian institutions, such as legislatures, has been growing; a "new" professionalism has thrust the armed forces into sweeping political roles.[24] When politicians seem bent on inflaming class strife, in the armed forces' view, members of the military are ready to impose their authoritarian solutions. Civilian control of the military remains the exceptional condition south of the Rio Grande, possible only with significant transformations in the entire political system.

Finally, there remains the handful of developing countries that had not, by late 1975, been subject to successful military intervention. It should not be assumed that Guyana, India, Lebanon, Malaysia, and the Philippines are "typical" of Third World countries. All have prided themselves on "democratic" political trappings; all have had competitive party systems; four of the five inherited American or British patterns of civil-military relations. Nor should it be assumed that civil-military relations since independence have been totally harmonious. The 1958 civilian coup in Lebanon, the disgruntlement of the Indian army in the 1962 border war with China, and the 1972 declaration of martial law in the Philippines, are noteworthy examples of tension. It should be noted, however, that the impetus for change in these three instances came from civilians: President Shamun, Defense Minister V. Krishna Menon, President Marcos. The restraint of the armed forces in what were provocative situations eased the respective countries through periods of civil-military acrimony. Did this restraint result more from an absence of military desire to exert power or from the legitimacy of the political institutions? No clear answer exists, since both were mixed in the three states.

Strategy 1 and Strategy 2 must be pursued concurrently. Military influence can be channelled in recognized and legitimatized ways, not undercutting the authority and autonomy of political institutions, *if the desire exists*. But to make civilian control work, it must be favored by officers, politicians, and the populace alike. It is thus far easier to preach than to practice the subordination of the military to governmental control.

Notes to Chapter 11
Welch, *Two Strategies of Civilian Control.*

1. Robert D. Putnam, "Toward Explaining Military Intervention in Latin American Politics," *World Politics* 20, 1 (1967): 83-110.
2. Samuel E. Finer, "The Man on Horseback—1974," *Armed Forces and Society* 1, 1 (1974): 19.
3. Edward Feit, *The Armed Bureaucrats: Military-Administrative Regimes and Political Development* (Boston: Houghton Mifflin, 1973), pp. 2-3.
3. Samuel E. Finer, *The Man on Horseback: The Role of the Military in Politics* (New York: Praeger, 1962), pp. 110-39.
5. Karl W. Deutsch, "Social Mobilization and Political Development," *American Political Science Review* 55, 3 (1961): 493-514.
6. Clifford Geertz, "The Integrative Revolution: Primordial Sentiments and Civic Politics in the New States," in Geertz, ed., *Old Societies and New States: The Quest for Modernity in Asia and Africa* (New York: Free Press of Glencoe, 1963).
7. See the prescriptions for slowing mobilization in Samuel P. Huntington, "Political Development and Political Decay," *World Politics* 17, 3 (1965): 386-430.
8. US Arms Control and Disarmament Agency, *World Military Expenditures and Arms Trade 1963-1973* (Washington: US Government Printing Office, 1974), p. 60.
9. Michael F. Lofchie, "The Uganda Coup—Class Action by the Military," *Journal of Modern African Studies* 10, 1 (1972): 19-35.

10. Samuel P. Huntington, *Political Order in Changing Societies* (New Haven: Yale University Press, 1968), p. 196. Note the omission of peasants from Huntington's social categories; the "Green uprising" occurs only under special conditions.

11. Karl W. Deutsch, *Nationalism and Social Communication: An Inquiry into the Foundations of Nationality,* 2nd edition (Cambridge: M.I.T. Press, 1966) p. 191.

12. Finer, "The Man on Horseback—1974," p. 15.

13. Claude E. Welch, Jr. and Arthur K. Smith, *Military Role and Rule: Perspectives on Civil-Military Relations* (North Scituate: Duxbury Press, 1974), pp. 39-42.

14. David B. Ralston, *The Army of the Republic: The Place of the Military in the Political Evolution of France, 1871-1914* (Cambridge: M.I.T. Press, 1967).

15. Martin C. Needler "Political Development and Military Intervention in Latin America," *American Political Science Review* 55, 3 (1966): 619-21. Cf. Kurt Lang, "The Military Putsch in a Developed Political Culture: Confrontations of Military and Civil Power in Germany and France," in Jacques van Doorn, ed., *Armed Forces and Society* (The Hague: Mouton, 1968), p. 228.

16. Bengt Abrahamson, *Military Professionalization and Political Power* (Beverly Hills: Sage, 1972).

17. Samuel P. Huntington, *The Soldier and the State: The Theory and Politics of Civil-Military Relations* (New York: Vintage, 1964), pp. 83-4.

18. Ralston, *The Army of the Republic,* p. 10.

19. Morris Janowitz, *The Professional Soldier: A Social and Political Portrait* (New York: Free Press of Glencoe, 1960), p. 435.

20. Seymour Martin Lipset, *Political Man* (London: Mercury Books, 1963), p. 77.

21. Huntington, *The Soldier and the State,* pp. 93-4, 97.

22. David C. Rapoport, "The Political Dimensions of Military Usurpation," *Political Science Quarterly* 83, 4 (1968), p. 569.

23. Welch and Smith, *Military Role and Rule,* p. 249.

INDEX

Delhumeau, Antonio, 217, 250

Deutsch, Karl W., 120, 315, 316, 326, 327

Diaz Ordaz, Gustavo, 221, 225, 230

Dishman, Robert B., 97

Dolian, James P., 25, 40, 214

Dominguez, Jorge I., 40

Dominican Republic, 214

Dreyer, Edward L., 40

Duque, Benjamin C., 121

Easton, David, 214, 217, 250

Echeverria, 215, 219, 220, 230, 245

Ecuador, 214

Edde, Raymond, 266, 267, 281, 282

Egypt, 268

El Salvador, 25, 214

Enckell, Carl, 212

Enloe, Cynthia H., 65, 95

Erikson, John, 20, 39

Estado Militar, 31

Europe, 214

Ezcurdia, Mario, 217, 250

Fagen, Richard R., 251

Faivovich, Jaime, 304

Fascist Party, 199

Feinberg, Richard E., 310

Feit, Edward, 326

Finer, S. E., 4, 26, 39, 40, 218, 250, 314, 318, 319, 326

Finland, x, xi, 12, 37, 187-212, 324

Fortescue, Sir John, 28, 41

France, 6, 11, 12, 25, 33, 159, 321

Franco, Francisco, 11

Franjieh, Suleiman, 274, 275

Frei, Eduardo, 289, 292, 296, 299, 302, 305, 306

French Revolution, 10, 11

Frunze, 20

Fuentealba, Renan, 295

Fu Ts'ung-pi, 129

Gandhi, Indira, 60, 61, 64

Garces, Juan, 304, 311

Gatmaitan, A. N., 121

GDF (see Guyana Defense Force)

Geertz, Clifford, 326

Geographic and Historical Factors, 24-30; (India), 50-53

Germany, 7, 25, 188, 206, 208

Ghana, 22, 23, 27, 320

Ghosh, K. K., 62

Gibbons, David S., 96

Gittings, John, 20, 39, 40, 142, 144, 145, 148

Glade, William P. 216, 249

Glorious Revolution, 28

Goldberg, Sherwood D., 35, 99, 119, 121

Gomez-Quinones, J., 231

Gott, Richard, 309

GPCR (see Great Proletarian Cultural Revolution)

Great Britain, 11, 27, 28, 55, 193

Great Proletarian Cultural Revolution (GPCR), 21, 123, 124, 127, 130, 131, 133, 134, 139, 141-3

Groener, Wilhelm, 183

Guatemala, 25, 214

Gurtov, Melvin, 145

Gutteridge, William, 95

Guyana, x, xi, 35, 36, 82-94, 215, 316, 319, 325

Guyana Defense Force (GDF), 82, 84, 85, 86, 87, 89, 90, 91, 92, 93

Guyot, James F., 95

Habron, John D., 308, 310

al-Hafiz, Amin, 274, 275

Haiti, 106, 222

Hannula, J. O., 208

Hansen, Roy Allen, 217, 250, 287, 307, 308, 311

Harding, Harry, 145

Harmaja, Leo, 211

Hare, Gertrude, E., 98, 307

Hawkins, David, 97

Hayden, Joseph R., 117, 118, 122

Heaphey, James J., 255

Helou, Charles, 266

Henderson, John, 95, 96

Heikinheimo, Oskari, 210, 212

Hibbs, Douglas A. Jr., 213, 253